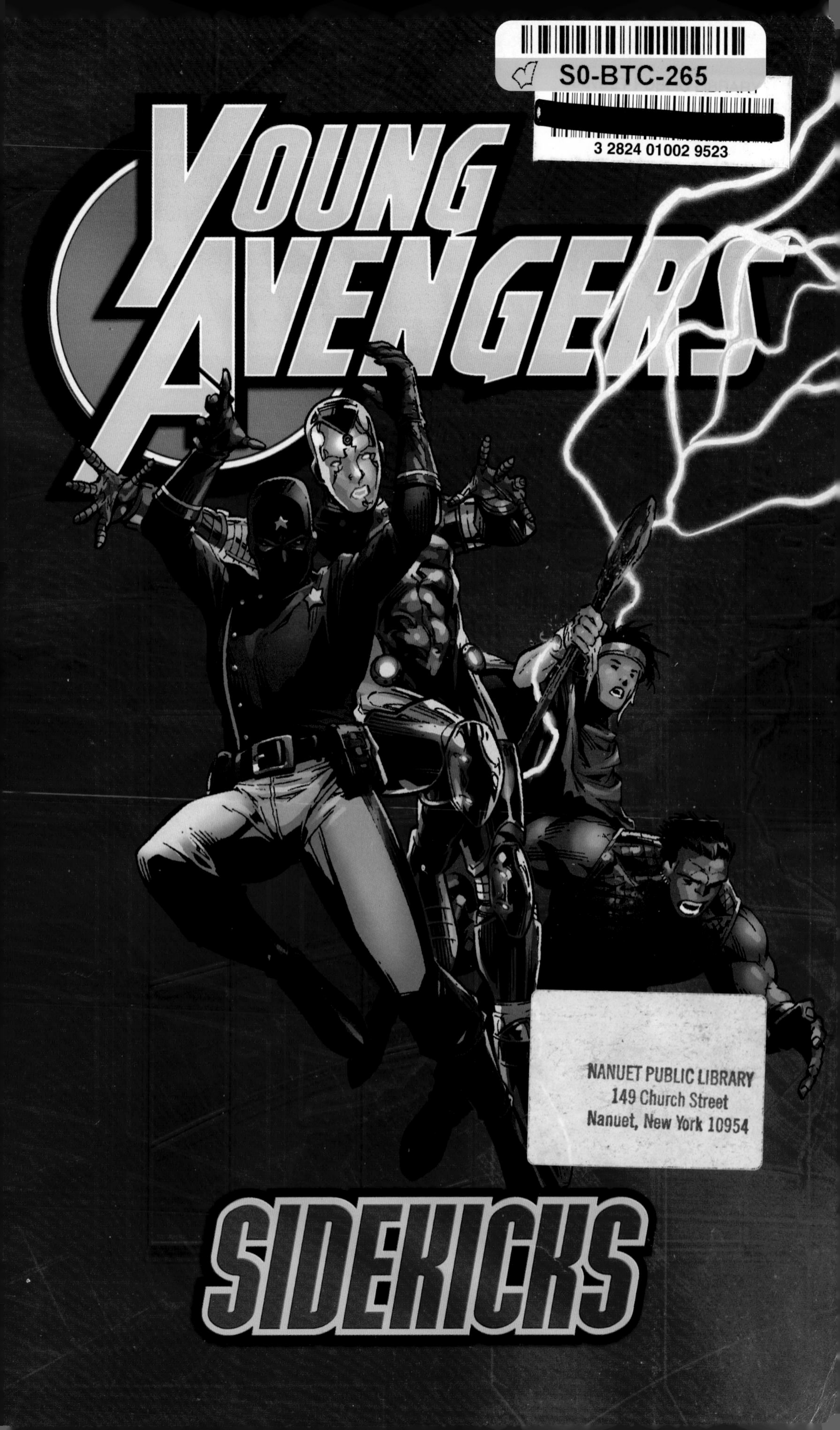
YOUNG AVENGERS
SIDEKICKS

YOUNG AVENGERS
SIDEKICKS

WRITER: **ALLAN HEINBERG**
PENCILS: **JIM CHEUNG**
INKS: **JOHN DELL, MARK MORALES & DREW GERACI**
COLORS: **JUSTIN PONSOR**
LETTERS: **VIRTUAL CALLIGRAPHY'S CORY PETIT**
ASSISTANT EDITORS: **STEPHANIE MOORE & MOLLY LAZER**
ASSOCIATE EDITOR: **ANDY SCHMIDT**
EDITOR: **TOM BREVOORT**

Young Avengers created by Allan Heinberg & Jim Cheung

COLLECTION EDITOR: **JENNIFER GRÜNWALD**
ASSISTANT EDITOR: **MICHAEL SHORT**
SENIOR EDITOR, SPECIAL PROJECTS: **JEFF YOUNGQUIST**
VICE PRESIDENT OF SALES: **DAVID GABRIEL**
BOOK DESIGNER: **PATRICK MCGRATH**
CREATIVE DIRECTOR: **TOM MARVELLI**

EDITOR IN CHIEF: **JOE QUESADA**
PUBLISHER: **DAN BUCKLEY**

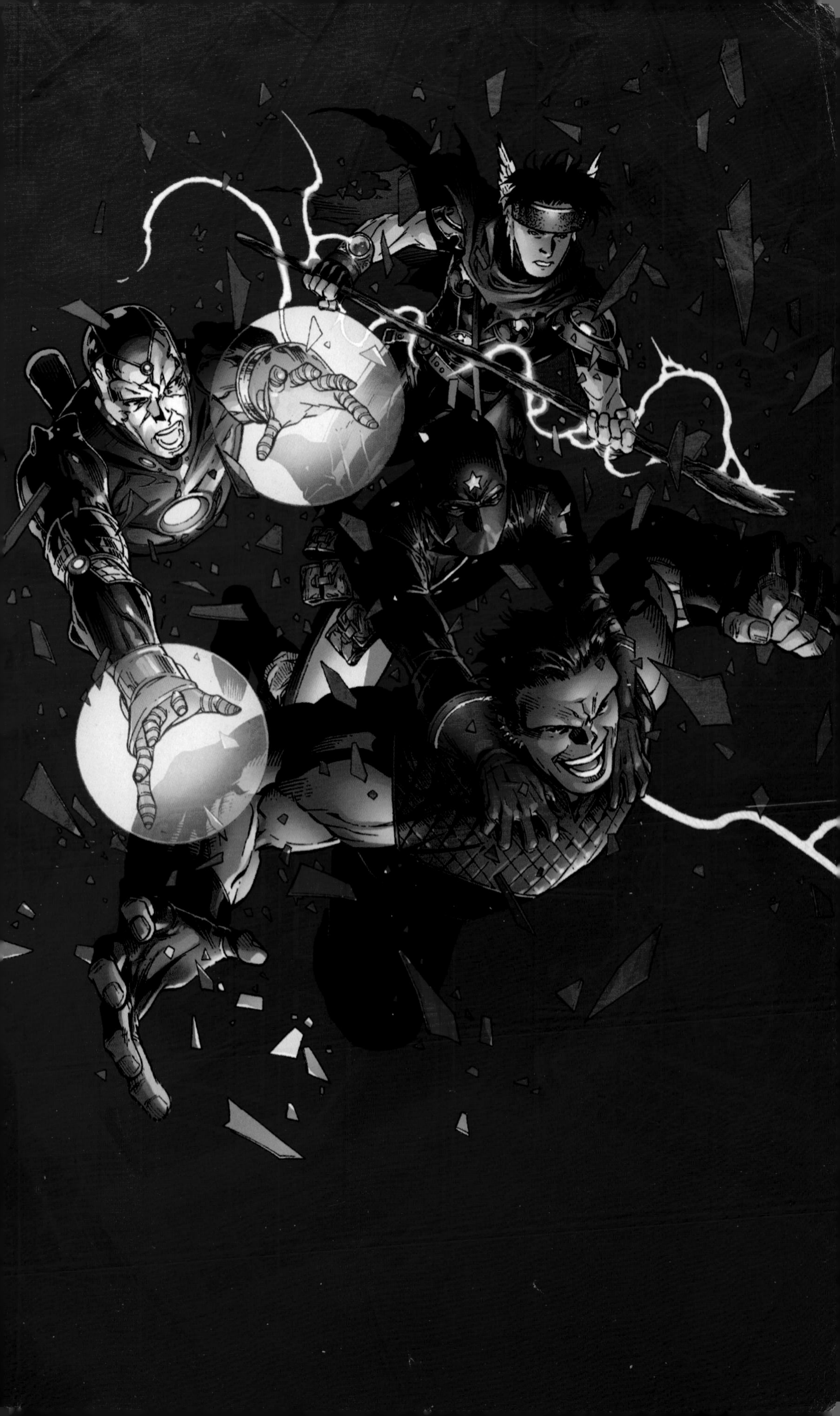

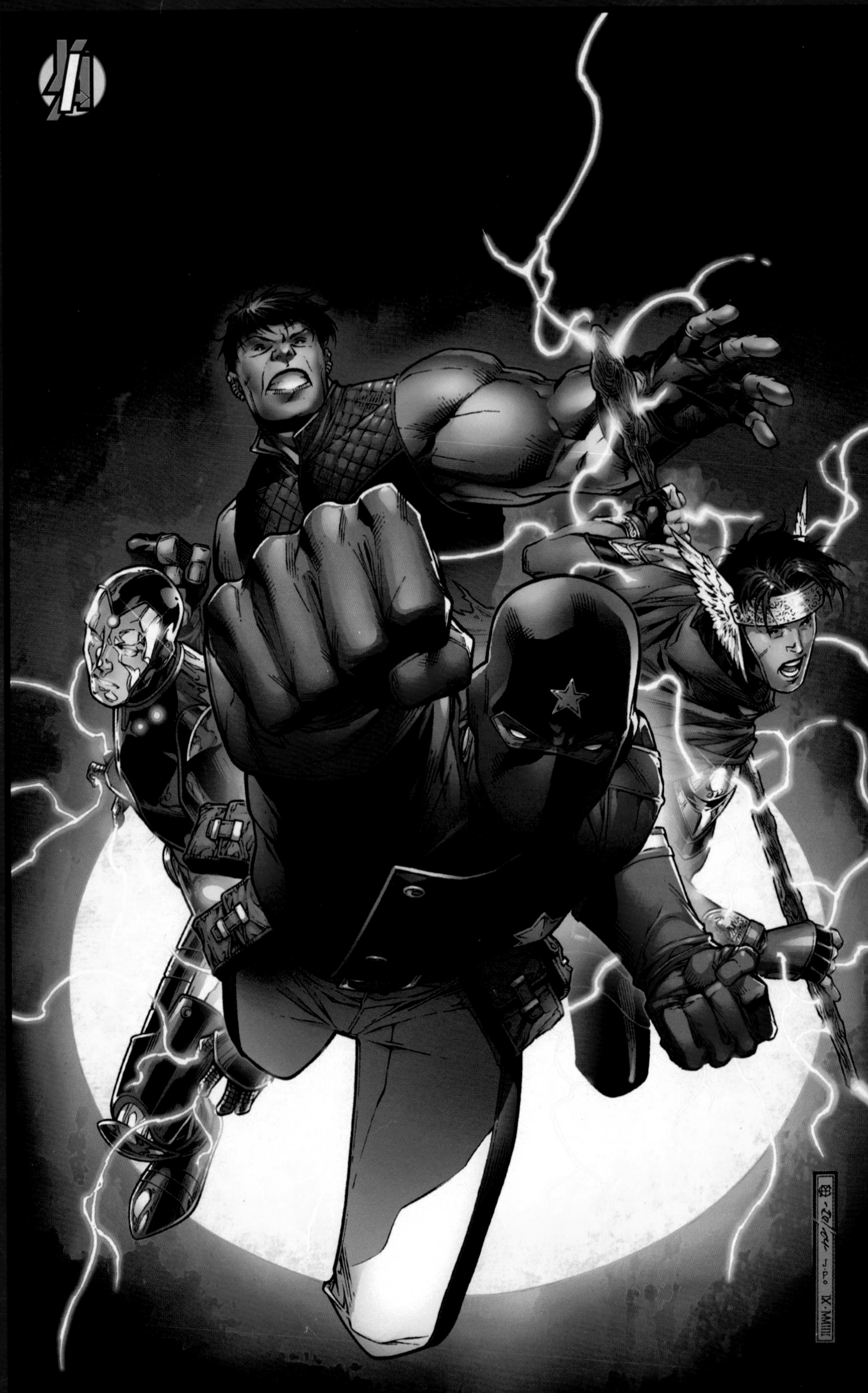

SIDEKICKS

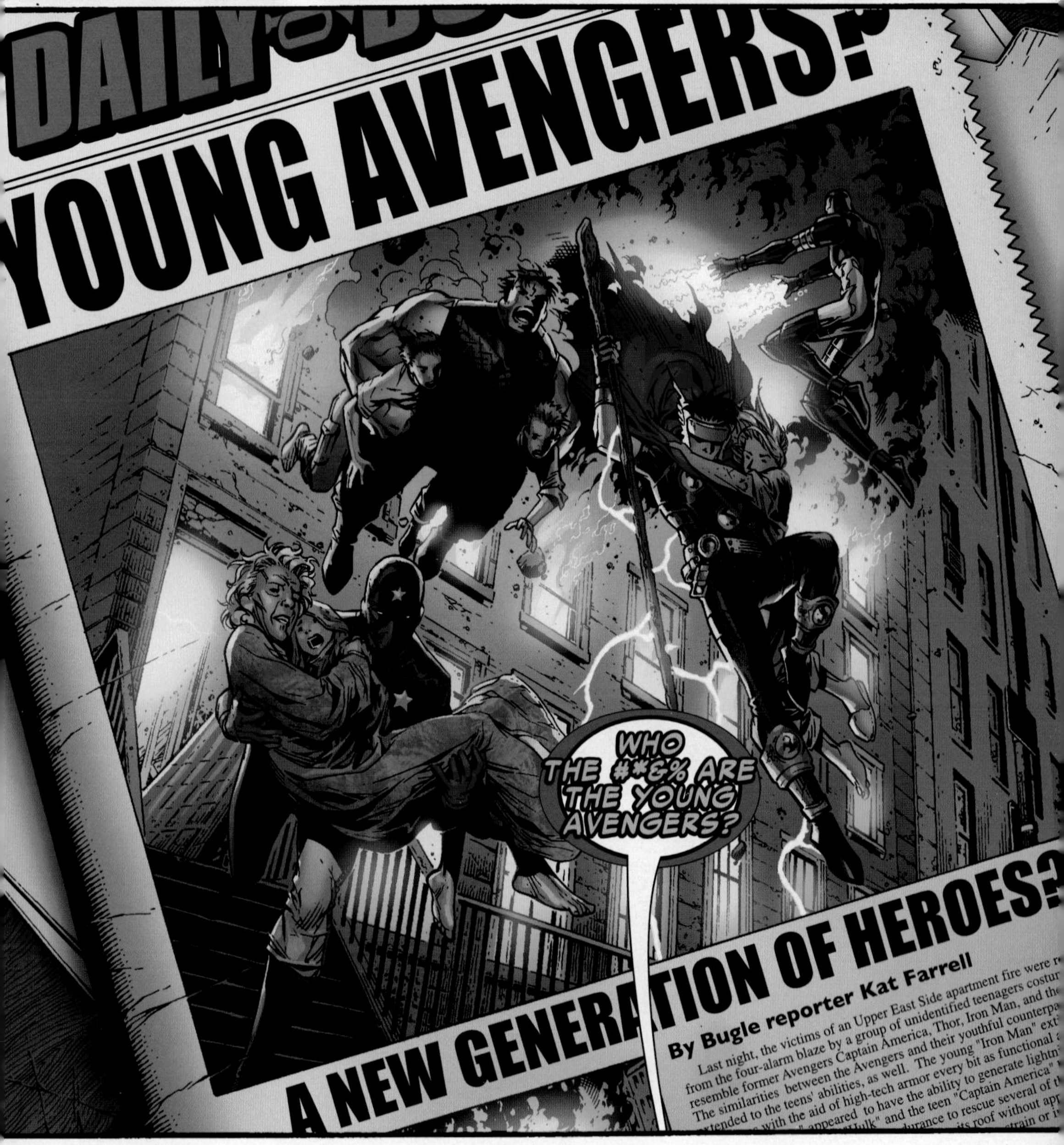
DAILY BUGLE
YOUNG AVENGERS?
WHO THE #*&% ARE THE YOUNG AVENGERS?
A NEW GENERATION OF HEROES?
By Bugle reporter Kat Farrell
Last night, the victims of an Upper East Side apartment fire were
from the four-alarm blaze by a group of unidentified teenagers costu
resemble former Avengers Captain America, Thor, Iron Man, and the
The similarities between the Avengers and their youthful counterpa
extended to the teens' abilities, as well. The young "Iron Man" ext
with the aid of high-tech armor every bit as functional
appeared to have the ability to generate lightn
"Hulk" and the teen "Captain America"
durance to rescue several of t
its roof without ap
strain or i

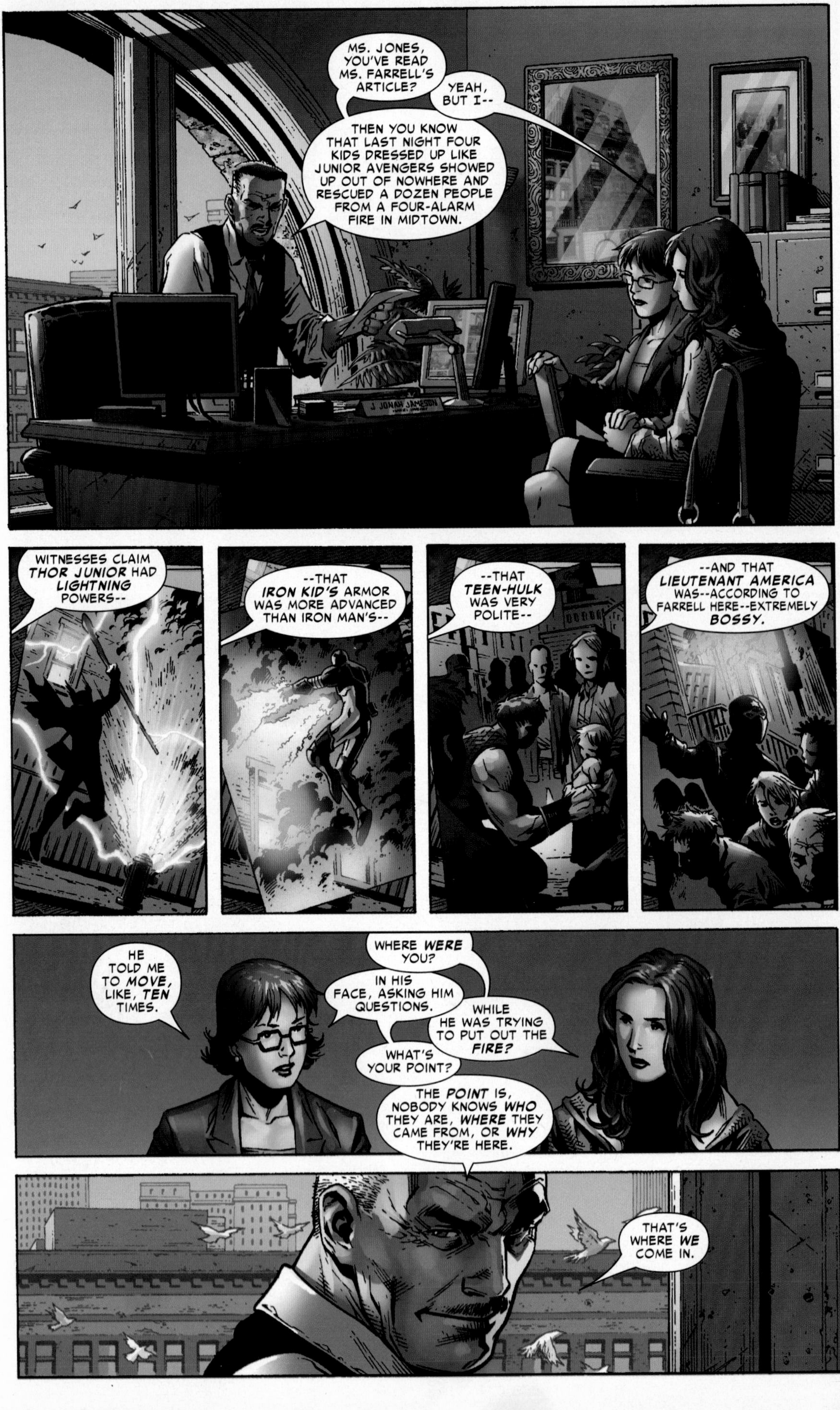
MS. JONES, YOU'VE READ MS. FARRELL'S ARTICLE?
YEAH, BUT I--
THEN YOU KNOW THAT LAST NIGHT FOUR KIDS DRESSED UP LIKE JUNIOR AVENGERS SHOWED UP OUT OF NOWHERE AND RESCUED A DOZEN PEOPLE FROM A FOUR-ALARM FIRE IN MIDTOWN.
J JONAH JAMESON
WITNESSES CLAIM THOR JUNIOR HAD LIGHTNING POWERS--
--THAT IRON KID'S ARMOR WAS MORE ADVANCED THAN IRON MAN'S--
--THAT TEEN-HULK WAS VERY POLITE--
--AND THAT LIEUTENANT AMERICA WAS--ACCORDING TO FARRELL HERE--EXTREMELY BOSSY.
HE TOLD ME TO MOVE, LIKE, TEN TIMES.
WHERE WERE YOU?
IN HIS FACE, ASKING HIM QUESTIONS.
WHILE HE WAS TRYING TO PUT OUT THE FIRE?
WHAT'S YOUR POINT?
THE POINT IS, NOBODY KNOWS WHO THEY ARE, WHERE THEY CAME FROM, OR WHY THEY'RE HERE.
THAT'S WHERE WE COME IN.

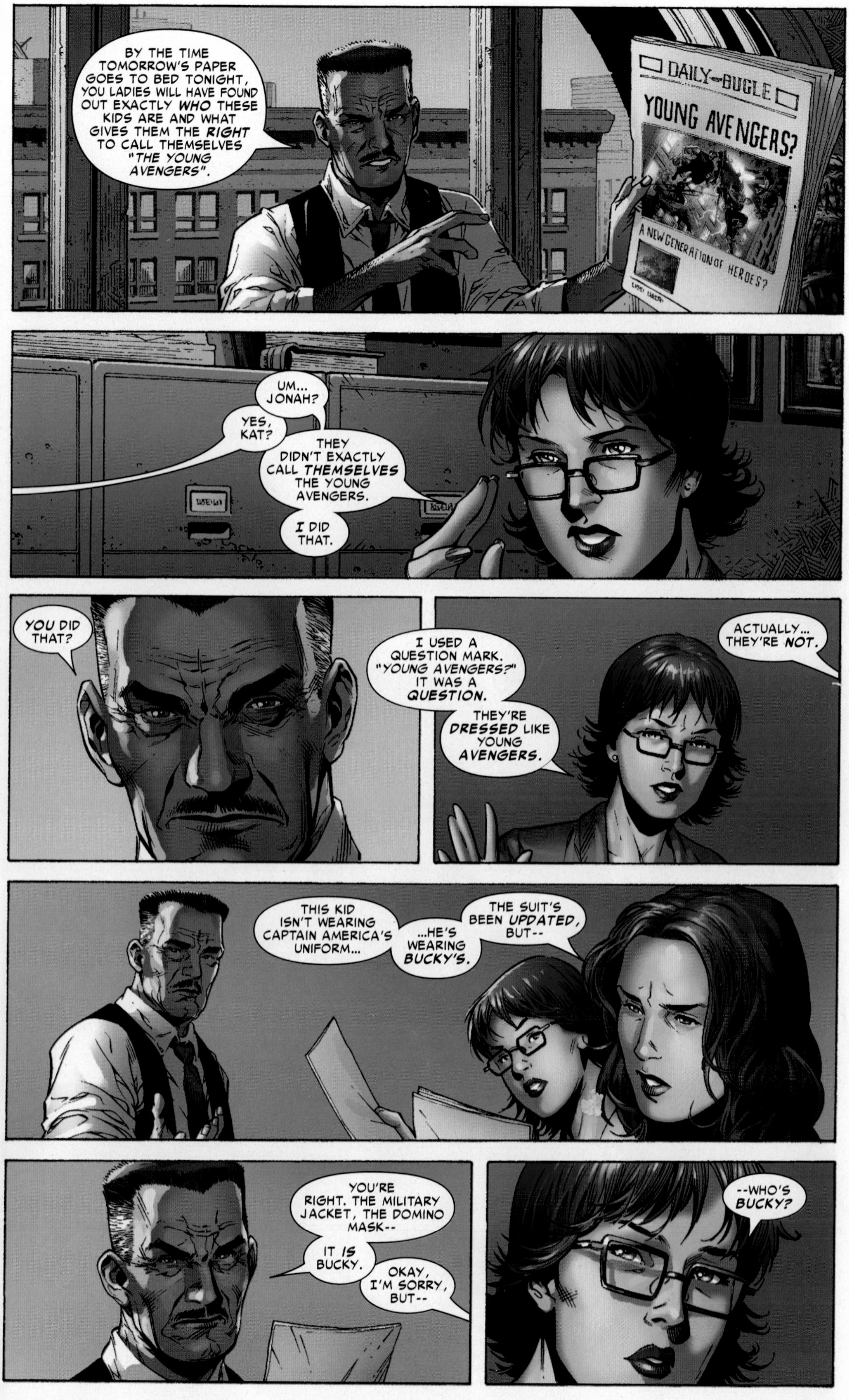
BY THE TIME TOMORROW'S PAPER GOES TO BED TONIGHT, YOU LADIES WILL HAVE FOUND OUT EXACTLY WHO THESE KIDS ARE AND WHAT GIVES THEM THE RIGHT TO CALL THEMSELVES "THE YOUNG AVENGERS".
DAILY BUGLE
YOUNG AVENGERS?
A NEW GENERATION OF HEROES?
UM... JONAH?
YES, KAT?
THEY DIDN'T EXACTLY CALL THEMSELVES THE YOUNG AVENGERS.
I DID THAT.
YOU DID THAT?
I USED A QUESTION MARK. "YOUNG AVENGERS?" IT WAS A QUESTION.
THEY'RE DRESSED LIKE YOUNG AVENGERS.
ACTUALLY... THEY'RE NOT.
THIS KID ISN'T WEARING CAPTAIN AMERICA'S UNIFORM...
...HE'S WEARING BUCKY'S.
THE SUIT'S BEEN UPDATED, BUT--
YOU'RE RIGHT. THE MILITARY JACKET, THE DOMINO MASK--
IT IS BUCKY.
OKAY, I'M SORRY, BUT--
--WHO'S BUCKY?

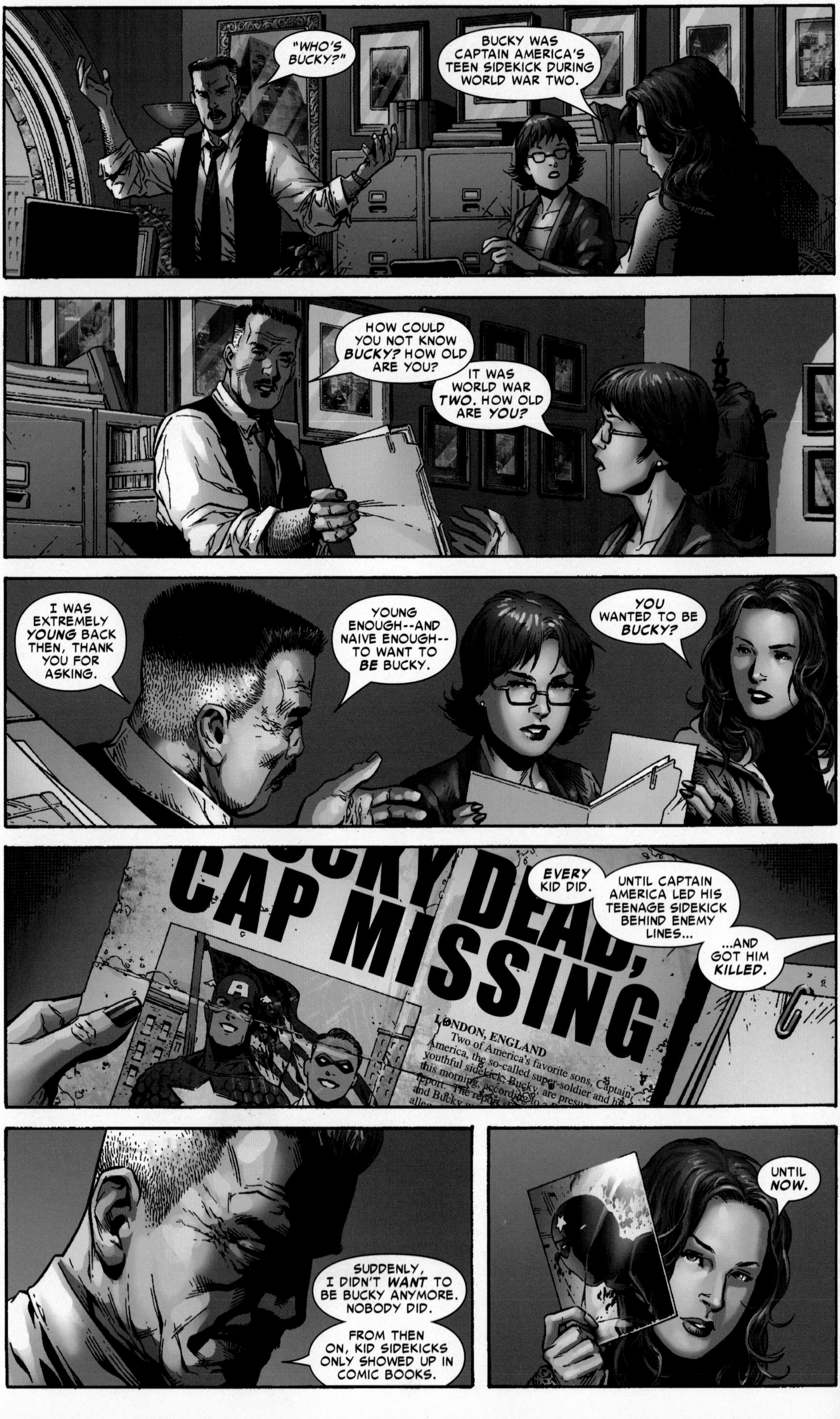
"WHO'S BUCKY?"
BUCKY WAS CAPTAIN AMERICA'S TEEN SIDEKICK DURING WORLD WAR TWO.
HOW COULD YOU NOT KNOW BUCKY? HOW OLD ARE YOU?
IT WAS WORLD WAR TWO. HOW OLD ARE YOU?
I WAS EXTREMELY YOUNG BACK THEN, THANK YOU FOR ASKING.
YOUNG ENOUGH--AND NAIVE ENOUGH--TO WANT TO BE BUCKY.
YOU WANTED TO BE BUCKY?
CAP MISSING
LONDON, ENGLAND
Two of America's favorite sons, Captain America, the so-called super-soldier and his youthful sidekick, Bucky, are presu
EVERY KID DID.
UNTIL CAPTAIN AMERICA LED HIS TEENAGE SIDEKICK BEHIND ENEMY LINES...
...AND GOT HIM KILLED.
SUDDENLY, I DIDN'T WANT TO BE BUCKY ANYMORE. NOBODY DID.
FROM THEN ON, KID SIDEKICKS ONLY SHOWED UP IN COMIC BOOKS.
UNTIL NOW.

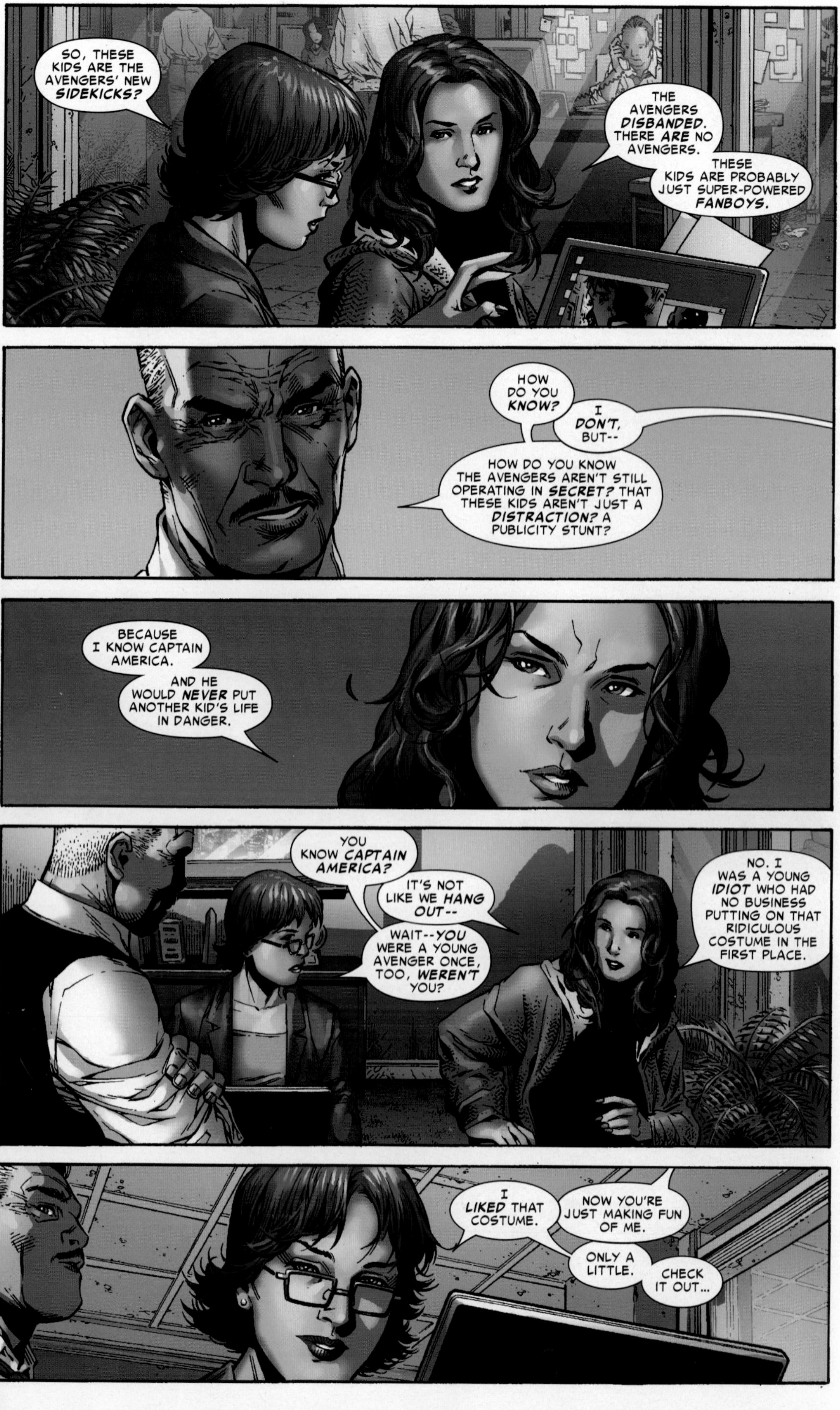
SO, THESE KIDS ARE THE AVENGERS' NEW SIDEKICKS?
THE AVENGERS DISBANDED. THERE ARE NO AVENGERS.
THESE KIDS ARE PROBABLY JUST SUPER-POWERED FANBOYS.
HOW DO YOU KNOW?
I DON'T, BUT--
HOW DO YOU KNOW THE AVENGERS AREN'T STILL OPERATING IN SECRET? THAT THESE KIDS AREN'T JUST A DISTRACTION? A PUBLICITY STUNT?
BECAUSE I KNOW CAPTAIN AMERICA.
AND HE WOULD NEVER PUT ANOTHER KID'S LIFE IN DANGER.
YOU KNOW CAPTAIN AMERICA?
IT'S NOT LIKE WE HANG OUT--
WAIT--YOU WERE A YOUNG AVENGER ONCE, TOO, WEREN'T YOU?
NO. I WAS A YOUNG IDIOT WHO HAD NO BUSINESS PUTTING ON THAT RIDICULOUS COSTUME IN THE FIRST PLACE.
I LIKED THAT COSTUME.
NOW YOU'RE JUST MAKING FUN OF ME.
ONLY A LITTLE.
CHECK IT OUT...

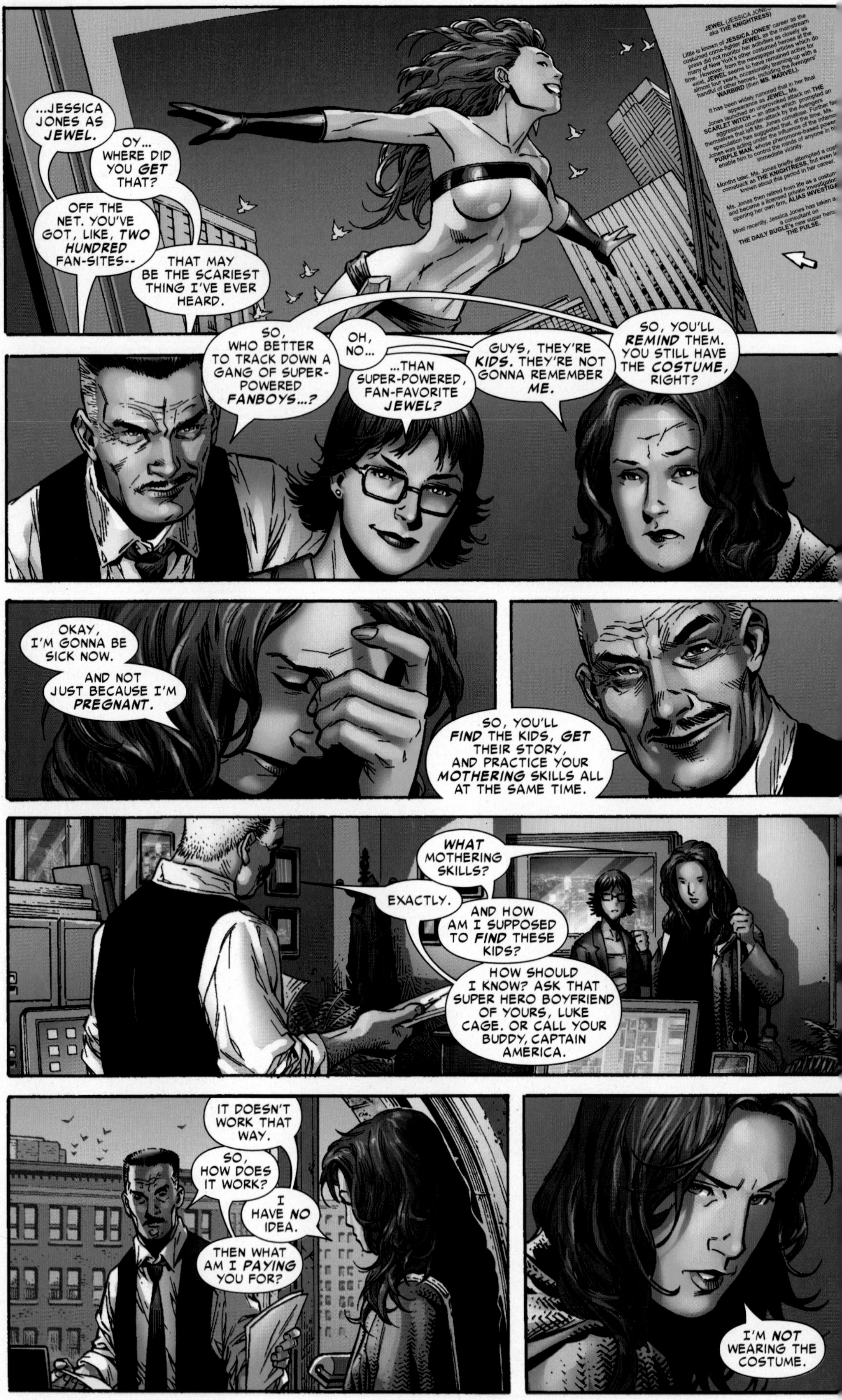
JEWEL (JESSICA JONES)
aka THE KNIGHTRESS)
Little is known of JESSICA JONES' career as the costumed crime-fighter JEWEL as the mainstream press did not monitor her activities as closely as many of New York's other costumed heroes at the time. However, from the newspaper articles which do exist, JEWEL seems to have remained active for almost four years, occasionally teaming-up with a handful of other heroes, including the Avengers' WARBIRD (then MS. MARVEL).
It has been widely rumored that in her final appearance as JEWEL, Ms. Jones launched an unprovoked attack on THE SCARLET WITCH – an attack which prompted an aggressive counter-attack by the Avengers themselves that left Ms. Jones comatose. Further speculation has suggested that, at the time, Ms. Jones was acting under the influence of the PURPLE MAN, whose pheromone-based power enable him to control the minds of anyone in immediate vicinity.
Months later, Ms. Jones briefly attempted a comeback as THE KNIGHTRESS, but even known about this period in her career.
Ms. Jones then retired from life as a and became a licensed private investigator opening her own firm, ALIAS INVESTIG
Most recently, Jessica Jones has taken a consultant on THE DAILY BUGLE's new super hero THE PULSE.
...JESSICA JONES AS *JEWEL.*
OY... WHERE DID YOU *GET* THAT?
OFF THE NET. YOU'VE GOT, LIKE, *TWO HUNDRED* FAN-SITES--
THAT MAY BE THE SCARIEST THING I'VE EVER HEARD.
SO, WHO BETTER TO TRACK DOWN A GANG OF SUPER-POWERED *FANBOYS...?*
OH, NO...
...THAN SUPER-POWERED, FAN-FAVORITE *JEWEL?*
GUYS, THEY'RE *KIDS.* THEY'RE NOT GONNA REMEMBER *ME.*
SO, YOU'LL *REMIND* THEM. YOU STILL HAVE THE *COSTUME,* RIGHT?
OKAY, I'M GONNA BE SICK NOW.
AND NOT JUST BECAUSE I'M *PREGNANT.*
SO, YOU'LL *FIND* THE KIDS, *GET* THEIR STORY, AND PRACTICE YOUR *MOTHERING* SKILLS ALL AT THE SAME TIME.
WHAT MOTHERING SKILLS?
EXACTLY.
AND HOW AM I SUPPOSED TO *FIND* THESE KIDS?
HOW SHOULD I KNOW? ASK THAT SUPER HERO BOYFRIEND OF YOURS, LUKE CAGE. OR CALL YOUR BUDDY, CAPTAIN AMERICA.
IT DOESN'T WORK THAT WAY.
SO, HOW DOES IT WORK?
I HAVE *NO* IDEA.
THEN WHAT AM I *PAYING* YOU FOR?
I'M *NOT* WEARING THE COSTUME.

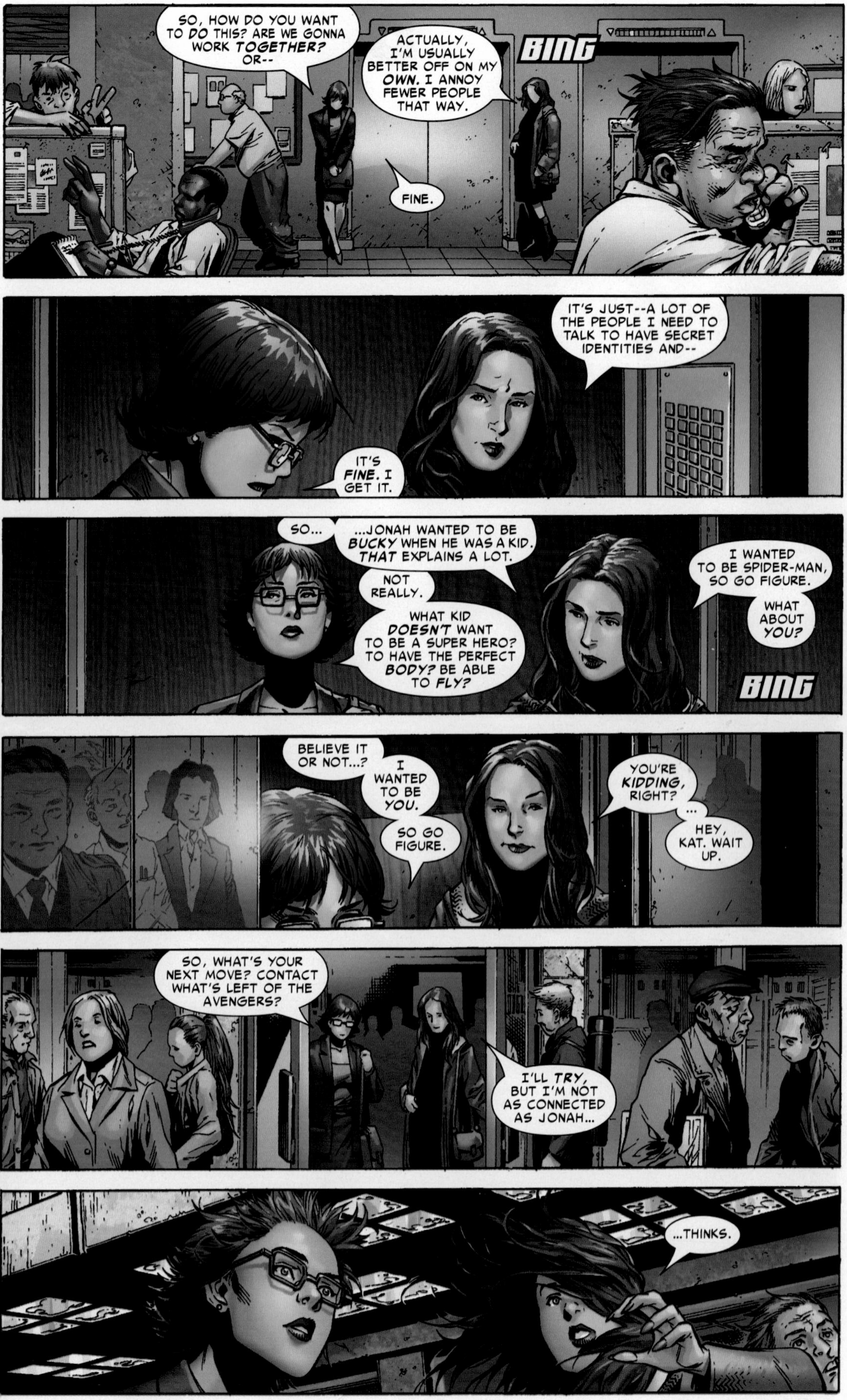
SO, HOW DO YOU WANT TO DO THIS? ARE WE GONNA WORK TOGETHER? OR--
ACTUALLY, I'M USUALLY BETTER OFF ON MY OWN. I ANNOY FEWER PEOPLE THAT WAY.
BING
FINE.
IT'S JUST--A LOT OF THE PEOPLE I NEED TO TALK TO HAVE SECRET IDENTITIES AND--
IT'S FINE. I GET IT.
SO...
...JONAH WANTED TO BE BUCKY WHEN HE WAS A KID. THAT EXPLAINS A LOT.
NOT REALLY.
WHAT KID DOESN'T WANT TO BE A SUPER HERO? TO HAVE THE PERFECT BODY? BE ABLE TO FLY?
I WANTED TO BE SPIDER-MAN, SO GO FIGURE.
WHAT ABOUT YOU?
BING
BELIEVE IT OR NOT...?
I WANTED TO BE YOU.
SO GO FIGURE.
YOU'RE KIDDING, RIGHT?
...
HEY, KAT. WAIT UP.
SO, WHAT'S YOUR NEXT MOVE? CONTACT WHAT'S LEFT OF THE AVENGERS?
I'LL TRY, BUT I'M NOT AS CONNECTED AS JONAH...
...THINKS.

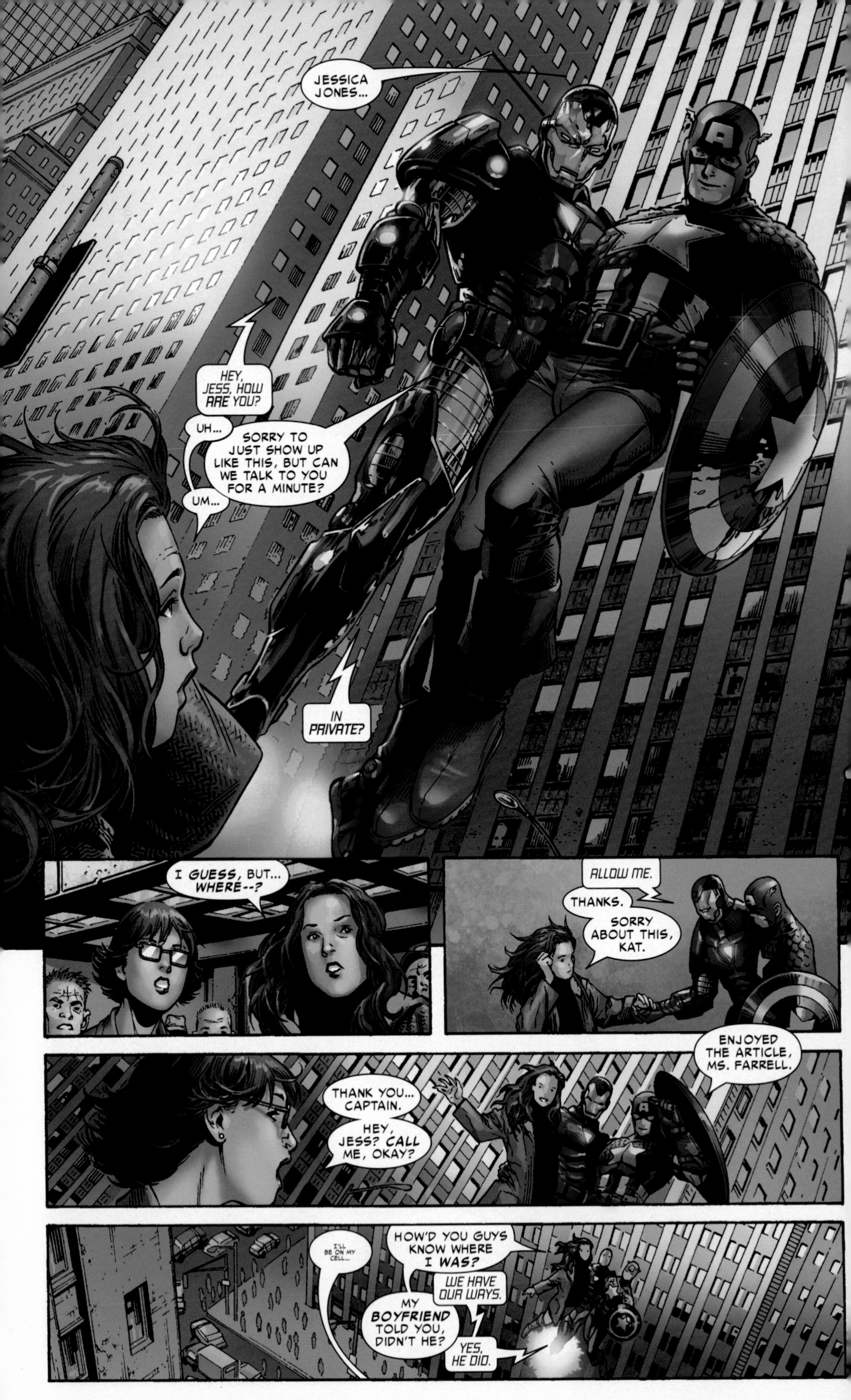
JESSICA JONES...
HEY, JESS, HOW ARE YOU?
UH...
SORRY TO JUST SHOW UP LIKE THIS, BUT CAN WE TALK TO YOU FOR A MINUTE?
UM...
IN PRIVATE?
I GUESS, BUT... WHERE--?
ALLOW ME.
THANKS.
SORRY ABOUT THIS, KAT.
ENJOYED THE ARTICLE, MS. FARRELL.
THANK YOU... CAPTAIN.
HEY, JESS? CALL ME, OKAY?
HOW'D YOU GUYS KNOW WHERE I WAS?
I'LL BE ON MY CELL...
WE HAVE OUR WAYS.
MY BOYFRIEND TOLD YOU, DIDN'T HE?
YES, HE DID.

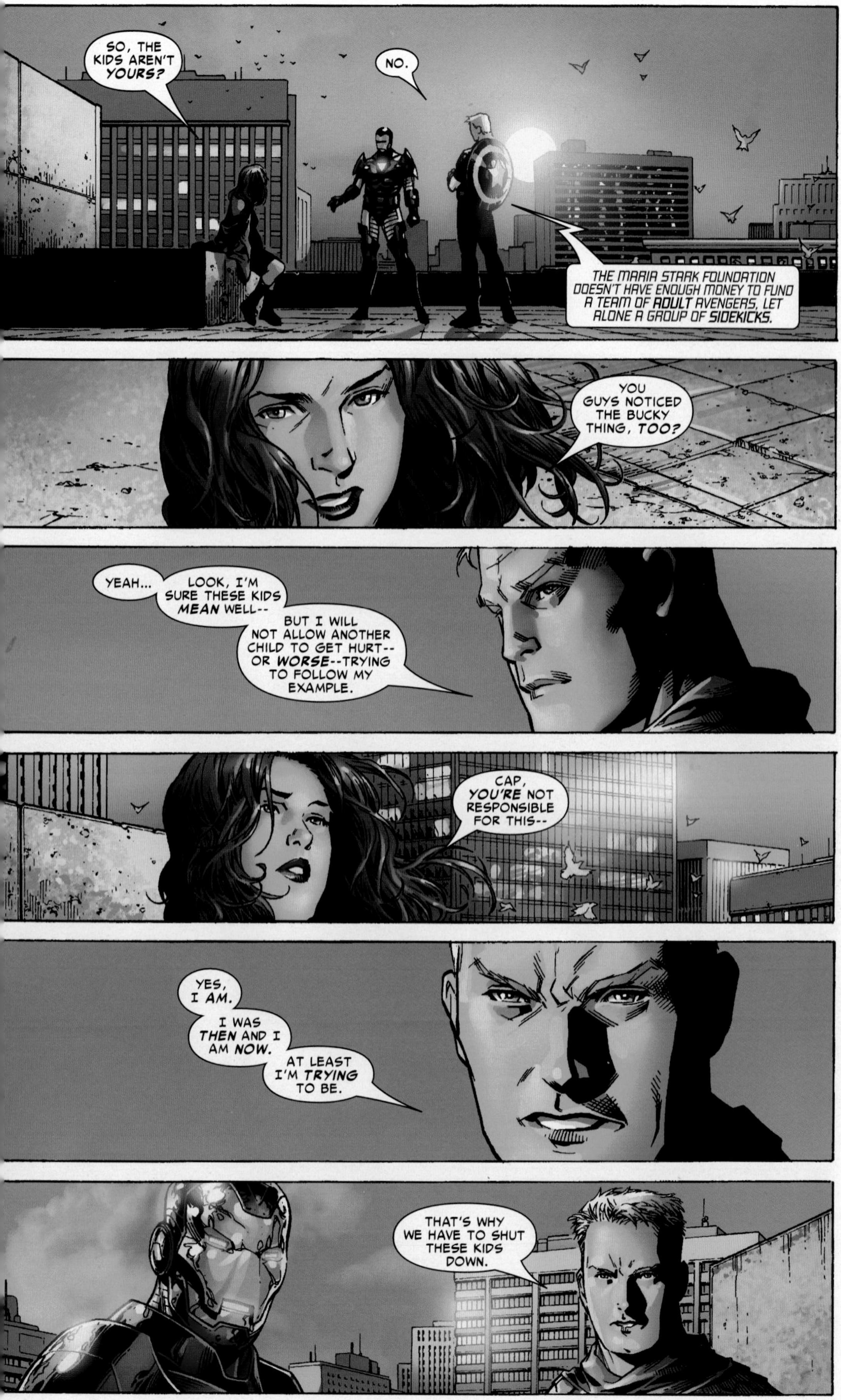
SO, THE KIDS AREN'T YOURS?
NO.
THE MARIA STARK FOUNDATION DOESN'T HAVE ENOUGH MONEY TO FUND A TEAM OF ADULT AVENGERS, LET ALONE A GROUP OF SIDEKICKS.
YOU GUYS NOTICED THE BUCKY THING, TOO?
YEAH...
LOOK, I'M SURE THESE KIDS MEAN WELL--
BUT I WILL NOT ALLOW ANOTHER CHILD TO GET HURT--OR WORSE--TRYING TO FOLLOW MY EXAMPLE.
CAP, YOU'RE NOT RESPONSIBLE FOR THIS--
YES, I AM.
I WAS THEN AND I AM NOW.
AT LEAST I'M TRYING TO BE.
THAT'S WHY WE HAVE TO SHUT THESE KIDS DOWN.

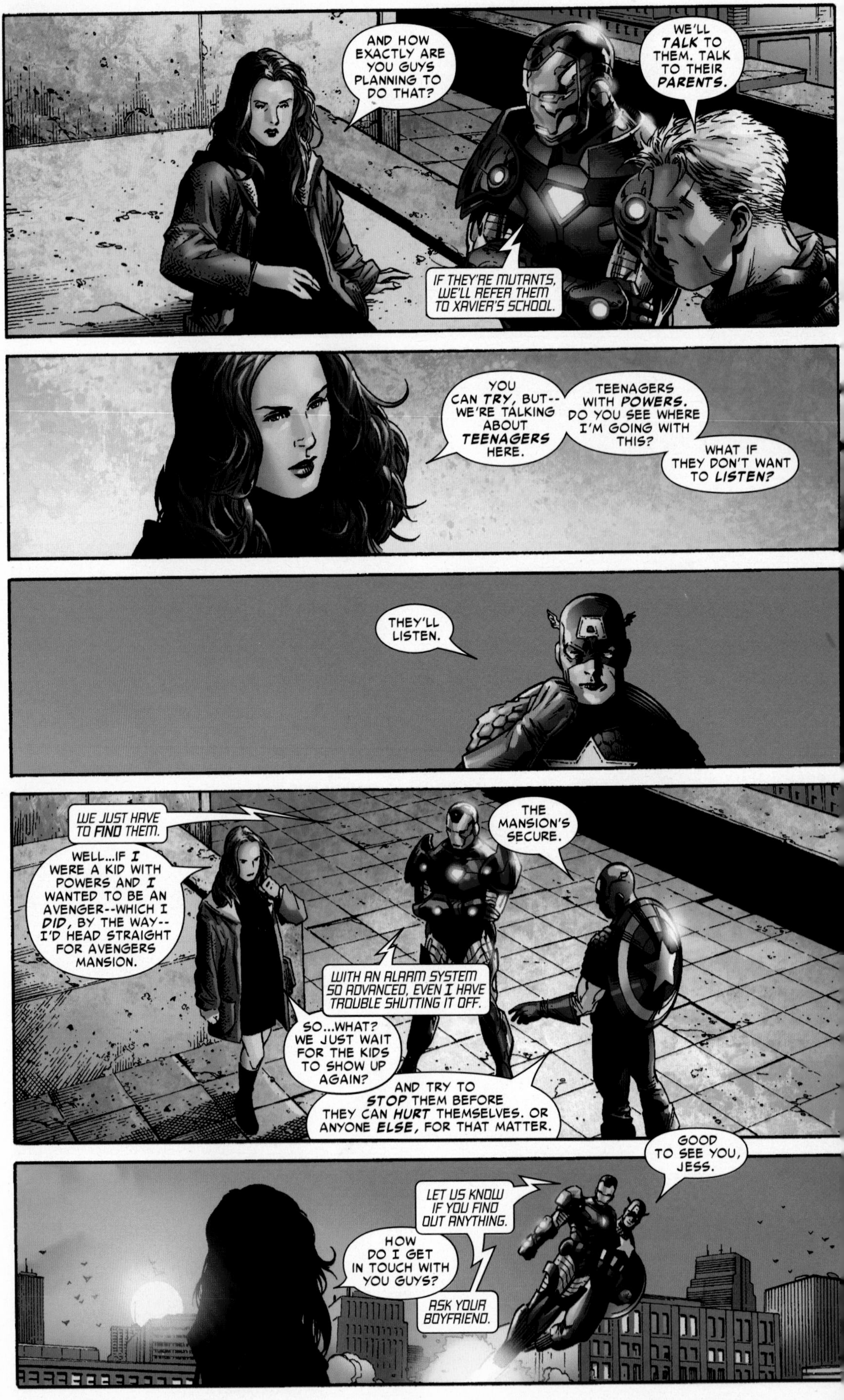
AND HOW EXACTLY ARE YOU GUYS PLANNING TO DO THAT?
WE'LL TALK TO THEM. TALK TO THEIR PARENTS.
IF THEY'RE MUTANTS, WE'LL REFER THEM TO XAVIER'S SCHOOL.
YOU CAN TRY, BUT-- WE'RE TALKING ABOUT TEENAGERS HERE.
TEENAGERS WITH POWERS. DO YOU SEE WHERE I'M GOING WITH THIS?
WHAT IF THEY DON'T WANT TO LISTEN?
THEY'LL LISTEN.
WE JUST HAVE TO FIND THEM.
WELL...IF I WERE A KID WITH POWERS AND I WANTED TO BE AN AVENGER--WHICH I DID, BY THE WAY--I'D HEAD STRAIGHT FOR AVENGERS MANSION.
THE MANSION'S SECURE.
WITH AN ALARM SYSTEM SO ADVANCED, EVEN I HAVE TROUBLE SHUTTING IT OFF.
SO...WHAT? WE JUST WAIT FOR THE KIDS TO SHOW UP AGAIN?
AND TRY TO STOP THEM BEFORE THEY CAN HURT THEMSELVES. OR ANYONE ELSE, FOR THAT MATTER.
GOOD TO SEE YOU, JESS.
LET US KNOW IF YOU FIND OUT ANYTHING.
HOW DO I GET IN TOUCH WITH YOU GUYS?
ASK YOUR BOYFRIEND.

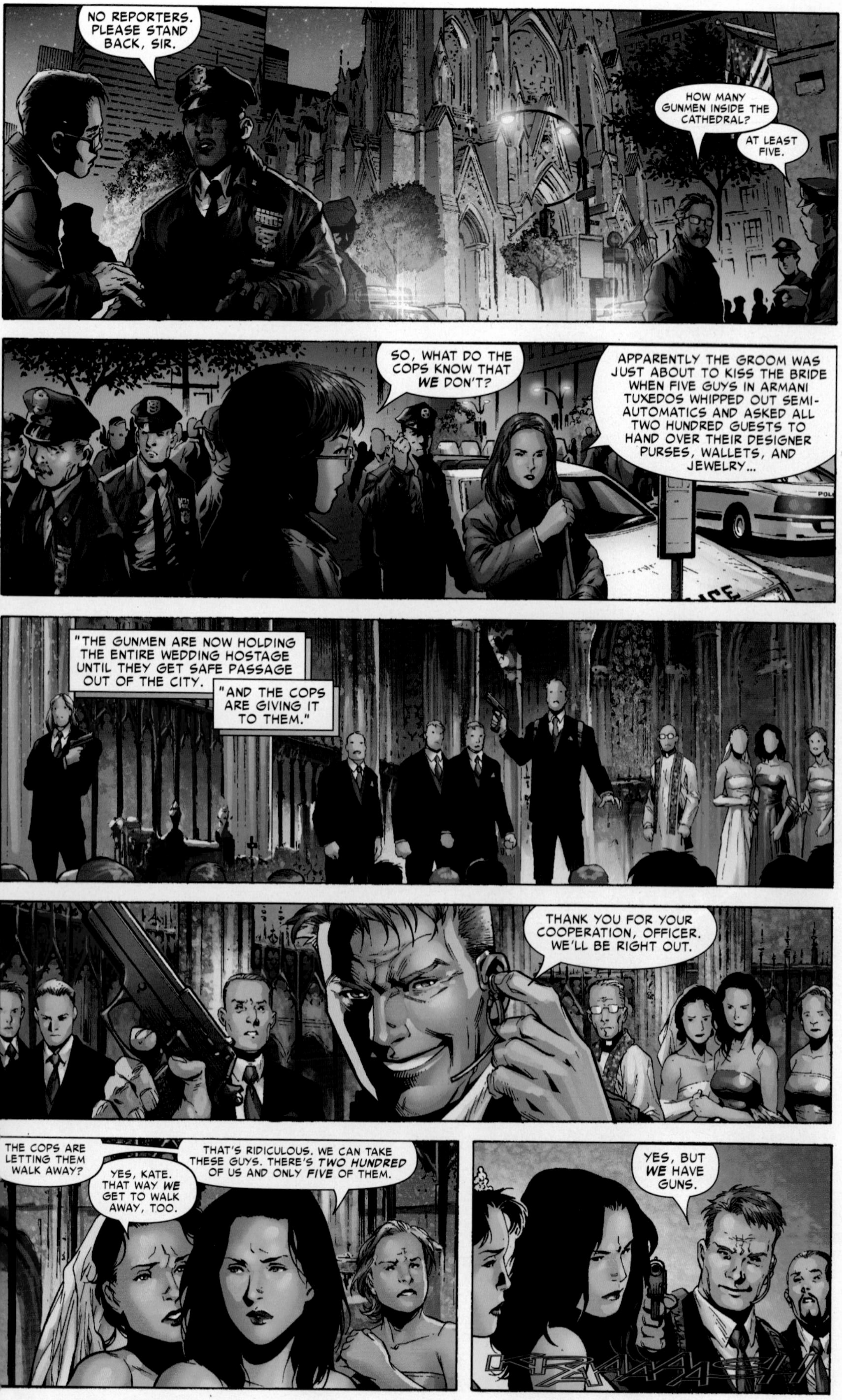
NO REPORTERS. PLEASE STAND BACK, SIR.
HOW MANY GUNMEN INSIDE THE CATHEDRAL?
AT LEAST FIVE.
SO, WHAT DO THE COPS KNOW THAT WE DON'T?
APPARENTLY THE GROOM WAS JUST ABOUT TO KISS THE BRIDE WHEN FIVE GUYS IN ARMANI TUXEDOS WHIPPED OUT SEMI-AUTOMATICS AND ASKED ALL TWO HUNDRED GUESTS TO HAND OVER THEIR DESIGNER PURSES, WALLETS, AND JEWELRY...
"THE GUNMEN ARE NOW HOLDING THE ENTIRE WEDDING HOSTAGE UNTIL THEY GET SAFE PASSAGE OUT OF THE CITY.
"AND THE COPS ARE GIVING IT TO THEM."
THANK YOU FOR YOUR COOPERATION, OFFICER. WE'LL BE RIGHT OUT.
THE COPS ARE LETTING THEM WALK AWAY?
YES, KATE. THAT WAY WE GET TO WALK AWAY, TOO.
THAT'S RIDICULOUS. WE CAN TAKE THESE GUYS. THERE'S TWO HUNDRED OF US AND ONLY FIVE OF THEM.
YES, BUT WE HAVE GUNS.

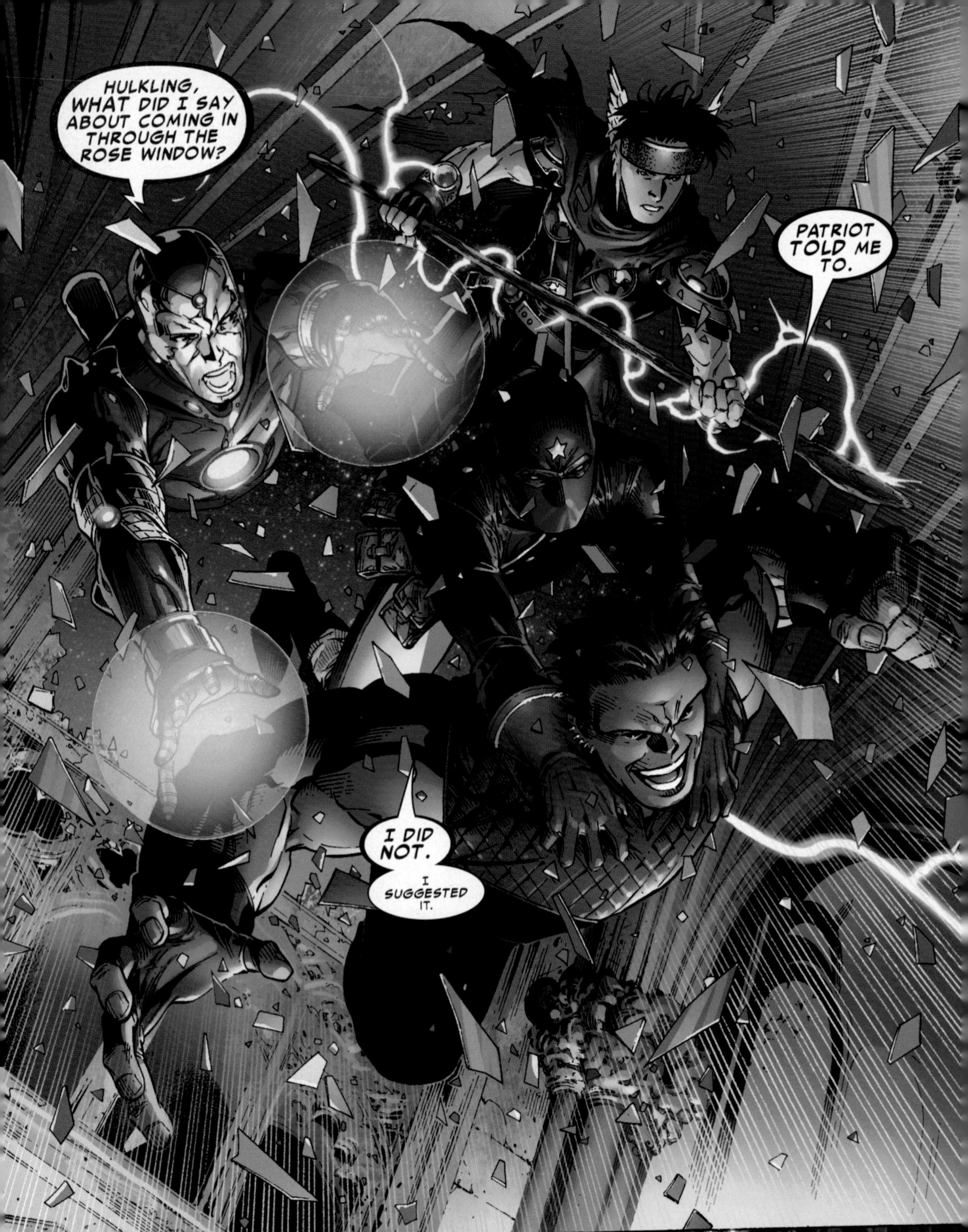
HULKLING, WHAT DID I SAY ABOUT COMING IN THROUGH THE ROSE WINDOW?
PATRIOT TOLD ME TO.
I DID NOT.
I SUGGESTED IT.
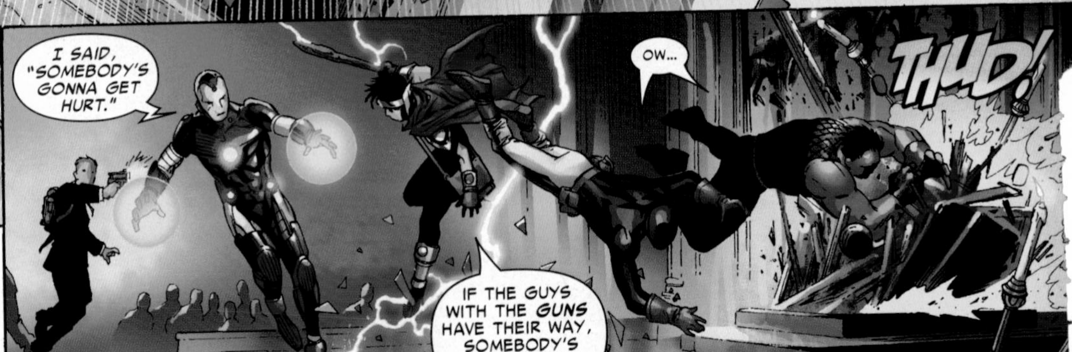
I SAID, "SOMEBODY'S GONNA GET HURT."
OW...
THUD!
IF THE GUYS WITH THE GUNS HAVE THEIR WAY, SOMEBODY'S GONNA GET KILLED.

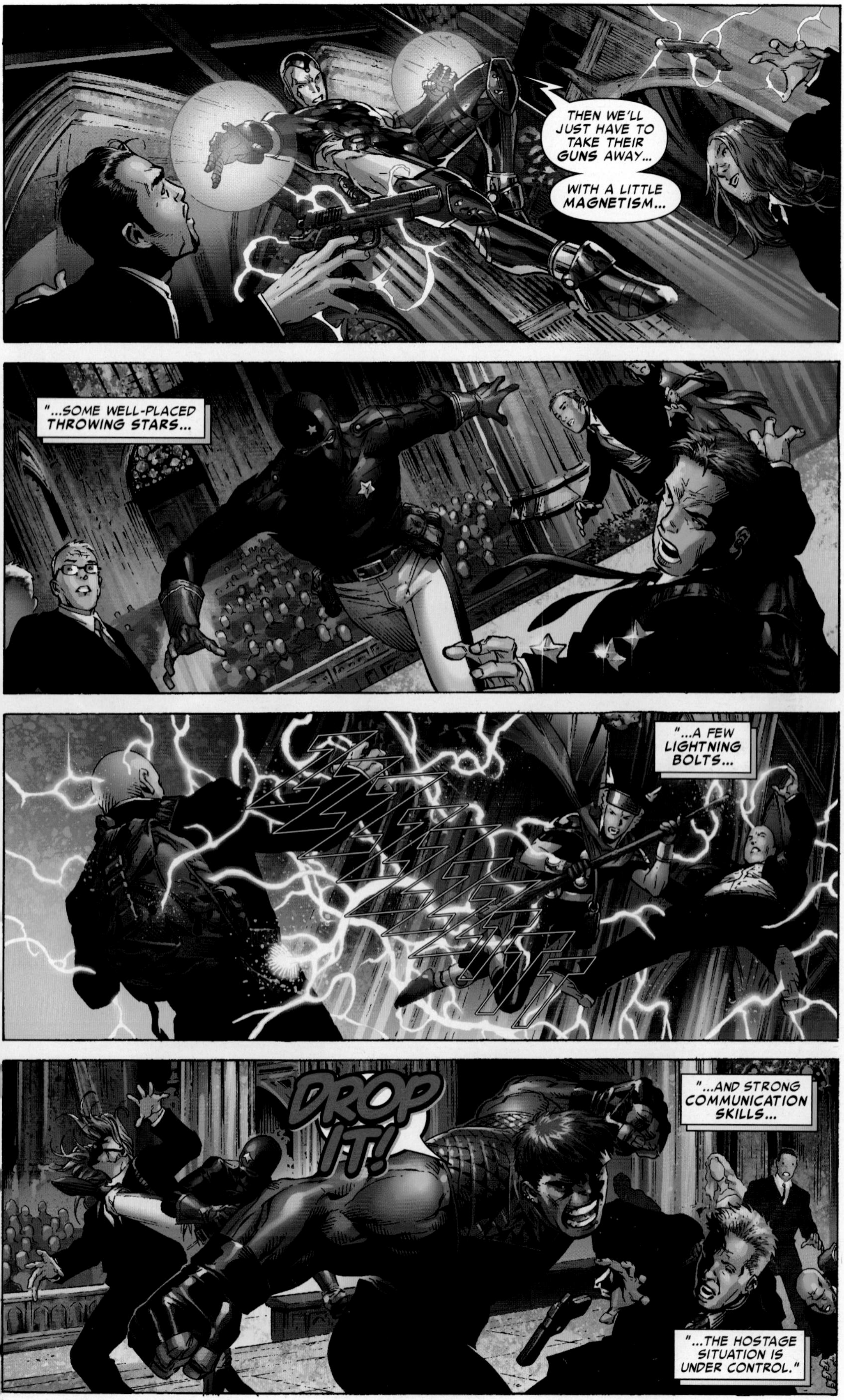

THEN WE'LL JUST HAVE TO TAKE THEIR GUNS AWAY...
WITH A LITTLE MAGNETISM...
"...SOME WELL-PLACED THROWING STARS...
"...A FEW LIGHTNING BOLTS...
DROP IT!
"...AND STRONG COMMUNICATION SKILLS...
"...THE HOSTAGE SITUATION IS UNDER CONTROL."

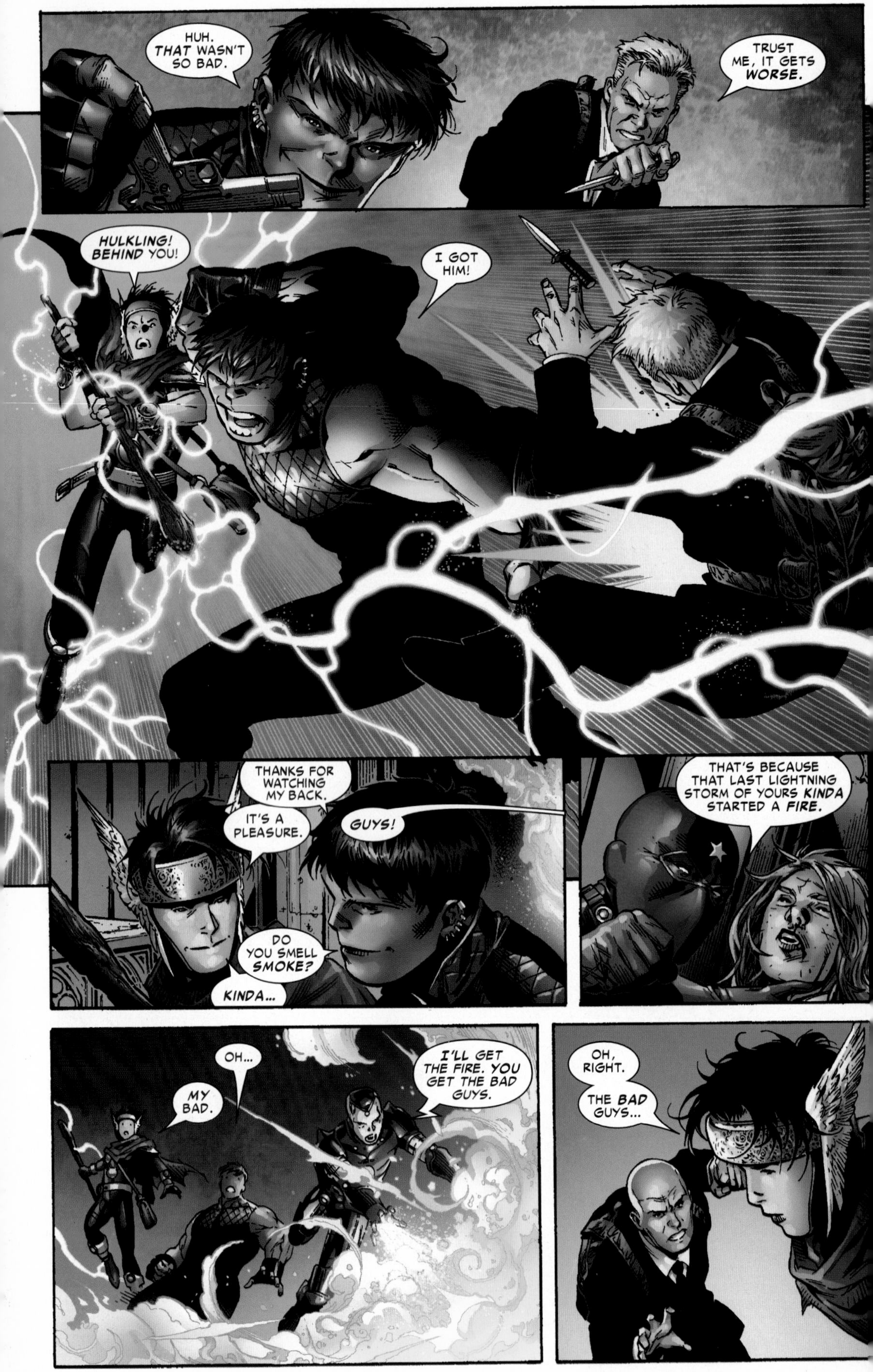
HUH. THAT WASN'T SO BAD.
TRUST ME, IT GETS WORSE.
HULKLING! BEHIND YOU!
I GOT HIM!
THANKS FOR WATCHING MY BACK.
IT'S A PLEASURE.
GUYS!
DO YOU SMELL SMOKE?
KINDA...
THAT'S BECAUSE THAT LAST LIGHTNING STORM OF YOURS KINDA STARTED A FIRE.
OH...
MY BAD.
I'LL GET THE FIRE. YOU GET THE BAD GUYS.
OH, RIGHT.
THE BAD GUYS...

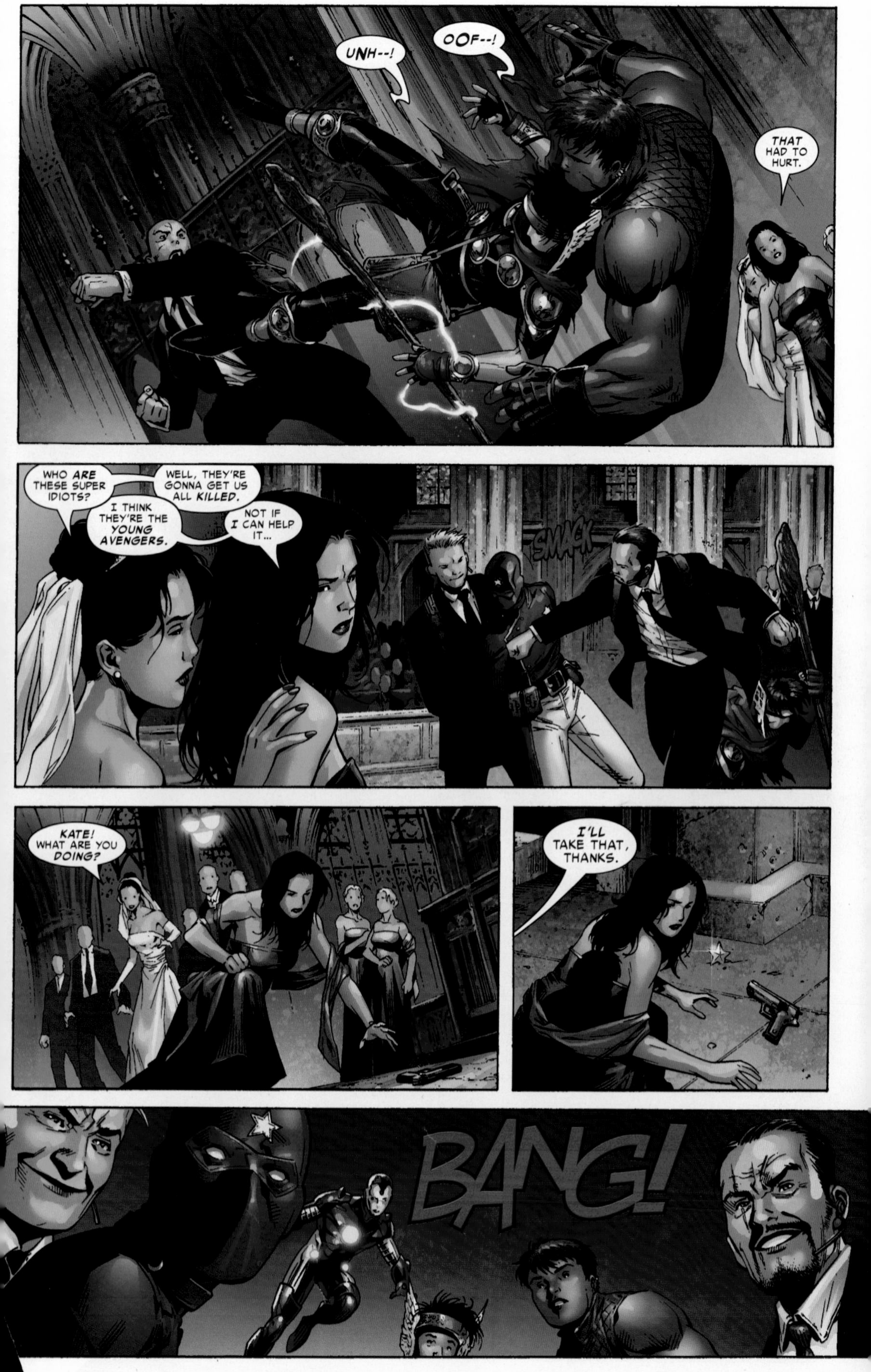
UNH--!
OOF--!
THAT HAD TO HURT.
WHO ARE THESE SUPER IDIOTS?
WELL, THEY'RE GONNA GET US ALL KILLED.
I THINK THEY'RE THE YOUNG AVENGERS.
NOT IF I CAN HELP IT...
SMACK
KATE! WHAT ARE YOU DOING?
I'LL TAKE THAT, THANKS.
BANG!

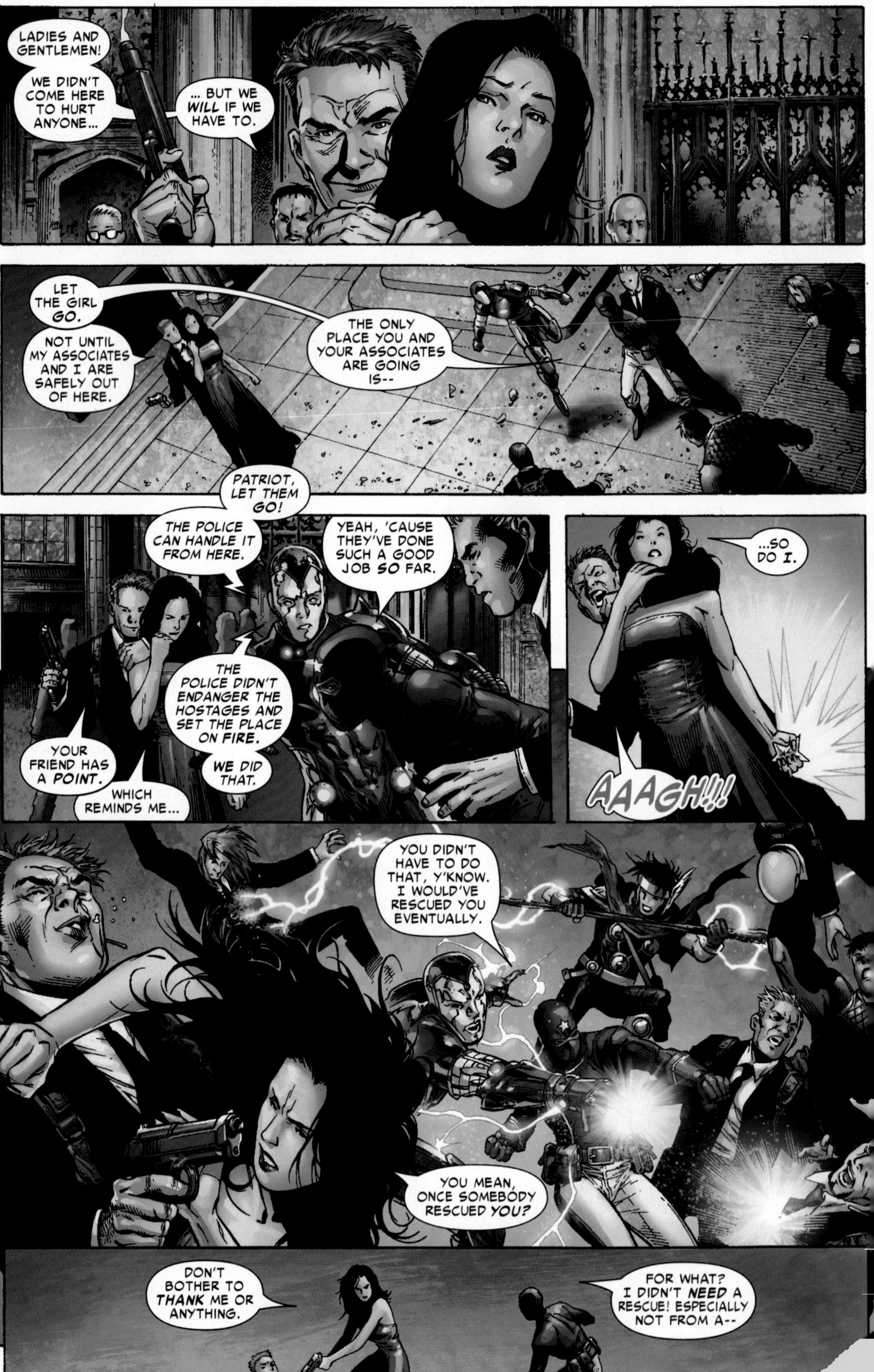
LADIES AND GENTLEMEN!
WE DIDN'T COME HERE TO HURT ANYONE...
... BUT WE *WILL* IF WE HAVE TO.
LET THE GIRL *GO*.
NOT UNTIL MY ASSOCIATES AND I ARE SAFELY OUT OF HERE.
THE ONLY PLACE YOU AND YOUR ASSOCIATES ARE GOING IS--
PATRIOT, LET THEM *GO*!
THE POLICE CAN HANDLE IT FROM HERE.
YEAH, 'CAUSE THEY'VE DONE SUCH A GOOD JOB *SO* FAR.
THE POLICE DIDN'T ENDANGER THE HOSTAGES AND SET THE PLACE ON *FIRE*.
WE DID THAT.
YOUR FRIEND HAS A *POINT*.
WHICH REMINDS ME...
...SO DO *I*.
AAAGH!!!
YOU DIDN'T HAVE TO DO THAT, Y'KNOW. I WOULD'VE RESCUED YOU EVENTUALLY.
YOU MEAN, ONCE SOMEBODY RESCUED *YOU*?
DON'T BOTHER TO *THANK* ME OR ANYTHING.
FOR WHAT? I DIDN'T *NEED* A RESCUE! ESPECIALLY NOT FROM A--
YOU *WILL* IF YOU FINISH THAT SENTENCE.

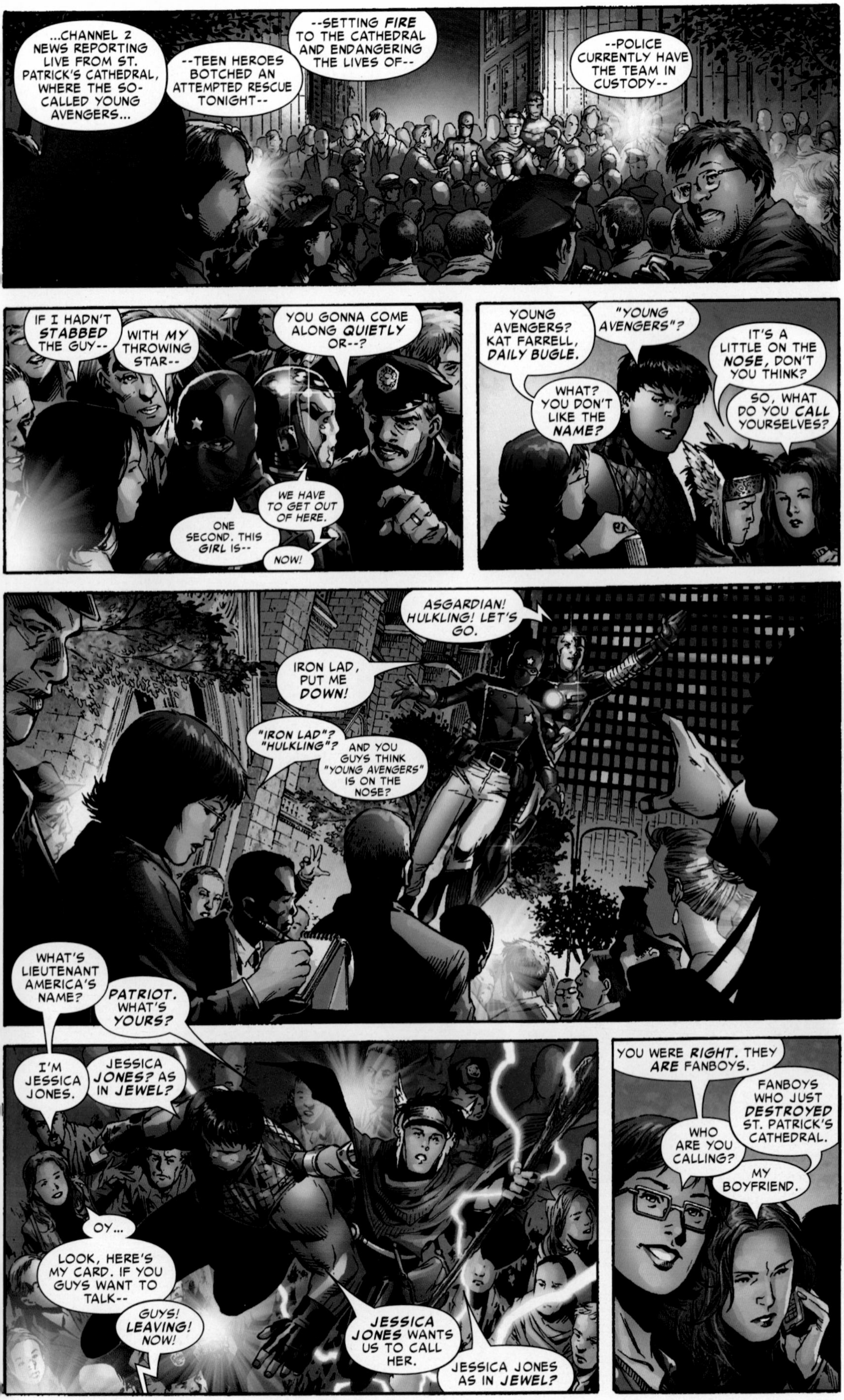
...CHANNEL 2 NEWS REPORTING LIVE FROM ST. PATRICK'S CATHEDRAL, WHERE THE SO-CALLED YOUNG AVENGERS...
--TEEN HEROES BOTCHED AN ATTEMPTED RESCUE TONIGHT--
--SETTING FIRE TO THE CATHEDRAL AND ENDANGERING THE LIVES OF--
--POLICE CURRENTLY HAVE THE TEAM IN CUSTODY--
IF I HADN'T STABBED THE GUY--
WITH MY THROWING STAR--
YOU GONNA COME ALONG QUIETLY OR--?
WE HAVE TO GET OUT OF HERE.
ONE SECOND. THIS GIRL IS--
NOW!
YOUNG AVENGERS? KAT FARRELL, DAILY BUGLE.
"YOUNG AVENGERS"?
WHAT? YOU DON'T LIKE THE NAME?
IT'S A LITTLE ON THE NOSE, DON'T YOU THINK?
SO, WHAT DO YOU CALL YOURSELVES?
ASGARDIAN! HULKLING! LET'S GO.
IRON LAD, PUT ME DOWN!
"IRON LAD"? "HULKLING"? AND YOU GUYS THINK "YOUNG AVENGERS" IS ON THE NOSE?
WHAT'S LIEUTENANT AMERICA'S NAME?
PATRIOT. WHAT'S YOURS?
I'M JESSICA JONES.
JESSICA JONES? AS IN JEWEL?
OY...
LOOK, HERE'S MY CARD. IF YOU GUYS WANT TO TALK--
GUYS! LEAVING! NOW!
JESSICA JONES WANTS US TO CALL HER.
JESSICA JONES AS IN JEWEL?
YOU WERE RIGHT. THEY ARE FANBOYS.
FANBOYS WHO JUST DESTROYED ST. PATRICK'S CATHEDRAL.
WHO ARE YOU CALLING?
MY BOYFRIEND.

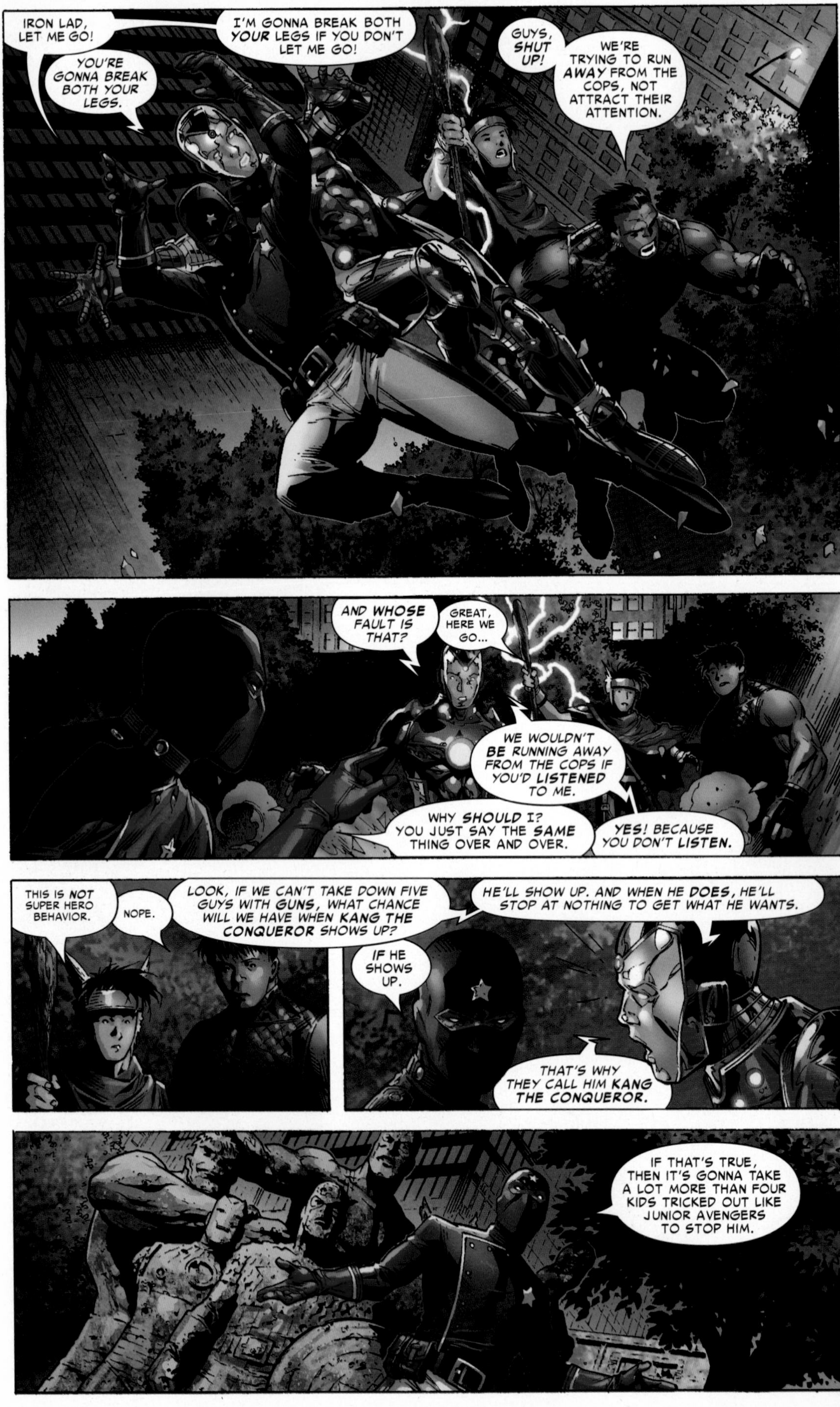
IRON LAD, LET ME GO!
I'M GONNA BREAK BOTH YOUR LEGS IF YOU DON'T LET ME GO!
YOU'RE GONNA BREAK BOTH YOUR LEGS.
GUYS, SHUT UP!
WE'RE TRYING TO RUN AWAY FROM THE COPS, NOT ATTRACT THEIR ATTENTION.
AND WHOSE FAULT IS THAT?
GREAT, HERE WE GO...
WE WOULDN'T BE RUNNING AWAY FROM THE COPS IF YOU'D LISTENED TO ME.
WHY SHOULD I? YOU JUST SAY THE SAME THING OVER AND OVER.
YES! BECAUSE YOU DON'T LISTEN.
THIS IS NOT SUPER HERO BEHAVIOR.
NOPE.
LOOK, IF WE CAN'T TAKE DOWN FIVE GUYS WITH GUNS, WHAT CHANCE WILL WE HAVE WHEN KANG THE CONQUEROR SHOWS UP?
IF HE SHOWS UP.
HE'LL SHOW UP. AND WHEN HE DOES, HE'LL STOP AT NOTHING TO GET WHAT HE WANTS.
THAT'S WHY THEY CALL HIM KANG THE CONQUEROR.
IF THAT'S TRUE, THEN IT'S GONNA TAKE A LOT MORE THAN FOUR KIDS TRICKED OUT LIKE JUNIOR AVENGERS TO STOP HIM.

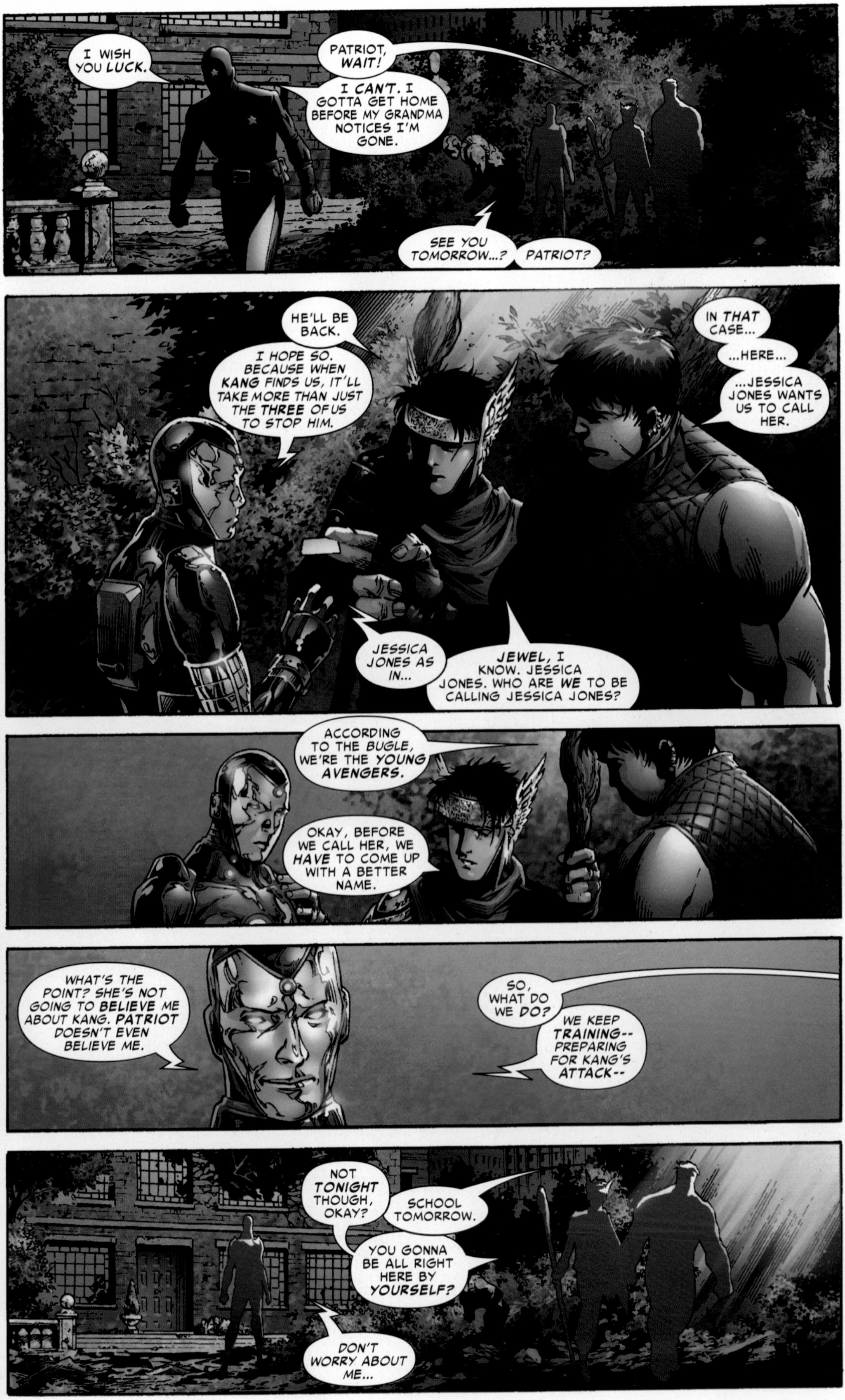
I WISH YOU LUCK.
PATRIOT, WAIT!
I CAN'T. I GOTTA GET HOME BEFORE MY GRANDMA NOTICES I'M GONE.
SEE YOU TOMORROW...?
PATRIOT?
HE'LL BE BACK.
I HOPE SO. BECAUSE WHEN KANG FINDS US, IT'LL TAKE MORE THAN JUST THE THREE OF US TO STOP HIM.
IN THAT CASE...
...HERE...
...JESSICA JONES WANTS US TO CALL HER.
JESSICA JONES AS IN...
JEWEL, I KNOW. JESSICA JONES. WHO ARE WE TO BE CALLING JESSICA JONES?
ACCORDING TO THE BUGLE, WE'RE THE YOUNG AVENGERS.
OKAY, BEFORE WE CALL HER, WE HAVE TO COME UP WITH A BETTER NAME.
WHAT'S THE POINT? SHE'S NOT GOING TO BELIEVE ME ABOUT KANG. PATRIOT DOESN'T EVEN BELIEVE ME.
SO, WHAT DO WE DO?
WE KEEP TRAINING-- PREPARING FOR KANG'S ATTACK--
NOT TONIGHT THOUGH, OKAY?
SCHOOL TOMORROW.
YOU GONNA BE ALL RIGHT HERE BY YOURSELF?
DON'T WORRY ABOUT ME...

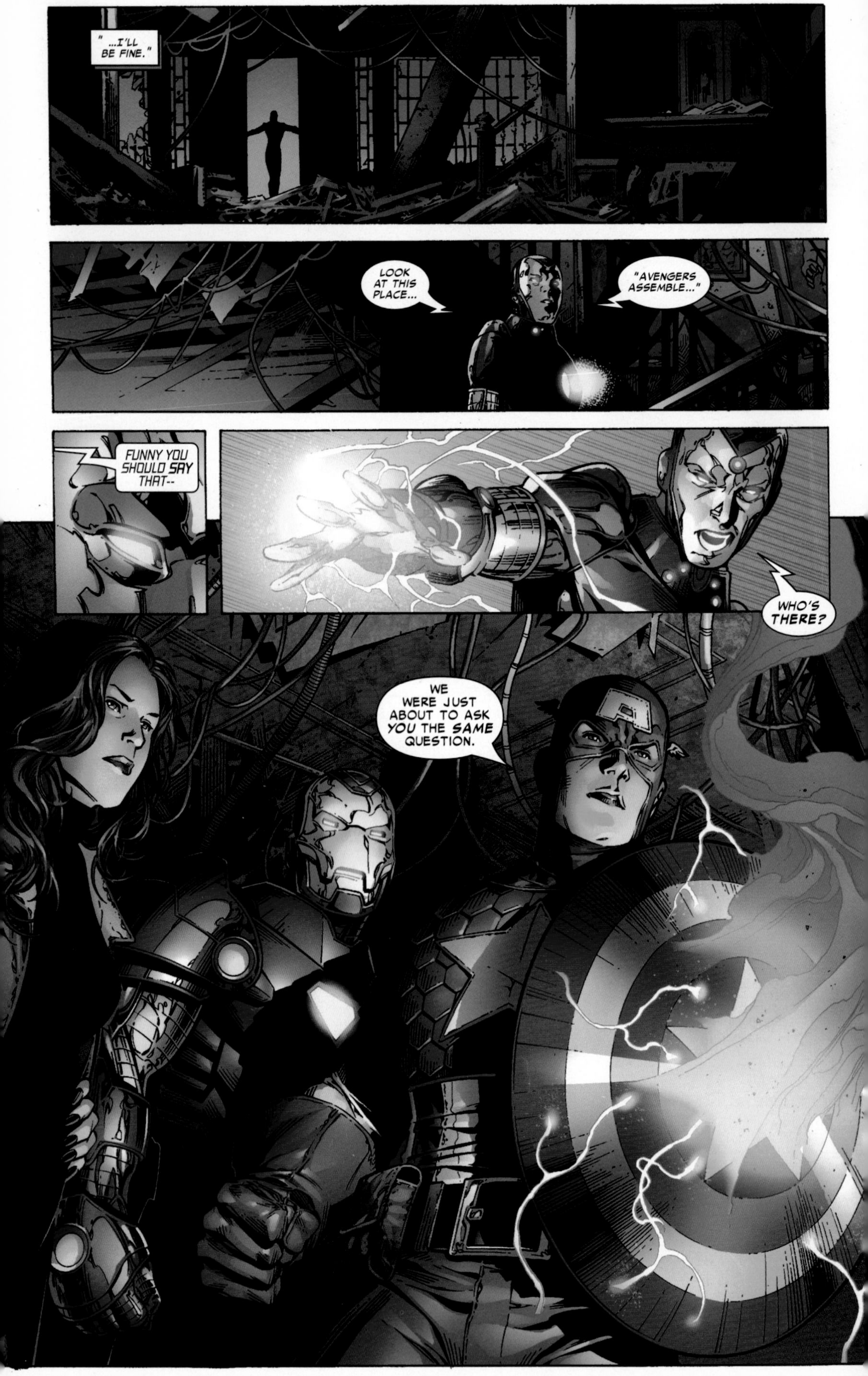
"...I'LL BE FINE."
LOOK AT THIS PLACE...
"AVENGERS ASSEMBLE..."
FUNNY YOU SHOULD SAY THAT--
WHO'S THERE?
WE WERE JUST ABOUT TO ASK YOU THE SAME QUESTION.

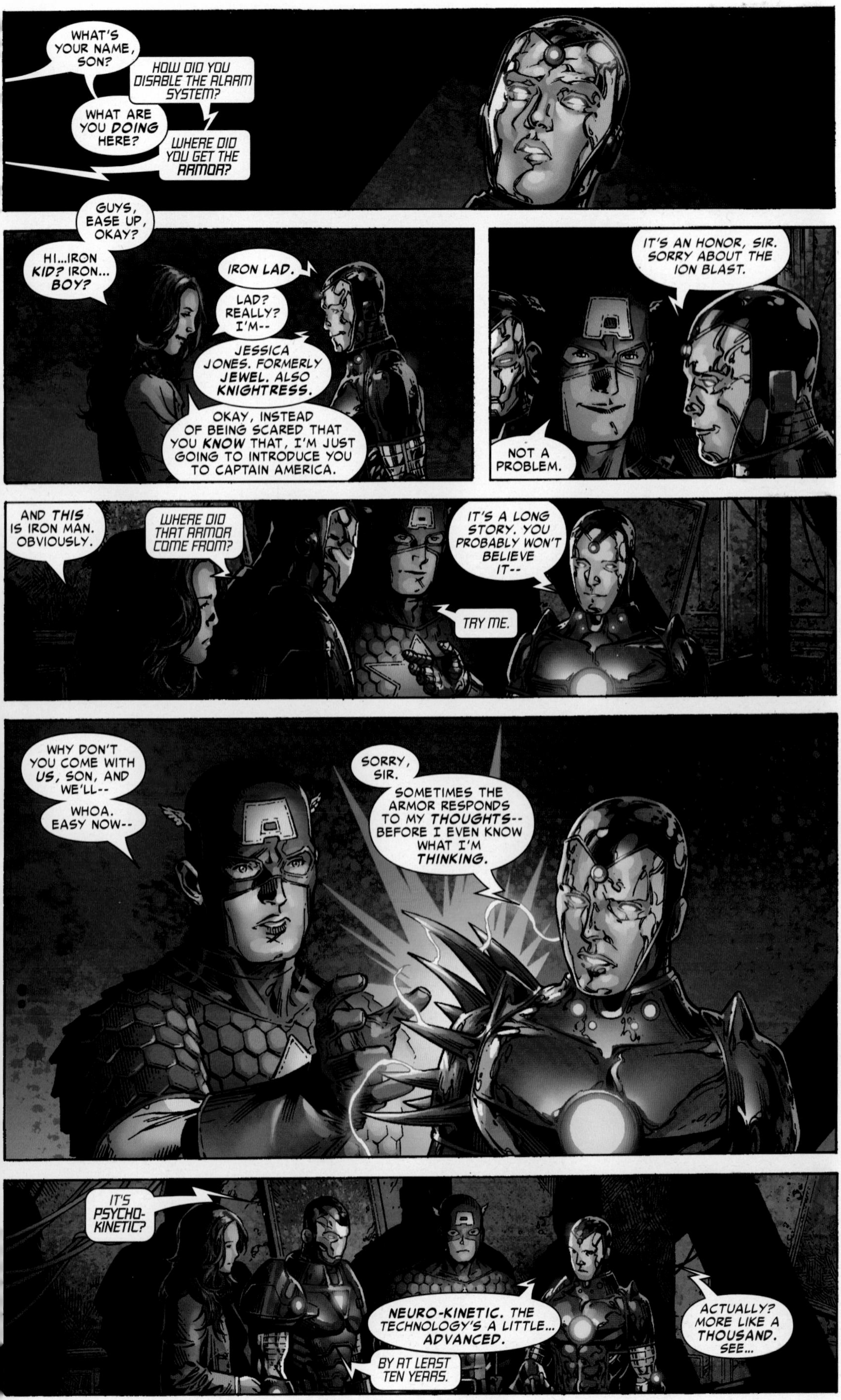
WHAT'S YOUR NAME, SON?
HOW DID YOU DISABLE THE ALARM SYSTEM?
WHAT ARE YOU DOING HERE?
WHERE DID YOU GET THE ARMOR?
GUYS, EASE UP, OKAY?
HI...IRON KID? IRON... BOY?
IRON LAD.
LAD? REALLY? I'M--
JESSICA JONES. FORMERLY JEWEL. ALSO KNIGHTRESS.
OKAY, INSTEAD OF BEING SCARED THAT YOU KNOW THAT, I'M JUST GOING TO INTRODUCE YOU TO CAPTAIN AMERICA.
IT'S AN HONOR, SIR. SORRY ABOUT THE ION BLAST.
NOT A PROBLEM.
AND THIS IS IRON MAN. OBVIOUSLY.
WHERE DID THAT ARMOR COME FROM?
IT'S A LONG STORY. YOU PROBABLY WON'T BELIEVE IT--
TRY ME.
WHY DON'T YOU COME WITH US, SON, AND WE'LL--
WHOA. EASY NOW--
SORRY, SIR.
SOMETIMES THE ARMOR RESPONDS TO MY THOUGHTS-- BEFORE I EVEN KNOW WHAT I'M THINKING.
IT'S PSYCHO-KINETIC?
NEURO-KINETIC. THE TECHNOLOGY'S A LITTLE... ADVANCED.
BY AT LEAST TEN YEARS.
ACTUALLY? MORE LIKE A THOUSAND. SEE...

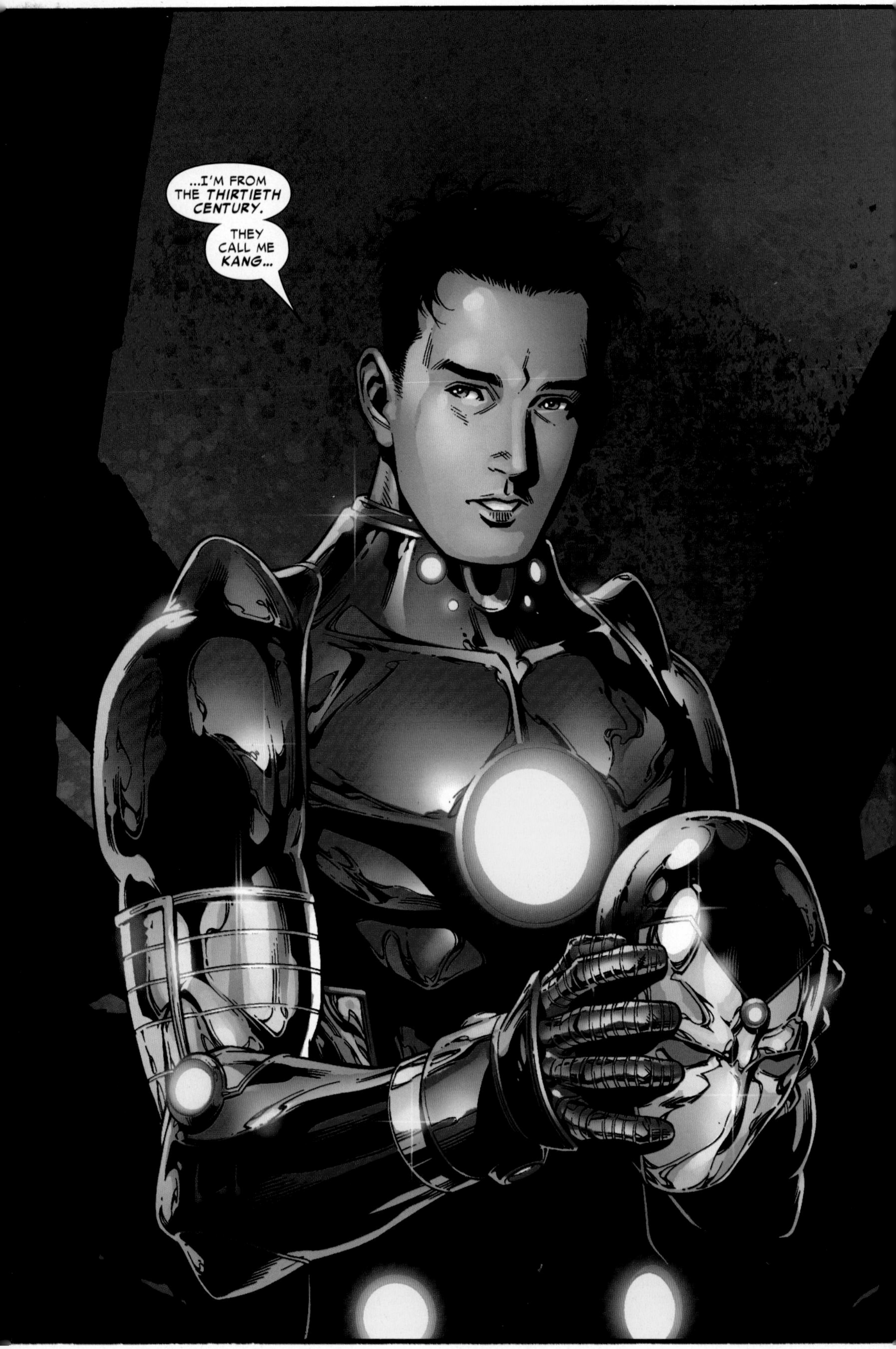
...I'M FROM THE *THIRTIETH CENTURY*.
THEY CALL ME *KANG*...

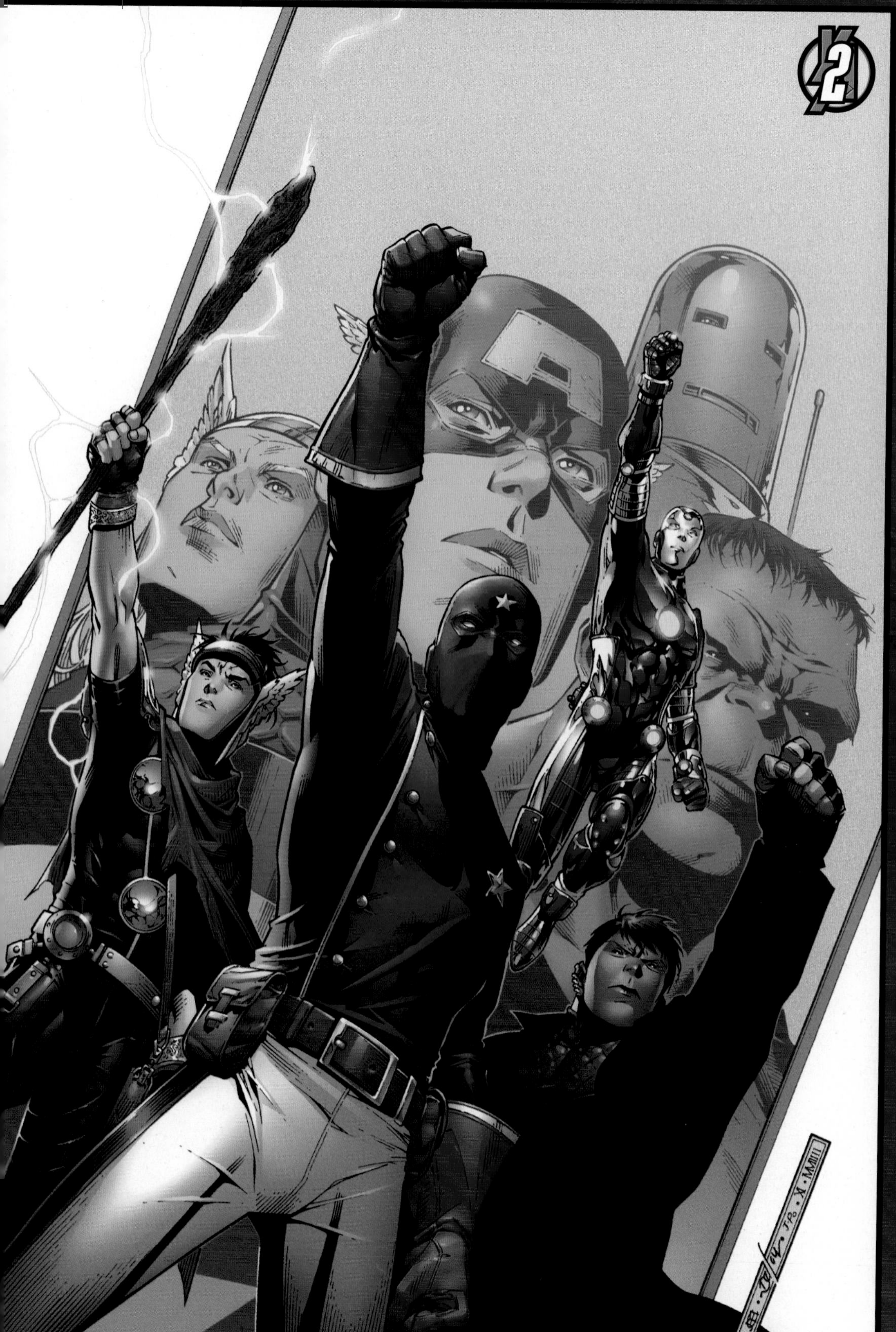

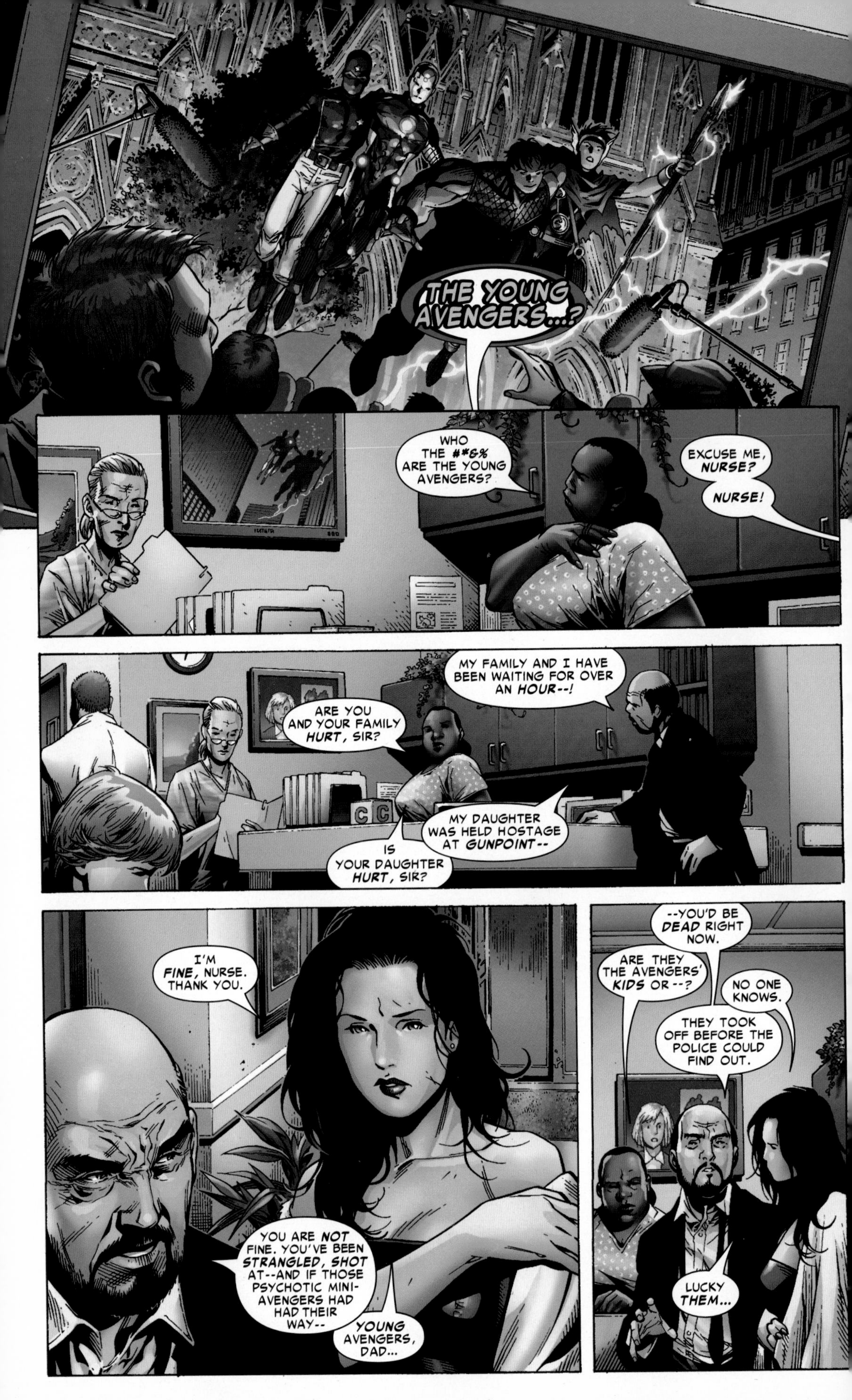
THE YOUNG AVENGERS...?
WHO THE #*&% ARE THE YOUNG AVENGERS?
EXCUSE ME, NURSE?
NURSE!
MY FAMILY AND I HAVE BEEN WAITING FOR OVER AN HOUR--!
ARE YOU AND YOUR FAMILY HURT, SIR?
MY DAUGHTER WAS HELD HOSTAGE AT GUNPOINT--
IS YOUR DAUGHTER HURT, SIR?
I'M FINE, NURSE. THANK YOU.
YOU ARE NOT FINE. YOU'VE BEEN STRANGLED, SHOT AT--AND IF THOSE PSYCHOTIC MINI-AVENGERS HAD HAD THEIR WAY--
YOUNG AVENGERS, DAD...
--YOU'D BE DEAD RIGHT NOW.
ARE THEY THE AVENGERS' KIDS OR--?
NO ONE KNOWS.
THEY TOOK OFF BEFORE THE POLICE COULD FIND OUT.
LUCKY THEM...

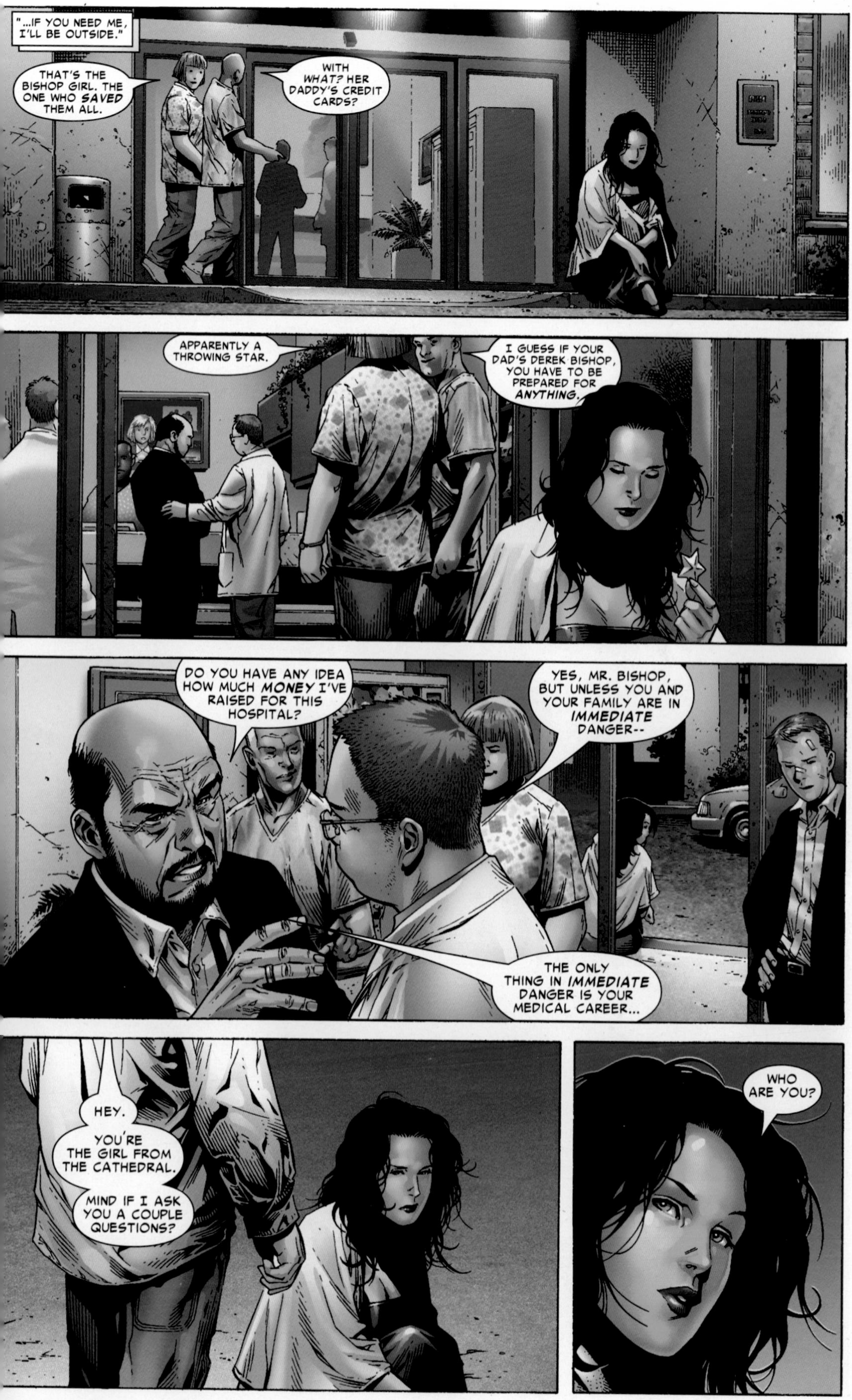
"...IF YOU NEED ME, I'LL BE OUTSIDE."
THAT'S THE BISHOP GIRL. THE ONE WHO SAVED THEM ALL.
WITH WHAT? HER DADDY'S CREDIT CARDS?
APPARENTLY A THROWING STAR.
I GUESS IF YOUR DAD'S DEREK BISHOP, YOU HAVE TO BE PREPARED FOR ANYTHING.
DO YOU HAVE ANY IDEA HOW MUCH MONEY I'VE RAISED FOR THIS HOSPITAL?
YES, MR. BISHOP, BUT UNLESS YOU AND YOUR FAMILY ARE IN IMMEDIATE DANGER--
THE ONLY THING IN IMMEDIATE DANGER IS YOUR MEDICAL CAREER...
HEY.
YOU'RE THE GIRL FROM THE CATHEDRAL.
MIND IF I ASK YOU A COUPLE QUESTIONS?
WHO ARE YOU?

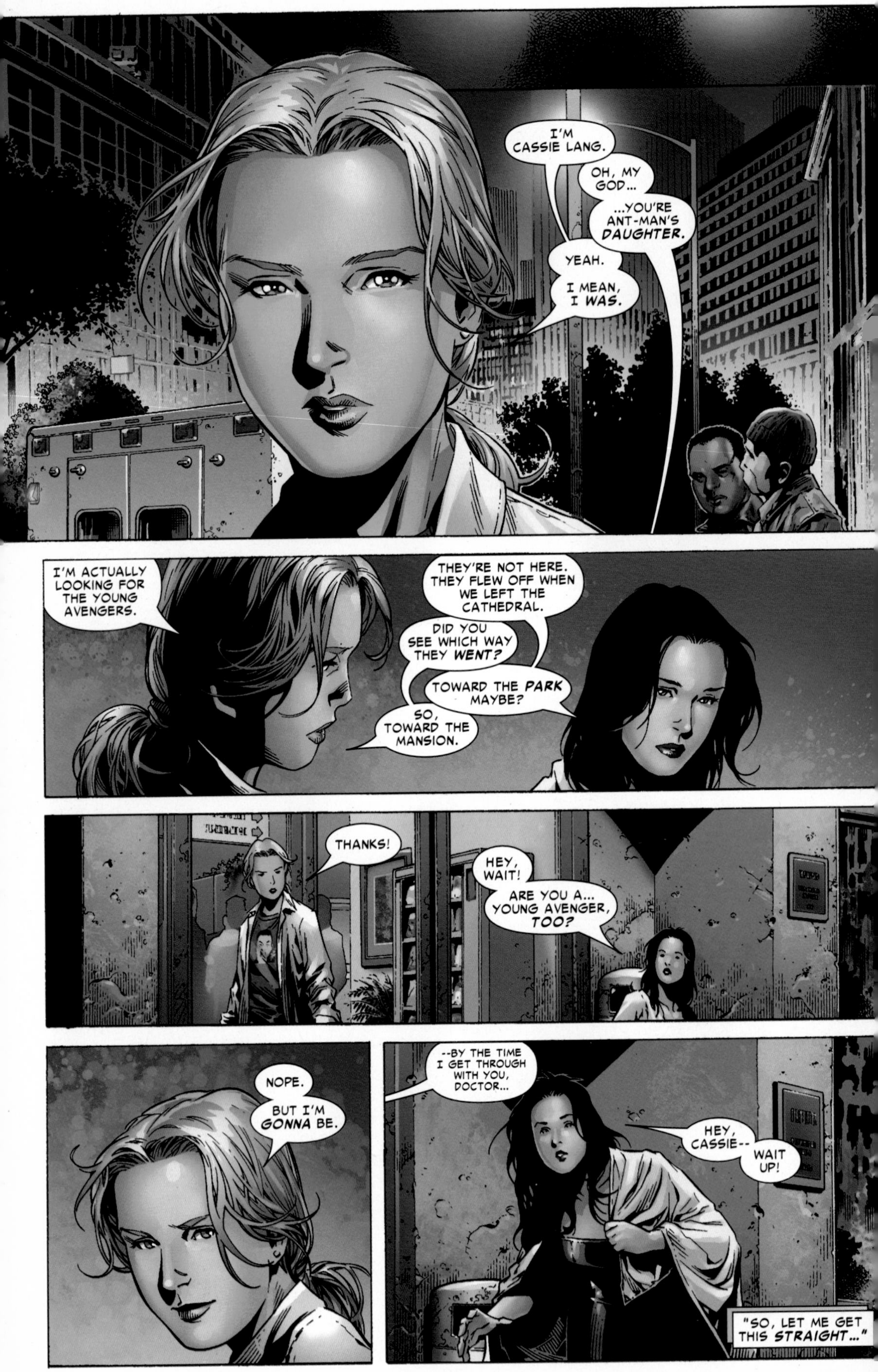
I'M CASSIE LANG.
OH, MY GOD...
...YOU'RE ANT-MAN'S DAUGHTER.
YEAH.
I MEAN, I WAS.
I'M ACTUALLY LOOKING FOR THE YOUNG AVENGERS.
THEY'RE NOT HERE. THEY FLEW OFF WHEN WE LEFT THE CATHEDRAL.
DID YOU SEE WHICH WAY THEY WENT?
TOWARD THE PARK MAYBE?
SO, TOWARD THE MANSION.
THANKS!
HEY, WAIT!
ARE YOU A... YOUNG AVENGER, TOO?
NOPE.
BUT I'M GONNA BE.
--BY THE TIME I GET THROUGH WITH YOU, DOCTOR...
HEY, CASSIE--
WAIT UP!
"SO, LET ME GET THIS STRAIGHT..."

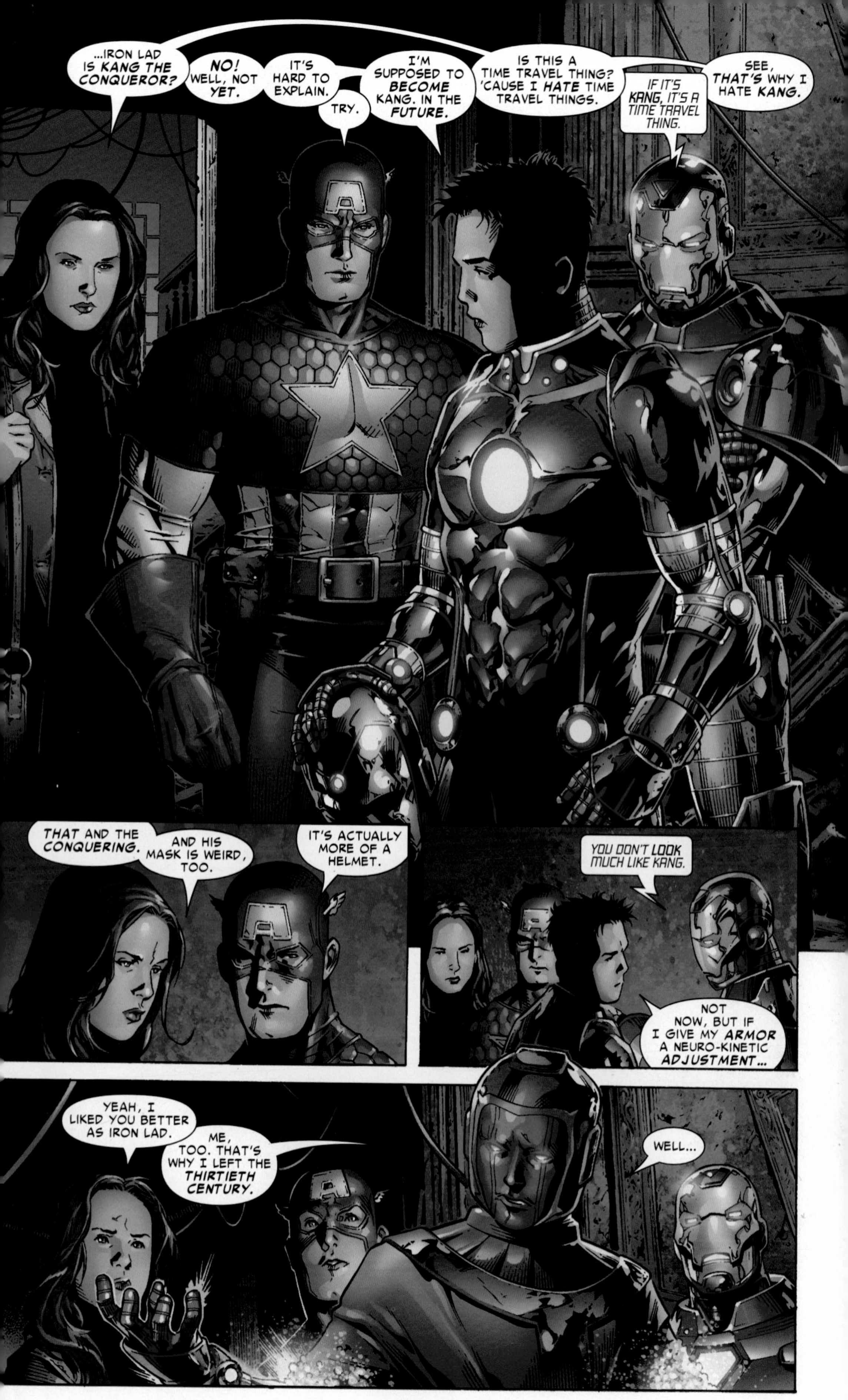

...IRON LAD IS KANG THE CONQUEROR?
NO! WELL, NOT YET.
IT'S HARD TO EXPLAIN.
TRY.
I'M SUPPOSED TO BECOME KANG. IN THE FUTURE.
IS THIS A TIME TRAVEL THING? 'CAUSE I HATE TIME TRAVEL THINGS.
IF IT'S KANG, IT'S A TIME TRAVEL THING.
SEE, THAT'S WHY I HATE KANG.
THAT AND THE CONQUERING.
AND HIS MASK IS WEIRD, TOO.
IT'S ACTUALLY MORE OF A HELMET.
YOU DON'T LOOK MUCH LIKE KANG.
NOT NOW, BUT IF I GIVE MY ARMOR A NEURO-KINETIC ADJUSTMENT...
YEAH, I LIKED YOU BETTER AS IRON LAD.
ME, TOO. THAT'S WHY I LEFT THE THIRTIETH CENTURY.
WELL...

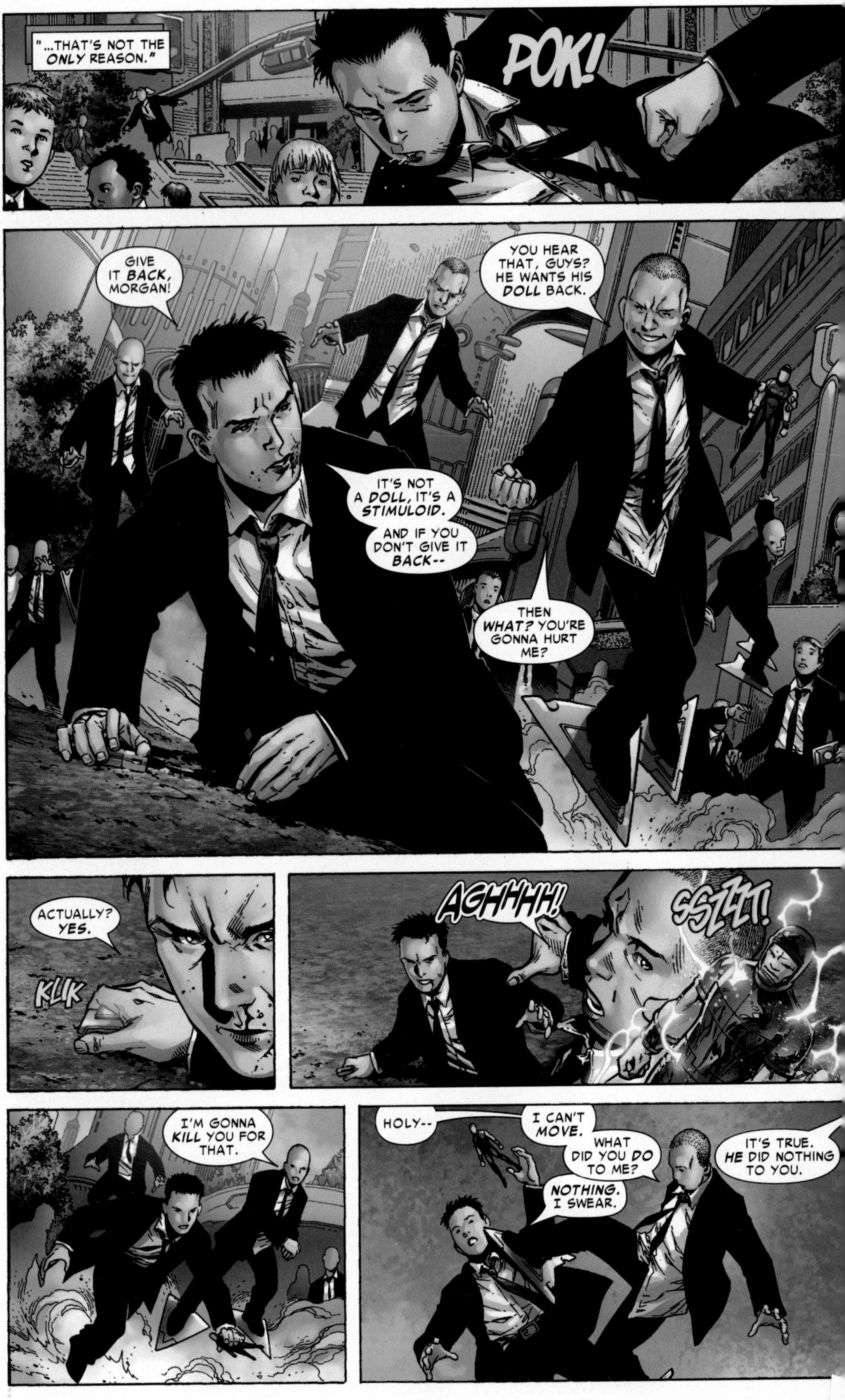
"...THAT'S NOT THE ONLY REASON."
POK!
GIVE IT BACK, MORGAN!
YOU HEAR THAT, GUYS? HE WANTS HIS DOLL BACK.
IT'S NOT A DOLL, IT'S A STIMULOID.
AND IF YOU DON'T GIVE IT BACK--
THEN WHAT? YOU'RE GONNA HURT ME?
ACTUALLY? YES.
KLIK
AGHHHH!
SSZZZT!
I'M GONNA KILL YOU FOR THAT.
HOLY--
I CAN'T MOVE.
WHAT DID YOU DO TO ME?
NOTHING. I SWEAR.
IT'S TRUE. HE DID NOTHING TO YOU.

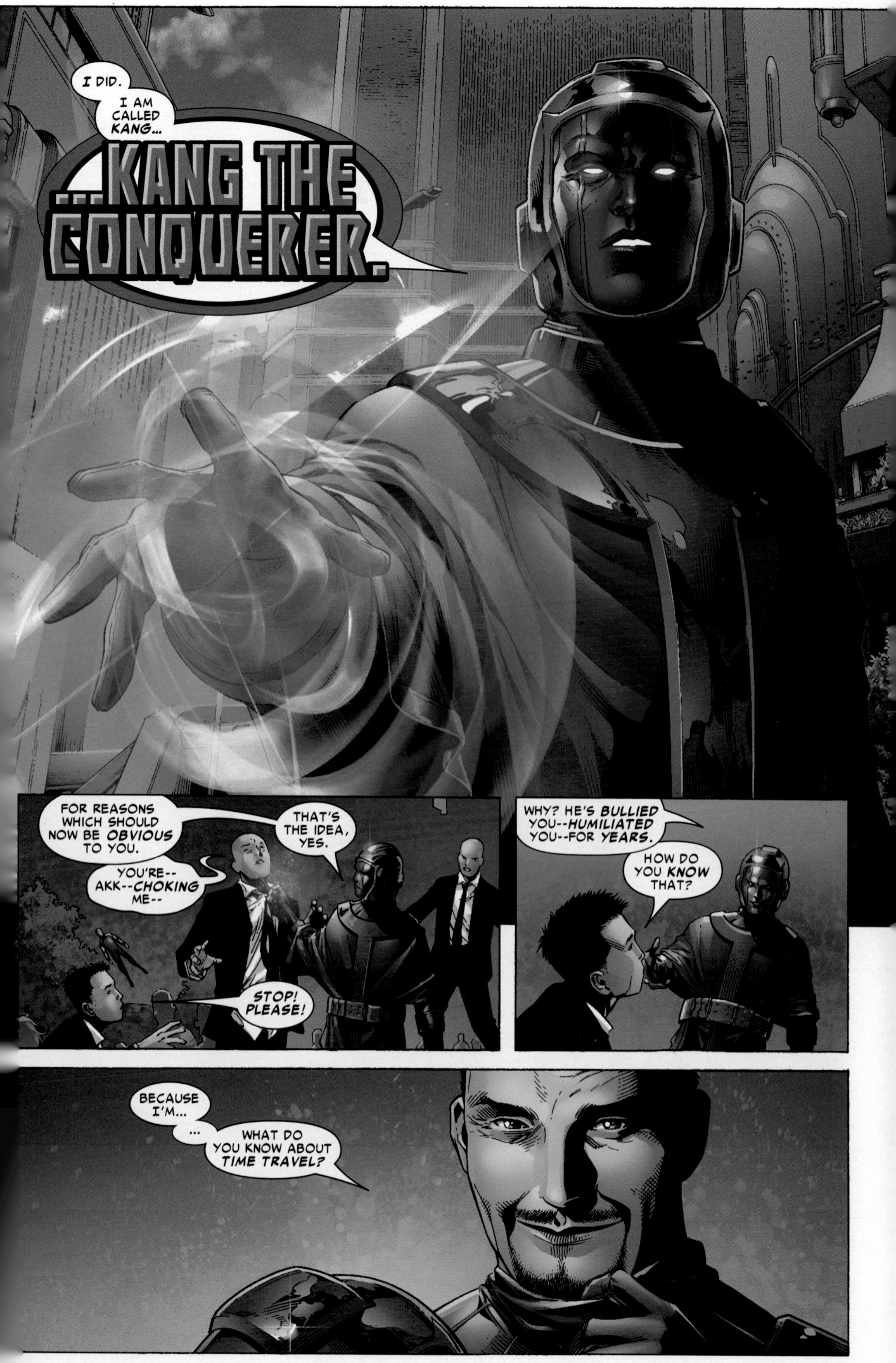
I DID.
I AM CALLED KANG...
...KANG THE CONQUERER.
FOR REASONS WHICH SHOULD NOW BE OBVIOUS TO YOU.
YOU'RE-- AKK--CHOKING ME--
THAT'S THE IDEA, YES.
STOP! PLEASE!
WHY? HE'S BULLIED YOU--HUMILIATED YOU--FOR YEARS.
HOW DO YOU KNOW THAT?
BECAUSE I'M...
...
WHAT DO YOU KNOW ABOUT TIME TRAVEL?

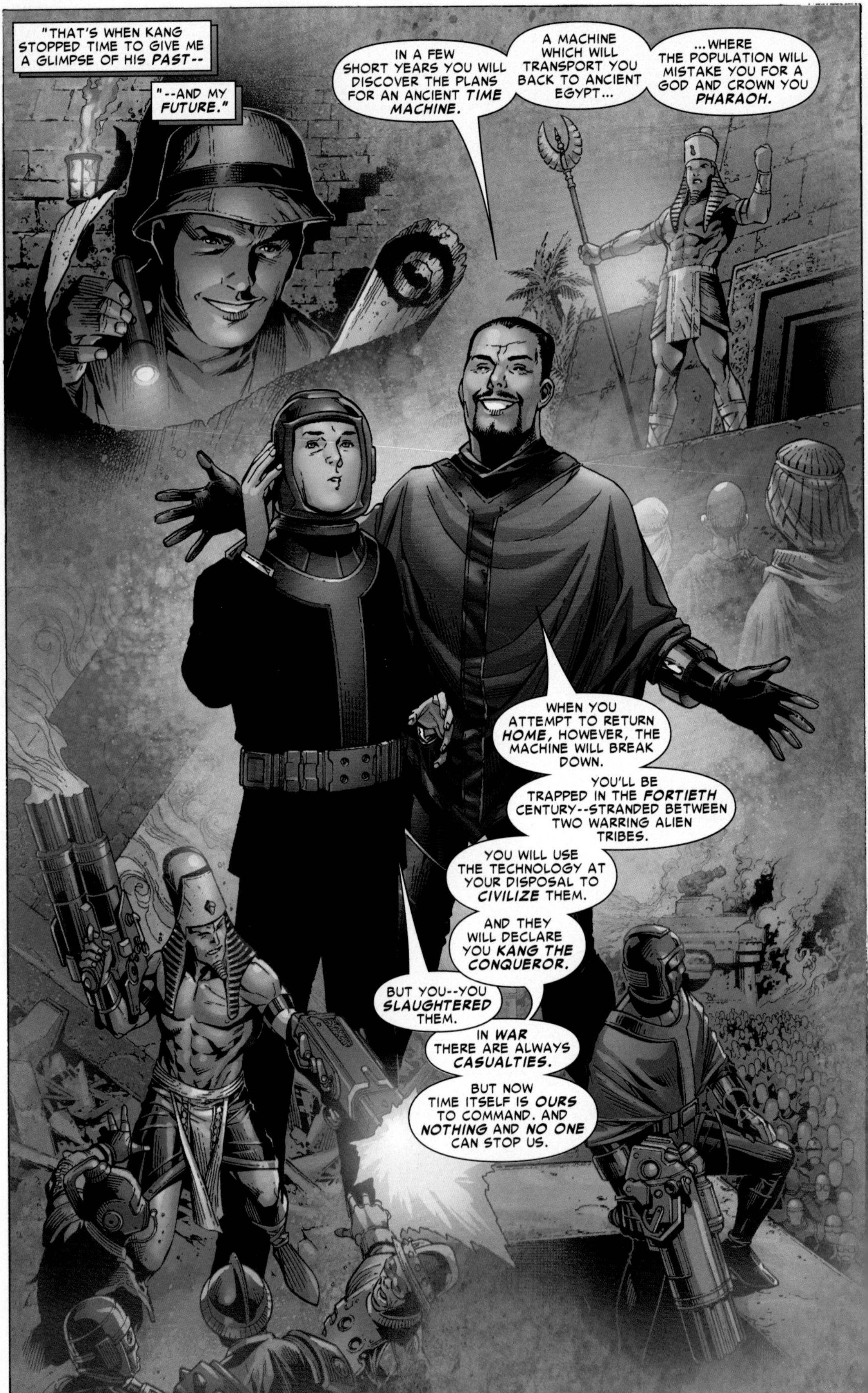
"THAT'S WHEN KANG STOPPED TIME TO GIVE ME A GLIMPSE OF HIS PAST--
"--AND MY FUTURE."
IN A FEW SHORT YEARS YOU WILL DISCOVER THE PLANS FOR AN ANCIENT TIME MACHINE.
A MACHINE WHICH WILL TRANSPORT YOU BACK TO ANCIENT EGYPT...
...WHERE THE POPULATION WILL MISTAKE YOU FOR A GOD AND CROWN YOU PHARAOH.
WHEN YOU ATTEMPT TO RETURN HOME, HOWEVER, THE MACHINE WILL BREAK DOWN.
YOU'LL BE TRAPPED IN THE FORTIETH CENTURY--STRANDED BETWEEN TWO WARRING ALIEN TRIBES.
YOU WILL USE THE TECHNOLOGY AT YOUR DISPOSAL TO CIVILIZE THEM.
AND THEY WILL DECLARE YOU KANG THE CONQUEROR.
BUT YOU--YOU SLAUGHTERED THEM.
IN WAR THERE ARE ALWAYS CASUALTIES.
BUT NOW TIME ITSELF IS OURS TO COMMAND. AND NOTHING AND NO ONE CAN STOP US.

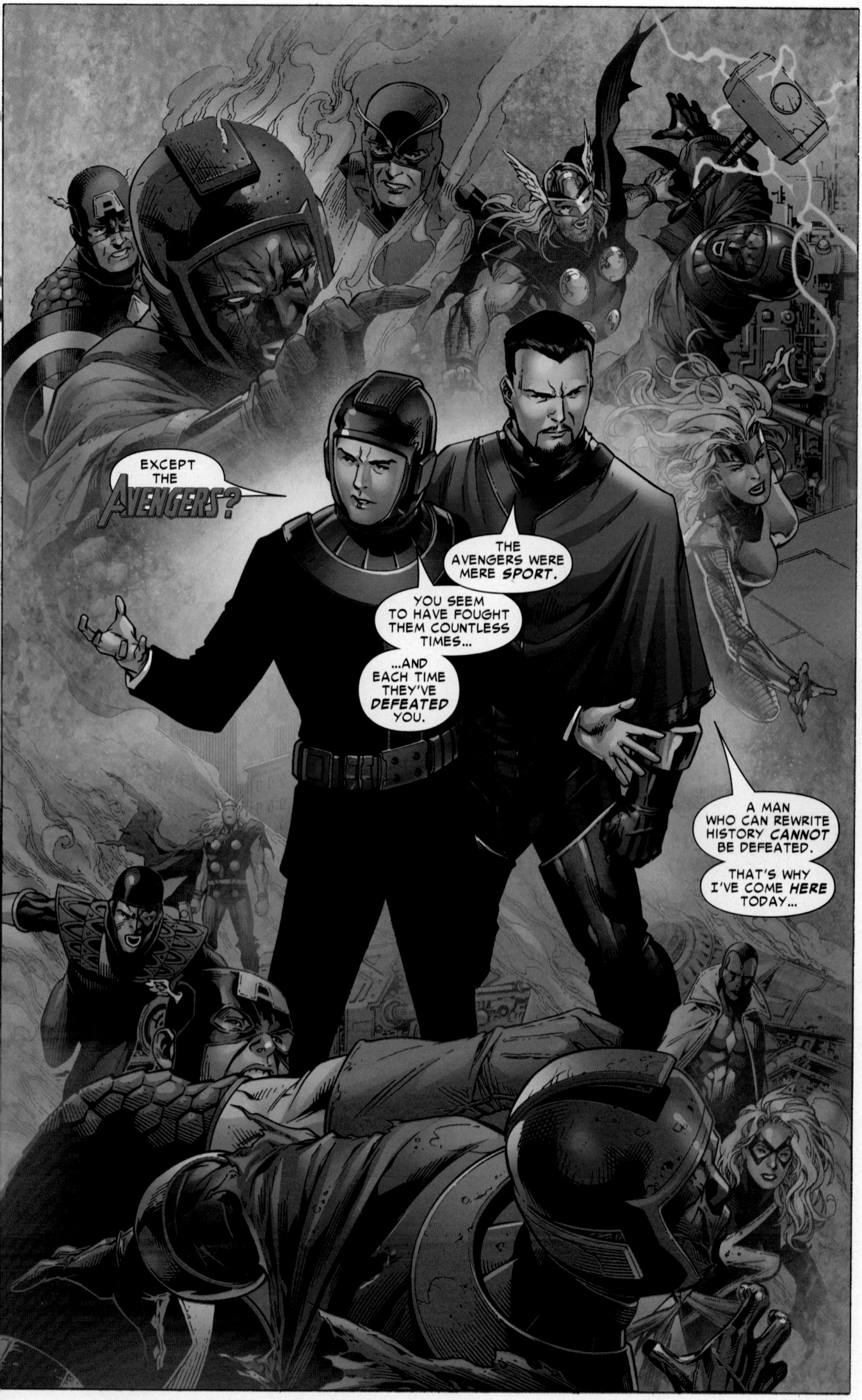
EXCEPT THE AVENGERS?
THE AVENGERS WERE MERE SPORT.
YOU SEEM TO HAVE FOUGHT THEM COUNTLESS TIMES...
...AND EACH TIME THEY'VE DEFEATED YOU.
A MAN WHO CAN REWRITE HISTORY CANNOT BE DEFEATED.
THAT'S WHY I'VE COME HERE TODAY...

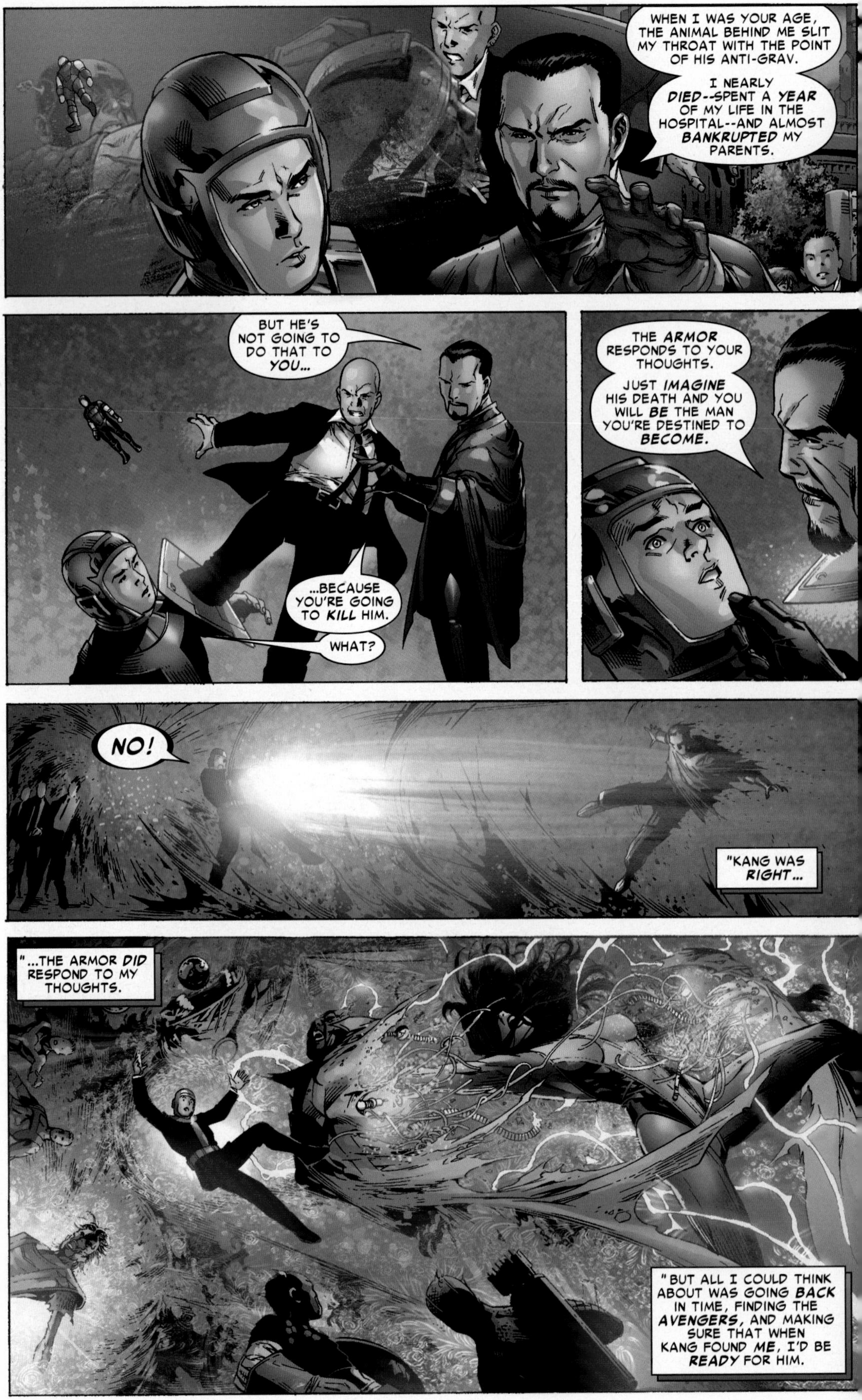

WHEN I WAS YOUR AGE, THE ANIMAL BEHIND ME SLIT MY THROAT WITH THE POINT OF HIS ANTI-GRAV.
I NEARLY DIED--SPENT A YEAR OF MY LIFE IN THE HOSPITAL--AND ALMOST BANKRUPTED MY PARENTS.
BUT HE'S NOT GOING TO DO THAT TO YOU...
...BECAUSE YOU'RE GOING TO KILL HIM.
WHAT?
THE ARMOR RESPONDS TO YOUR THOUGHTS.
JUST IMAGINE HIS DEATH AND YOU WILL BE THE MAN YOU'RE DESTINED TO BECOME.
NO!
"KANG WAS RIGHT...
"...THE ARMOR DID RESPOND TO MY THOUGHTS.
"BUT ALL I COULD THINK ABOUT WAS GOING BACK IN TIME, FINDING THE AVENGERS, AND MAKING SURE THAT WHEN KANG FOUND ME, I'D BE READY FOR HIM.

"HOWEVER, WHEN I ARRIVED, I DISCOVERED THE AVENGERS HAD *DISBANDED*.

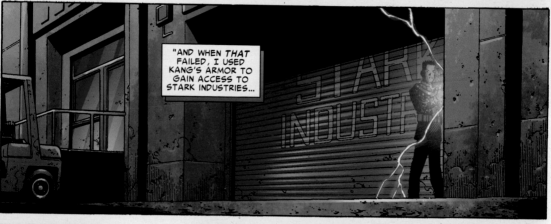

"I TRIED TO CONTACT AS MANY *FORMER* AVENGERS AS I COULD...

MR. STARK! ONE SECOND! *PLEASE--!*

MR. STARK DOESN'T HAVE TIME FOR AUTOGRAPHS, KID.

"AND WHEN *THAT* FAILED, I USED KANG'S ARMOR TO GAIN ACCESS TO STARK INDUSTRIES...

"...WHERE I FINALLY *DID* FIND SOMEONE WHO COULD HELP ME."

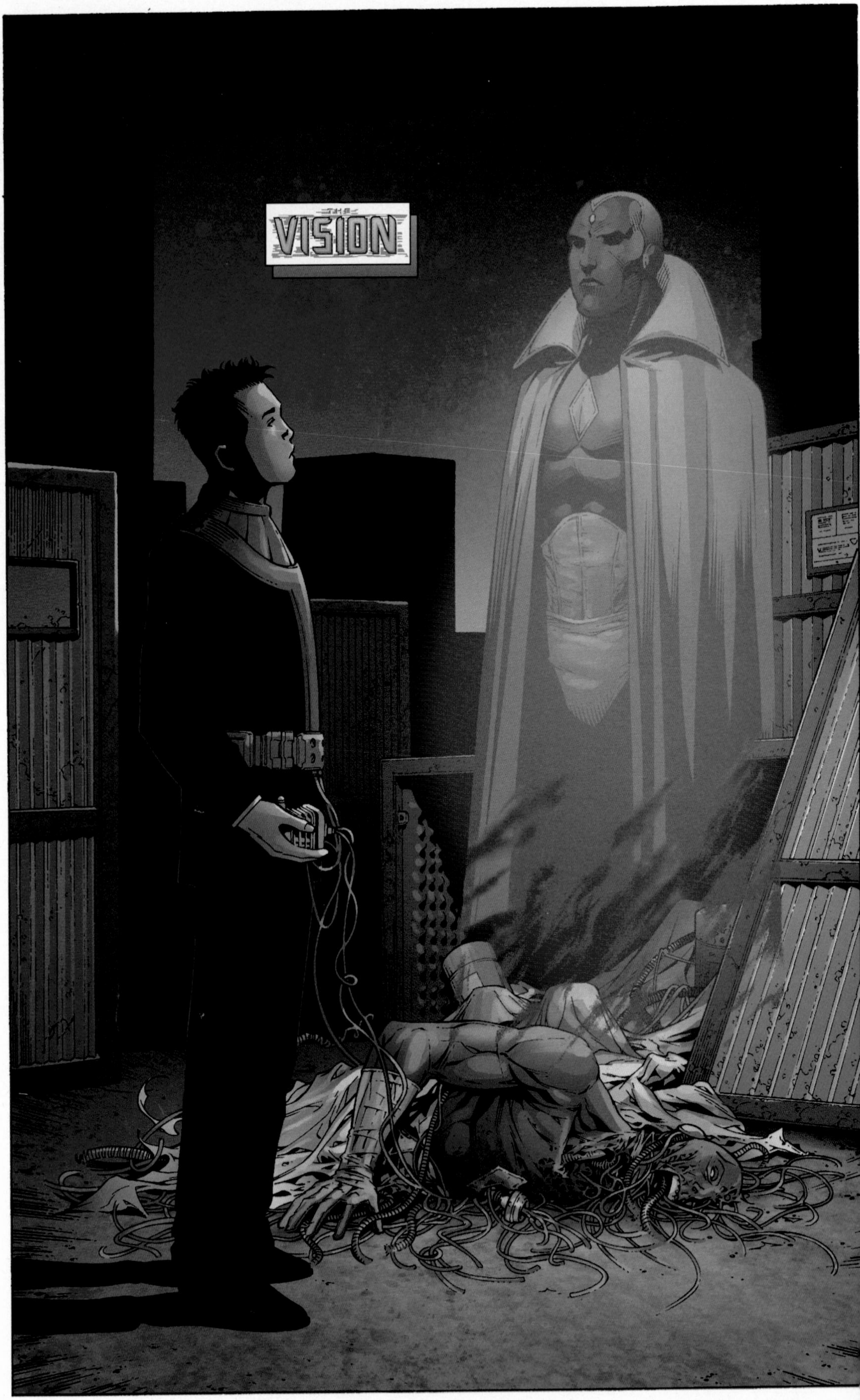
THE VISION

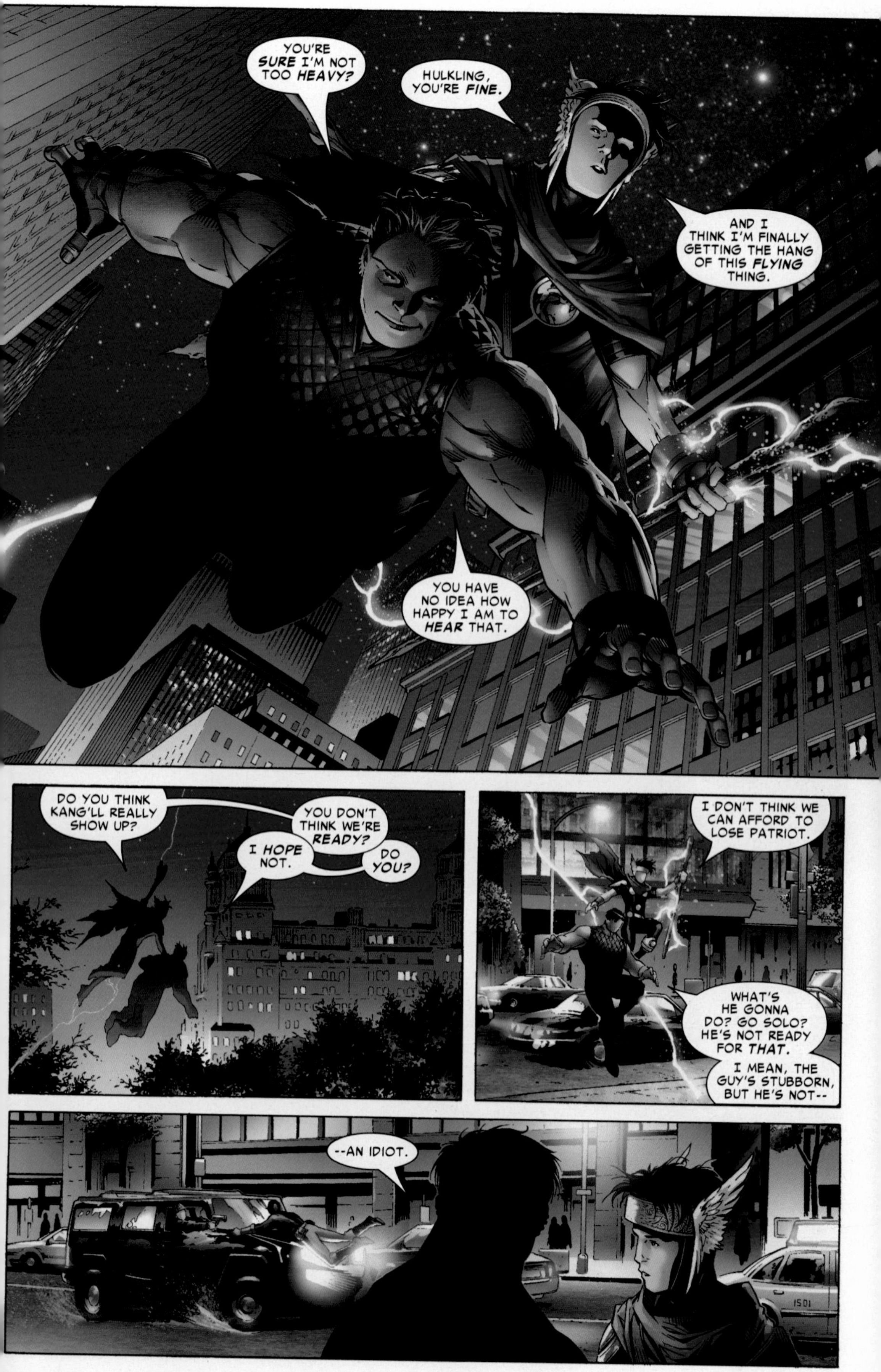
YOU'RE SURE I'M NOT TOO HEAVY?
HULKLING, YOU'RE FINE.
AND I THINK I'M FINALLY GETTING THE HANG OF THIS FLYING THING.
YOU HAVE NO IDEA HOW HAPPY I AM TO HEAR THAT.
DO YOU THINK KANG'LL REALLY SHOW UP?
YOU DON'T THINK WE'RE READY?
I HOPE NOT.
DO YOU?
I DON'T THINK WE CAN AFFORD TO LOSE PATRIOT.
WHAT'S HE GONNA DO? GO SOLO? HE'S NOT READY FOR THAT.
I MEAN, THE GUY'S STUBBORN, BUT HE'S NOT--
--AN IDIOT.

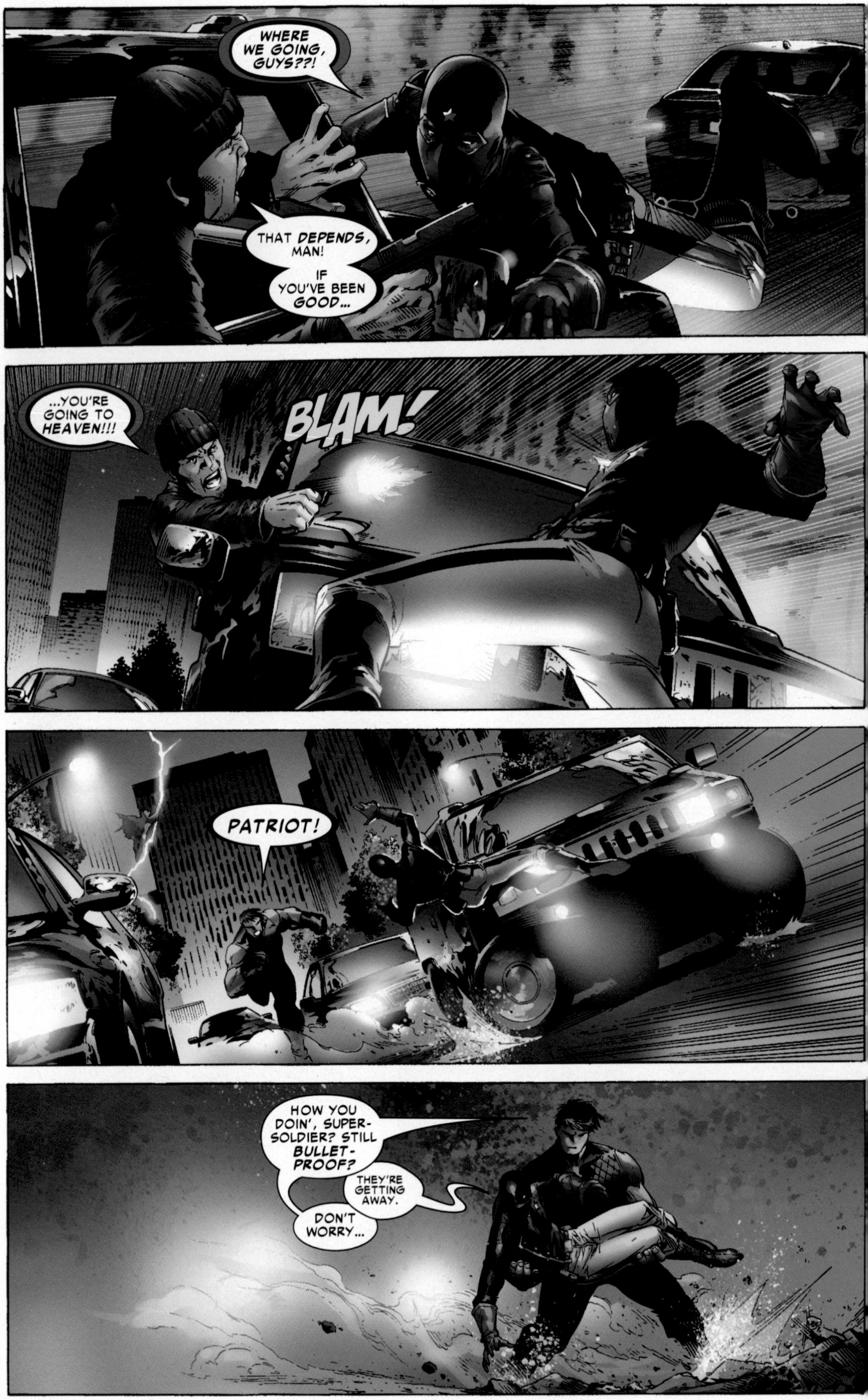
WHERE WE GOING, GUYS??!
THAT DEPENDS, MAN!
IF YOU'VE BEEN GOOD...
...YOU'RE GOING TO HEAVEN!!!
BLAM!
PATRIOT!
HOW YOU DOIN', SUPER-SOLDIER? STILL BULLET-PROOF?
THEY'RE GETTING AWAY.
DON'T WORRY...

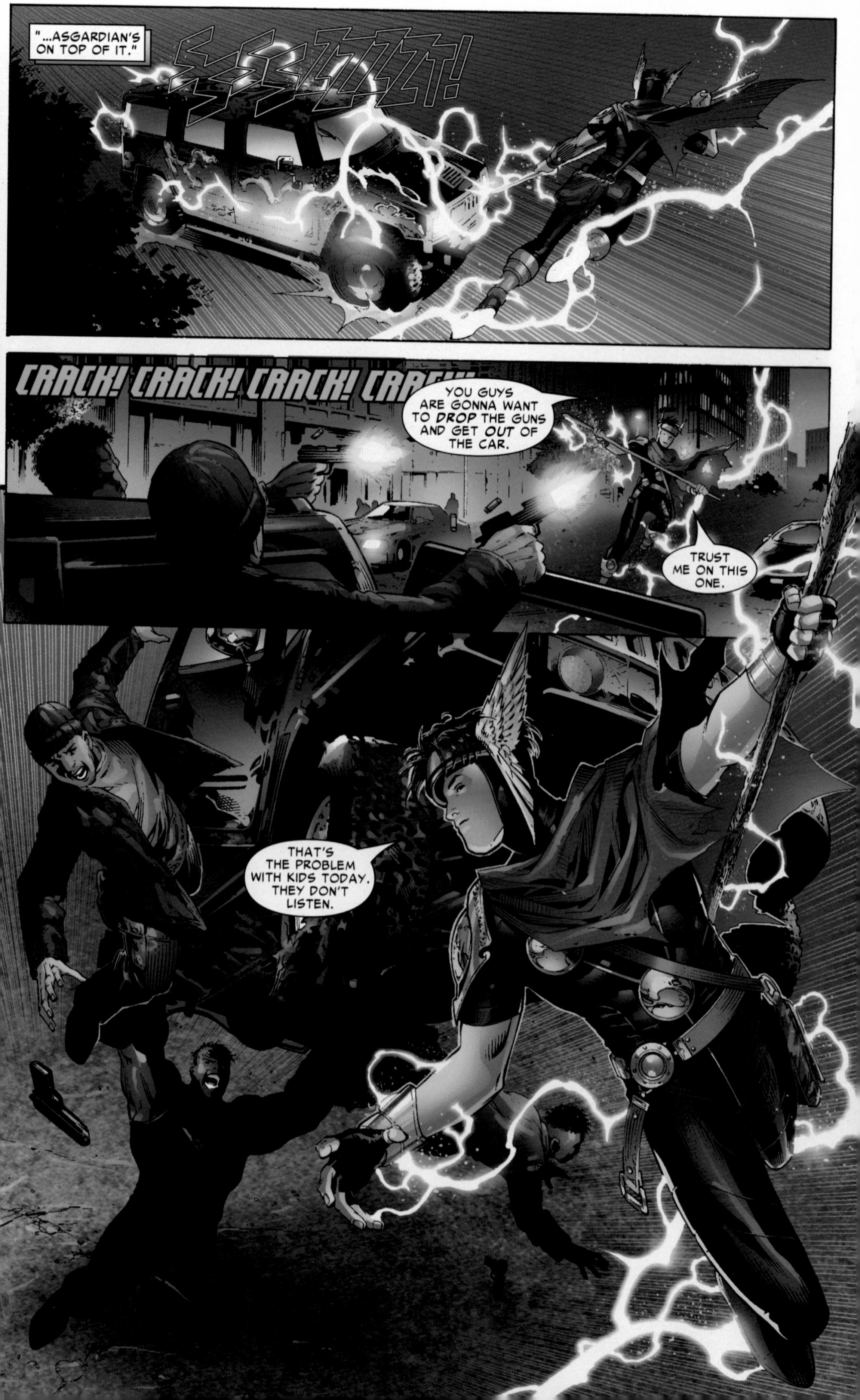
"...ASGARDIAN'S ON TOP OF IT."
CRACK! CRACK! CRACK!
YOU GUYS ARE GONNA WANT TO *DROP* THE GUNS AND GET *OUT* OF THE CAR.
TRUST ME ON THIS ONE.
THAT'S THE PROBLEM WITH KIDS TODAY. THEY DON'T LISTEN.

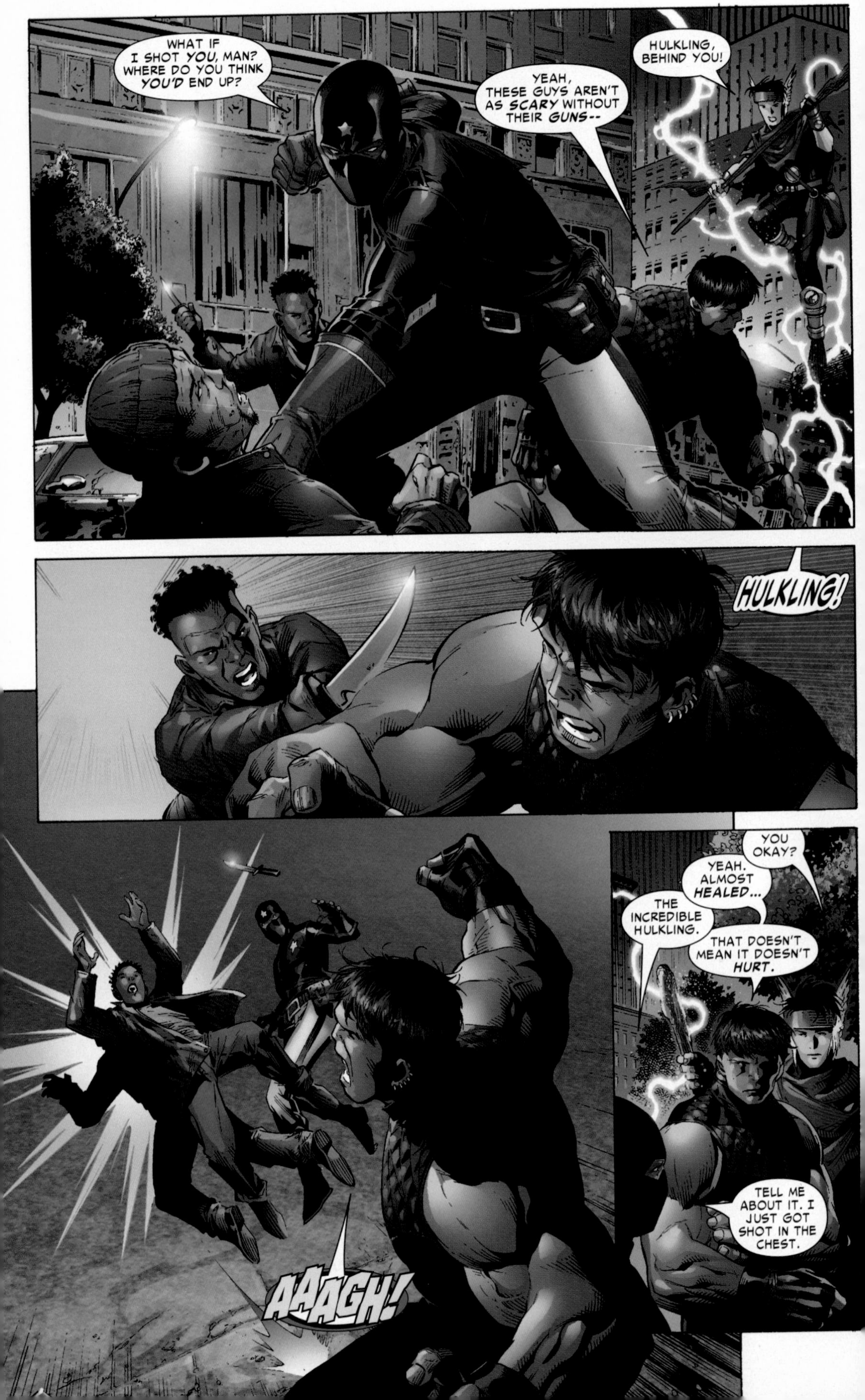
WHAT IF I SHOT YOU, MAN? WHERE DO YOU THINK YOU'D END UP?
YEAH, THESE GUYS AREN'T AS SCARY WITHOUT THEIR GUNS--
HULKLING, BEHIND YOU!
HULKLING!
AAAGH!
YOU OKAY?
YEAH. ALMOST HEALED...
THAT DOESN'T MEAN IT DOESN'T HURT.
THE INCREDIBLE HULKLING.
TELL ME ABOUT IT. I JUST GOT SHOT IN THE CHEST.

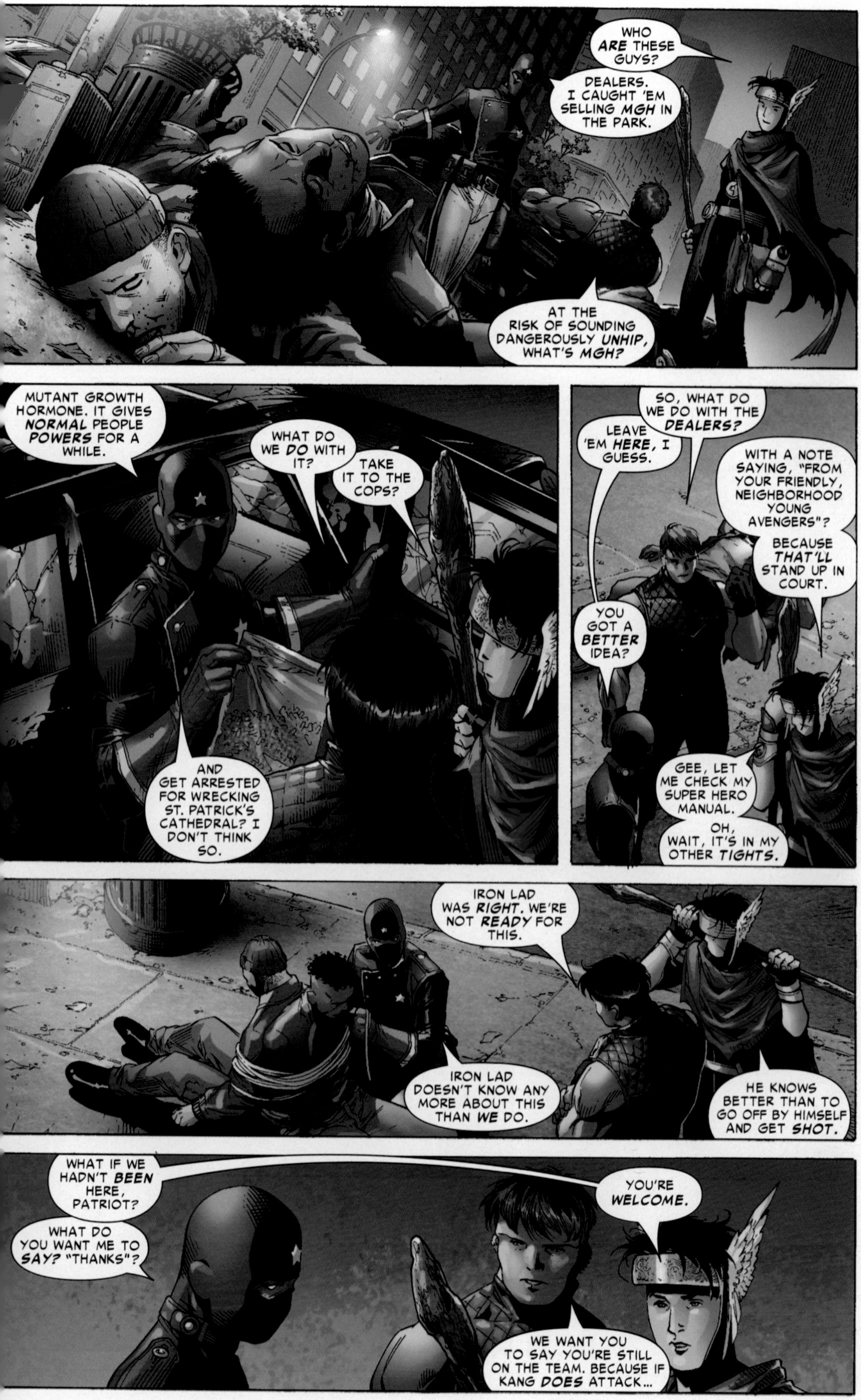
WHO ARE THESE GUYS?
DEALERS. I CAUGHT 'EM SELLING MGH IN THE PARK.
AT THE RISK OF SOUNDING DANGEROUSLY UNHIP, WHAT'S MGH?
MUTANT GROWTH HORMONE. IT GIVES NORMAL PEOPLE POWERS FOR A WHILE.
WHAT DO WE DO WITH IT?
TAKE IT TO THE COPS?
AND GET ARRESTED FOR WRECKING ST. PATRICK'S CATHEDRAL? I DON'T THINK SO.
SO, WHAT DO WE DO WITH THE DEALERS?
LEAVE 'EM HERE, I GUESS.
WITH A NOTE SAYING, "FROM YOUR FRIENDLY, NEIGHBORHOOD YOUNG AVENGERS"?
BECAUSE THAT'LL STAND UP IN COURT.
YOU GOT A BETTER IDEA?
GEE, LET ME CHECK MY SUPER HERO MANUAL.
OH, WAIT, IT'S IN MY OTHER TIGHTS.
IRON LAD WAS RIGHT. WE'RE NOT READY FOR THIS.
IRON LAD DOESN'T KNOW ANY MORE ABOUT THIS THAN WE DO.
HE KNOWS BETTER THAN TO GO OFF BY HIMSELF AND GET SHOT.
WHAT IF WE HADN'T BEEN HERE, PATRIOT?
YOU'RE WELCOME.
WHAT DO YOU WANT ME TO SAY? "THANKS"?
WE WANT YOU TO SAY YOU'RE STILL ON THE TEAM. BECAUSE IF KANG DOES ATTACK...

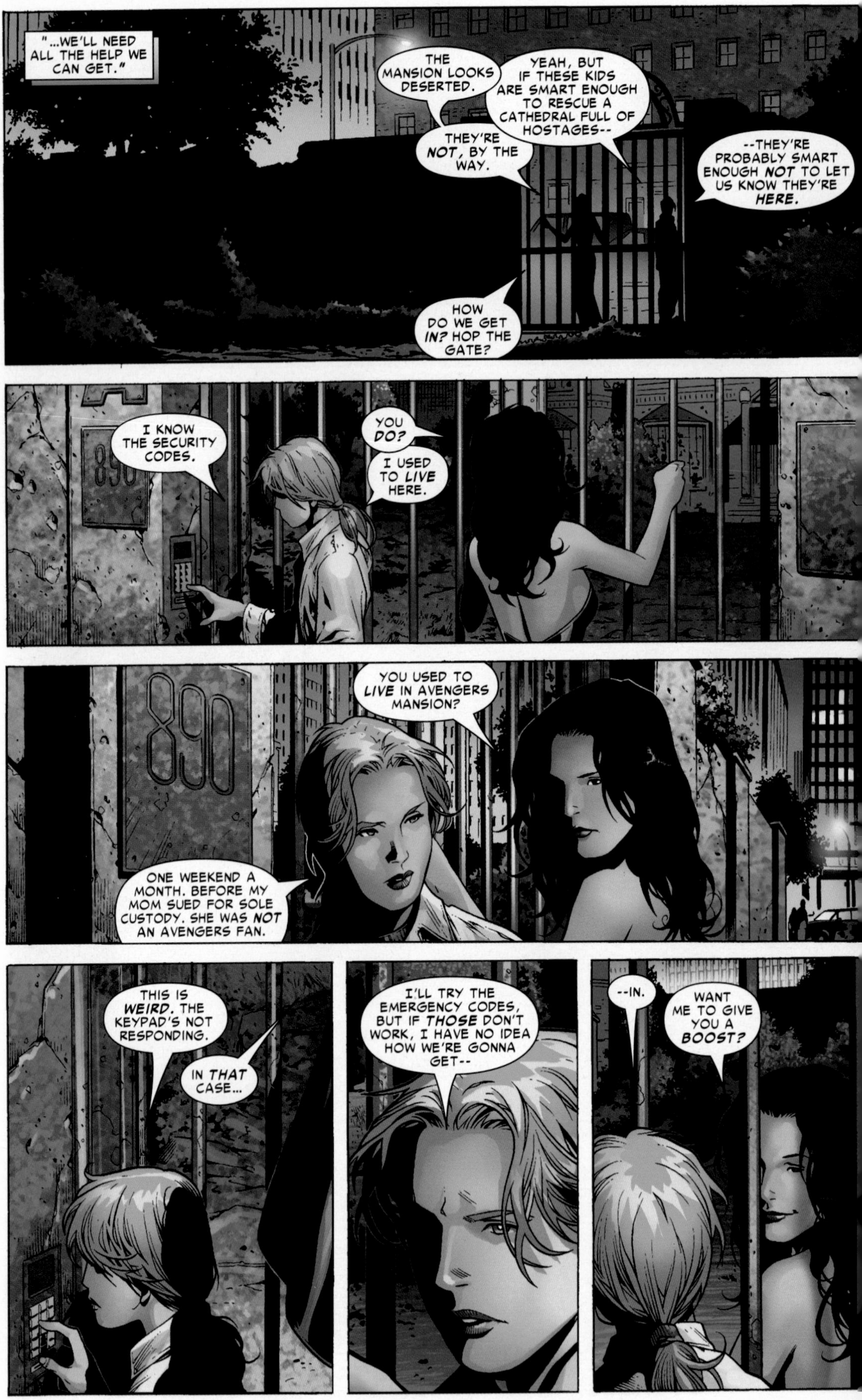
"...WE'LL NEED ALL THE HELP WE CAN GET."
THE MANSION LOOKS DESERTED.
YEAH, BUT IF THESE KIDS ARE SMART ENOUGH TO RESCUE A CATHEDRAL FULL OF HOSTAGES--
THEY'RE NOT, BY THE WAY.
--THEY'RE PROBABLY SMART ENOUGH NOT TO LET US KNOW THEY'RE HERE.
HOW DO WE GET IN? HOP THE GATE?
I KNOW THE SECURITY CODES.
YOU DO?
I USED TO LIVE HERE.
890
YOU USED TO LIVE IN AVENGERS MANSION?
ONE WEEKEND A MONTH. BEFORE MY MOM SUED FOR SOLE CUSTODY. SHE WAS NOT AN AVENGERS FAN.
THIS IS WEIRD. THE KEYPAD'S NOT RESPONDING.
IN THAT CASE...
I'LL TRY THE EMERGENCY CODES, BUT IF THOSE DON'T WORK, I HAVE NO IDEA HOW WE'RE GONNA GET--
--IN.
WANT ME TO GIVE YOU A BOOST?

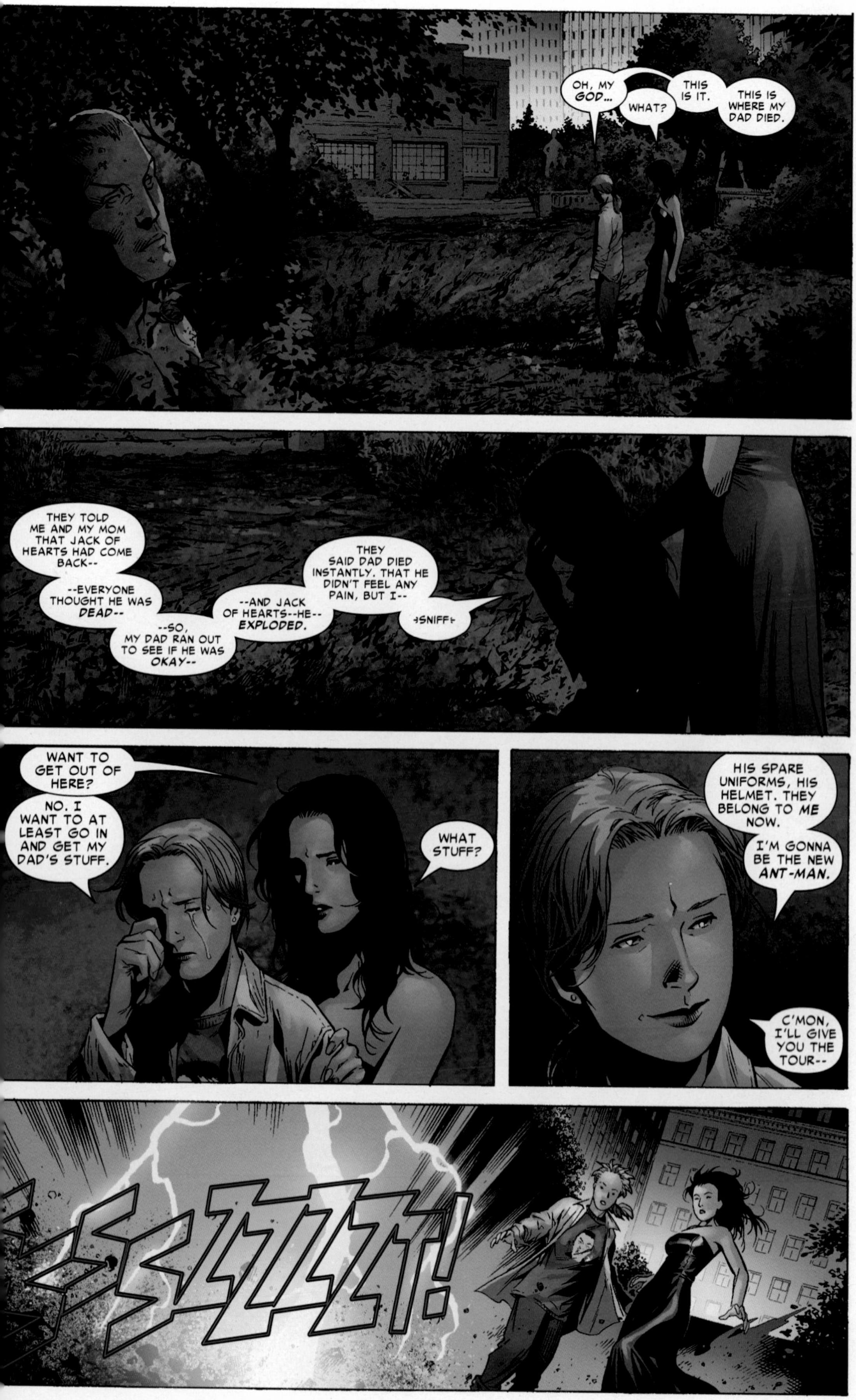
OH, MY GOD...
WHAT?
THIS IS IT.
THIS IS WHERE MY DAD DIED.
THEY TOLD ME AND MY MOM THAT JACK OF HEARTS HAD COME BACK--
--EVERYONE THOUGHT HE WAS DEAD--
--SO, MY DAD RAN OUT TO SEE IF HE WAS OKAY--
--AND JACK OF HEARTS--HE--EXPLODED.
THEY SAID DAD DIED INSTANTLY. THAT HE DIDN'T FEEL ANY PAIN, BUT I--
SNIFF
WANT TO GET OUT OF HERE?
NO. I WANT TO AT LEAST GO IN AND GET MY DAD'S STUFF.
WHAT STUFF?
HIS SPARE UNIFORMS, HIS HELMET. THEY BELONG TO ME NOW.
I'M GONNA BE THE NEW ANT-MAN.
C'MON, I'LL GIVE YOU THE TOUR--
SSZZZT!

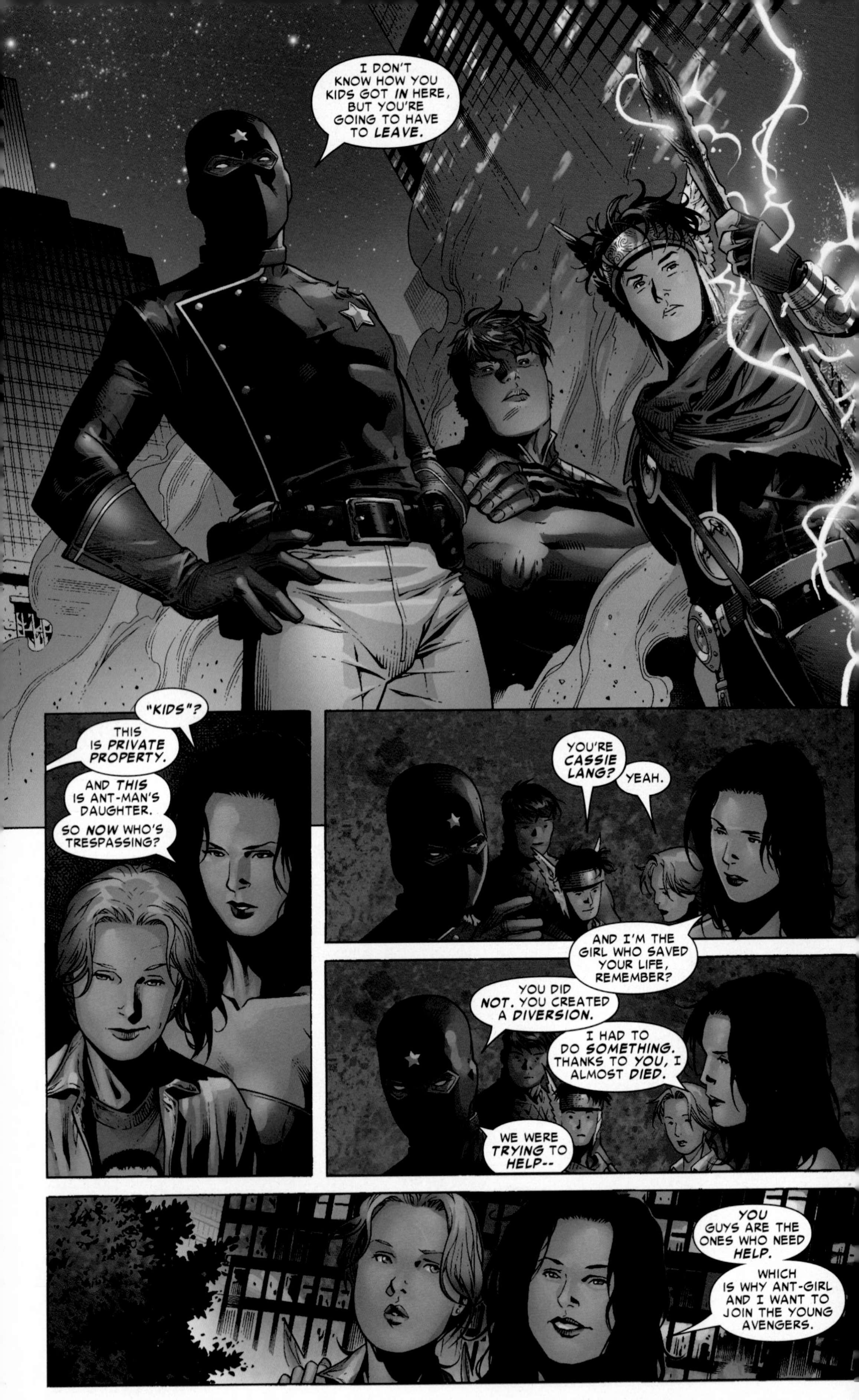

I DON'T KNOW HOW YOU KIDS GOT IN HERE, BUT YOU'RE GOING TO HAVE TO LEAVE.
"KIDS"?
THIS IS PRIVATE PROPERTY.
AND THIS IS ANT-MAN'S DAUGHTER.
SO NOW WHO'S TRESPASSING?
YOU'RE CASSIE LANG?
YEAH.
AND I'M THE GIRL WHO SAVED YOUR LIFE, REMEMBER?
YOU DID NOT. YOU CREATED A DIVERSION.
I HAD TO DO SOMETHING. THANKS TO YOU, I ALMOST DIED.
WE WERE TRYING TO HELP--
YOU GUYS ARE THE ONES WHO NEED HELP.
WHICH IS WHY ANT-GIRL AND I WANT TO JOIN THE YOUNG AVENGERS.

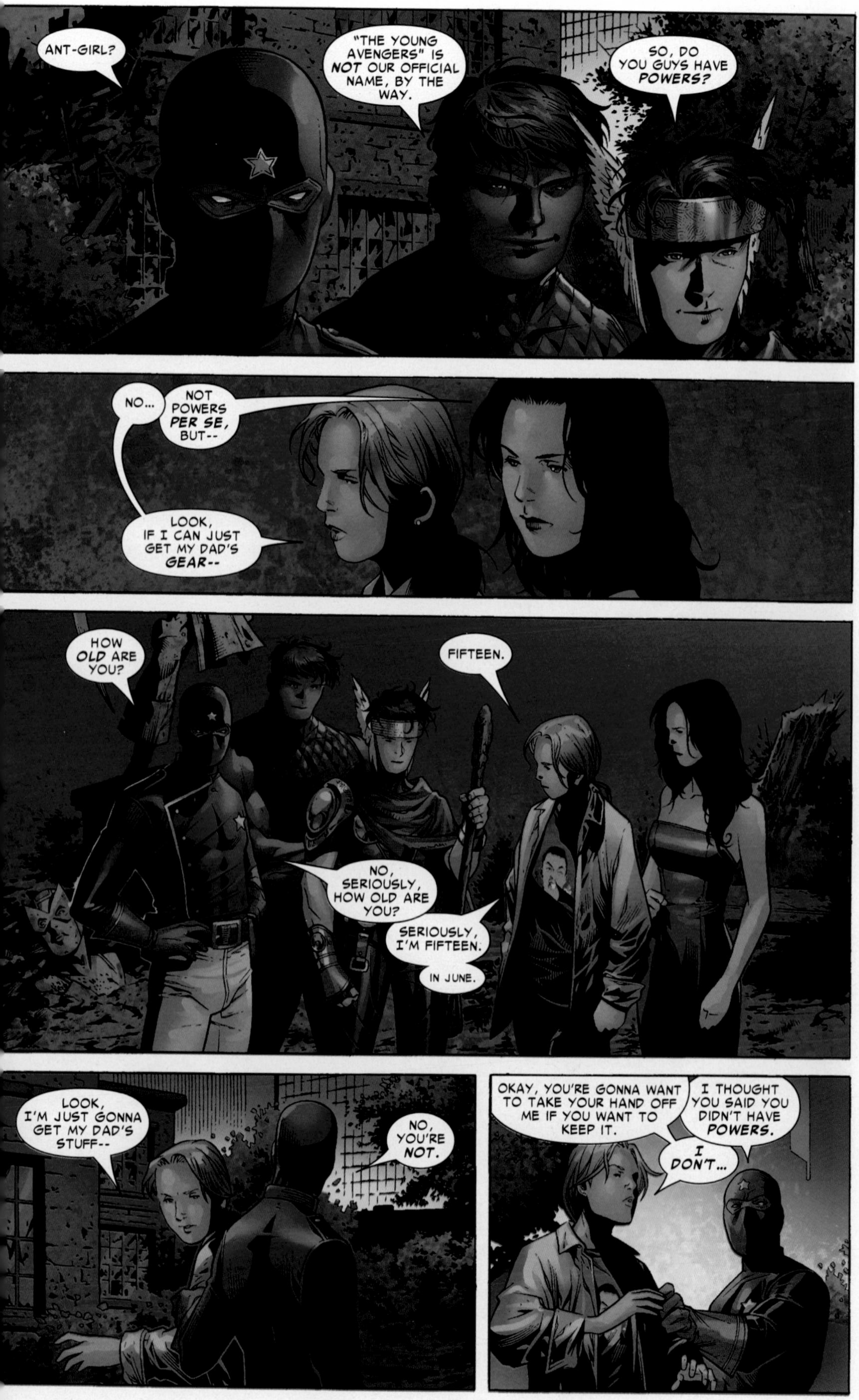
ANT-GIRL?
"THE YOUNG AVENGERS" IS NOT OUR OFFICIAL NAME, BY THE WAY.
SO, DO YOU GUYS HAVE POWERS?
NO...
NOT POWERS PER SE, BUT--
LOOK, IF I CAN JUST GET MY DAD'S GEAR--
HOW OLD ARE YOU?
FIFTEEN.
NO, SERIOUSLY, HOW OLD ARE YOU?
SERIOUSLY, I'M FIFTEEN.
IN JUNE.
LOOK, I'M JUST GONNA GET MY DAD'S STUFF--
NO, YOU'RE NOT.
OKAY, YOU'RE GONNA WANT TO TAKE YOUR HAND OFF ME IF YOU WANT TO KEEP IT.
I THOUGHT YOU SAID YOU DIDN'T HAVE POWERS.
I DON'T...

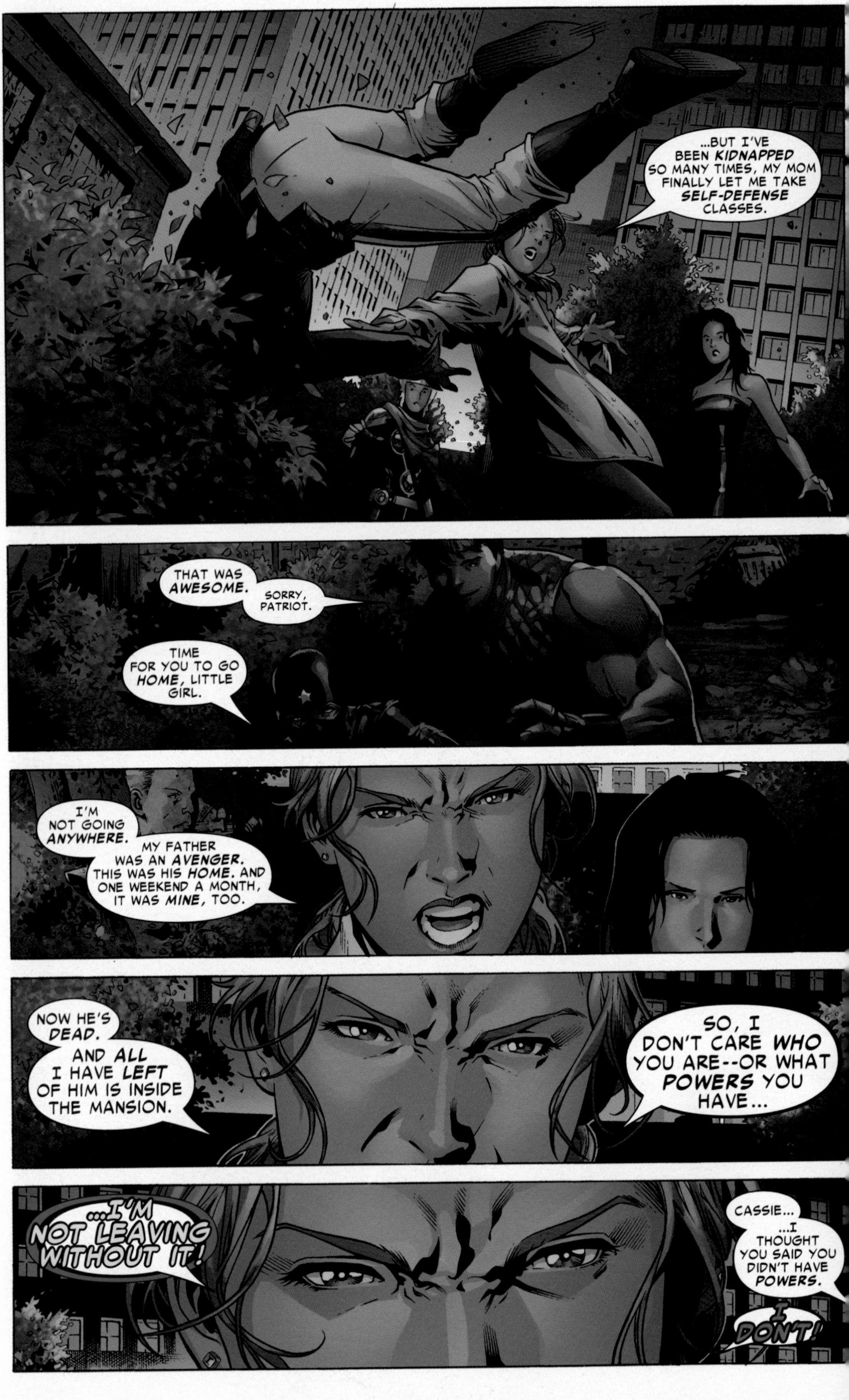
...BUT I'VE BEEN KIDNAPPED SO MANY TIMES, MY MOM FINALLY LET ME TAKE SELF-DEFENSE CLASSES.
THAT WAS AWESOME.
SORRY, PATRIOT.
TIME FOR YOU TO GO HOME, LITTLE GIRL.
I'M NOT GOING ANYWHERE.
MY FATHER WAS AN AVENGER. THIS WAS HIS HOME. AND ONE WEEKEND A MONTH, IT WAS MINE, TOO.
NOW HE'S DEAD.
AND ALL I HAVE LEFT OF HIM IS INSIDE THE MANSION.
SO, I DON'T CARE WHO YOU ARE--OR WHAT POWERS YOU HAVE...
...I'M NOT LEAVING WITHOUT IT!
CASSIE...
...I THOUGHT YOU SAID YOU DIDN'T HAVE POWERS.
I DON'T!

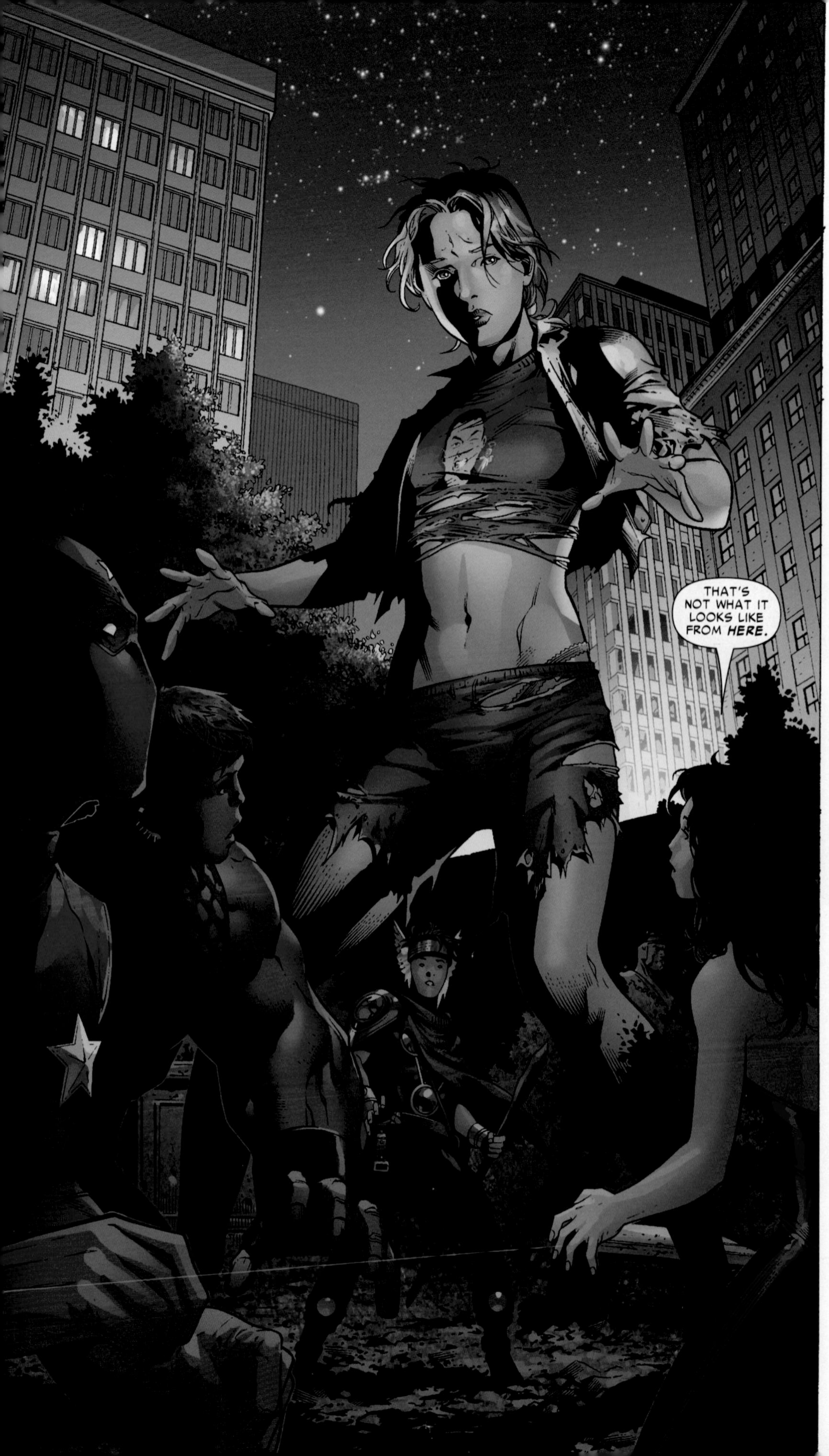
THAT'S NOT WHAT IT LOOKS LIKE FROM *HERE*.

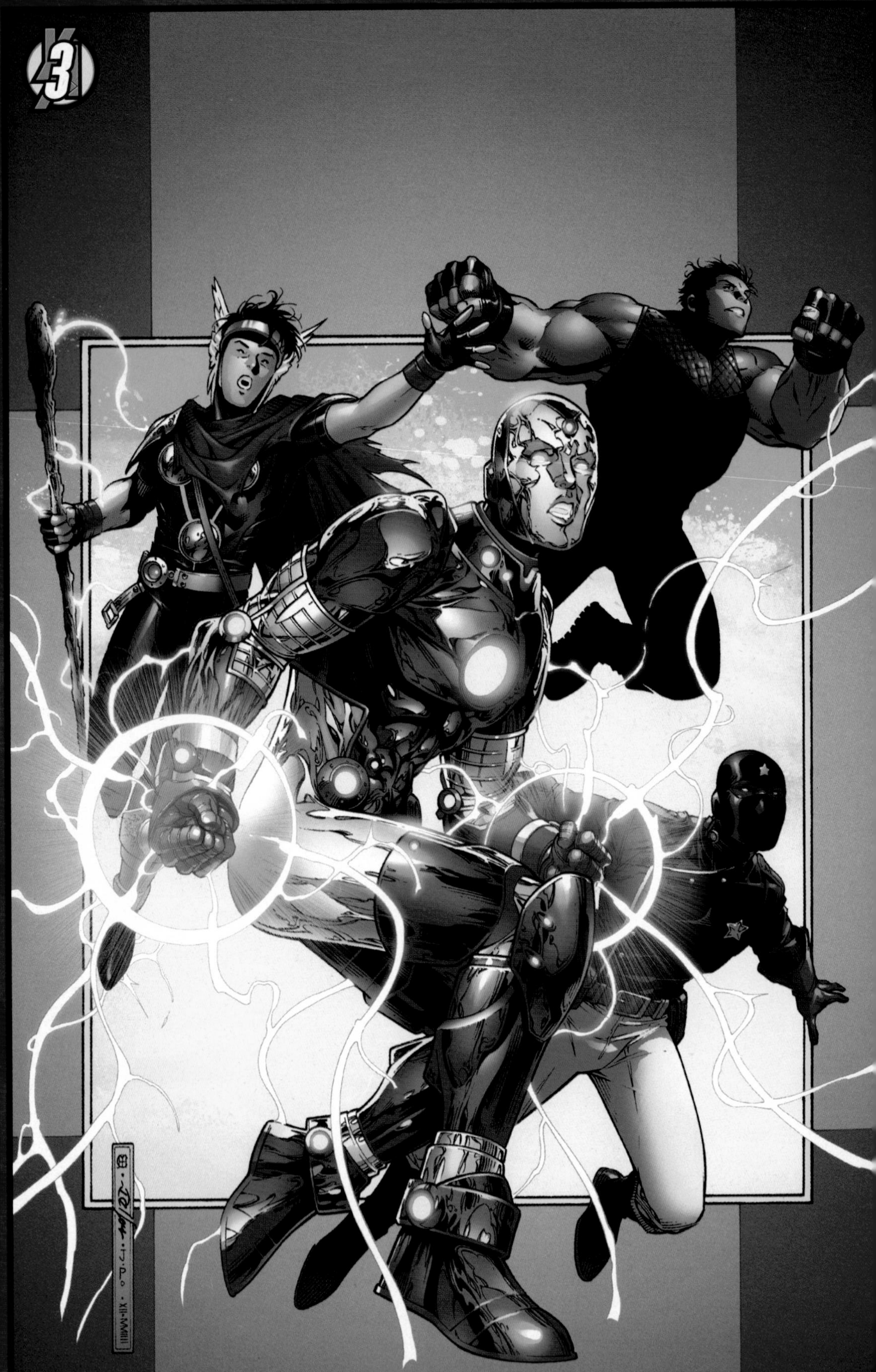

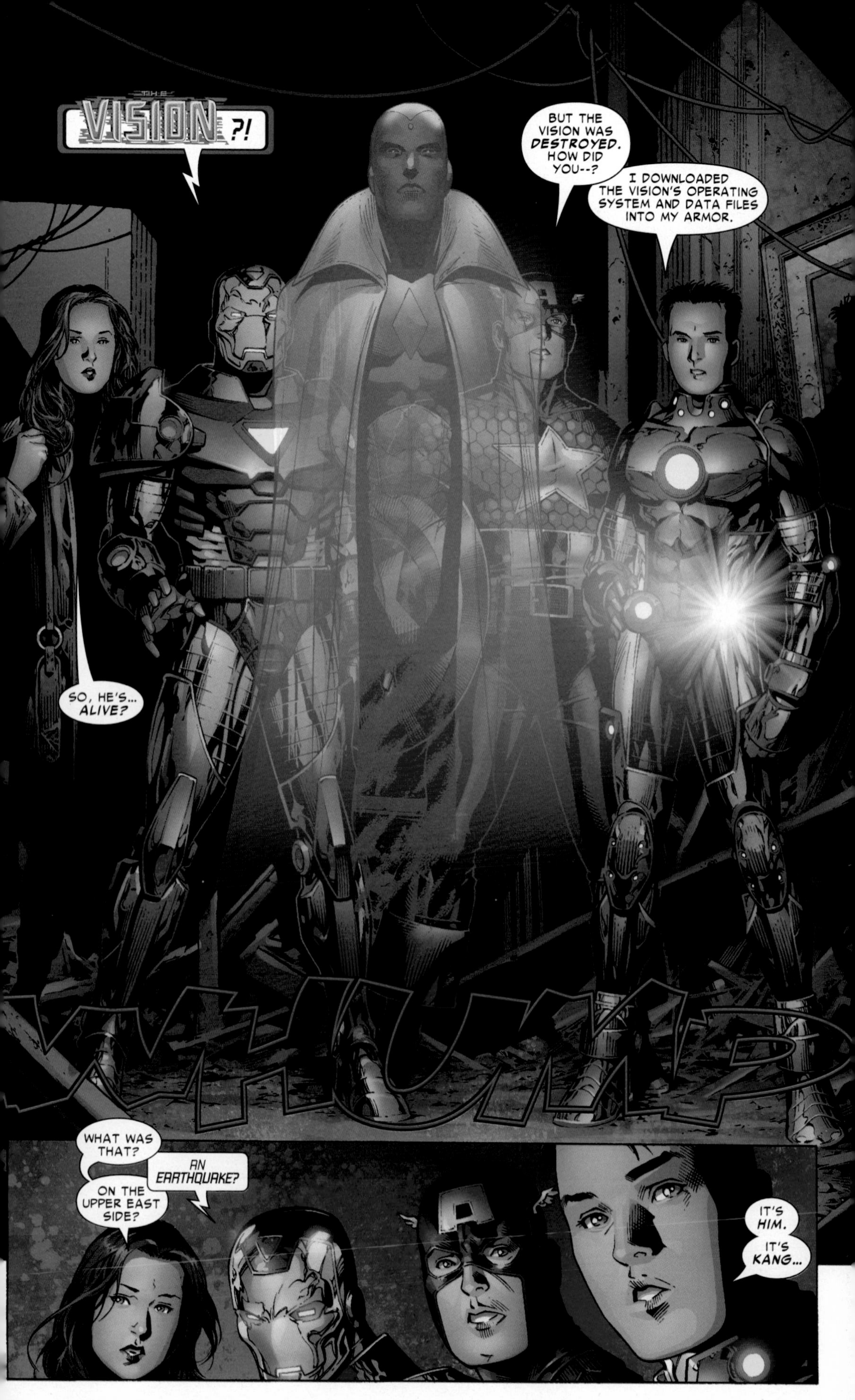
THE VISION ?!
BUT THE VISION WAS DESTROYED. HOW DID YOU--?
I DOWNLOADED THE VISION'S OPERATING SYSTEM AND DATA FILES INTO MY ARMOR.
SO, HE'S... ALIVE?
WHAT WAS THAT?
AN EARTHQUAKE?
ON THE UPPER EAST SIDE?
IT'S HIM. IT'S KANG...

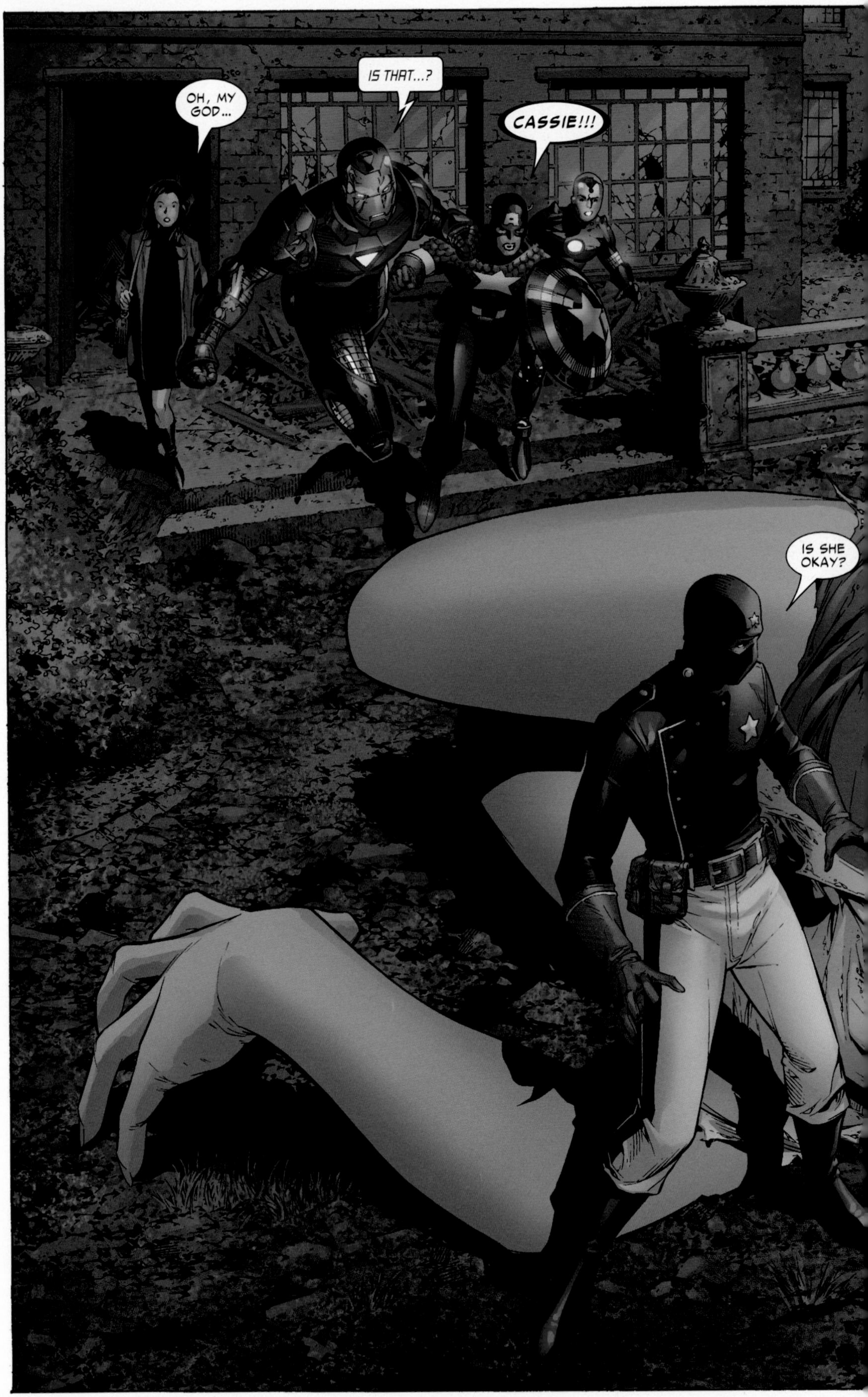
OH, MY GOD...
IS THAT...?
CASSIE!!!
IS SHE OKAY?

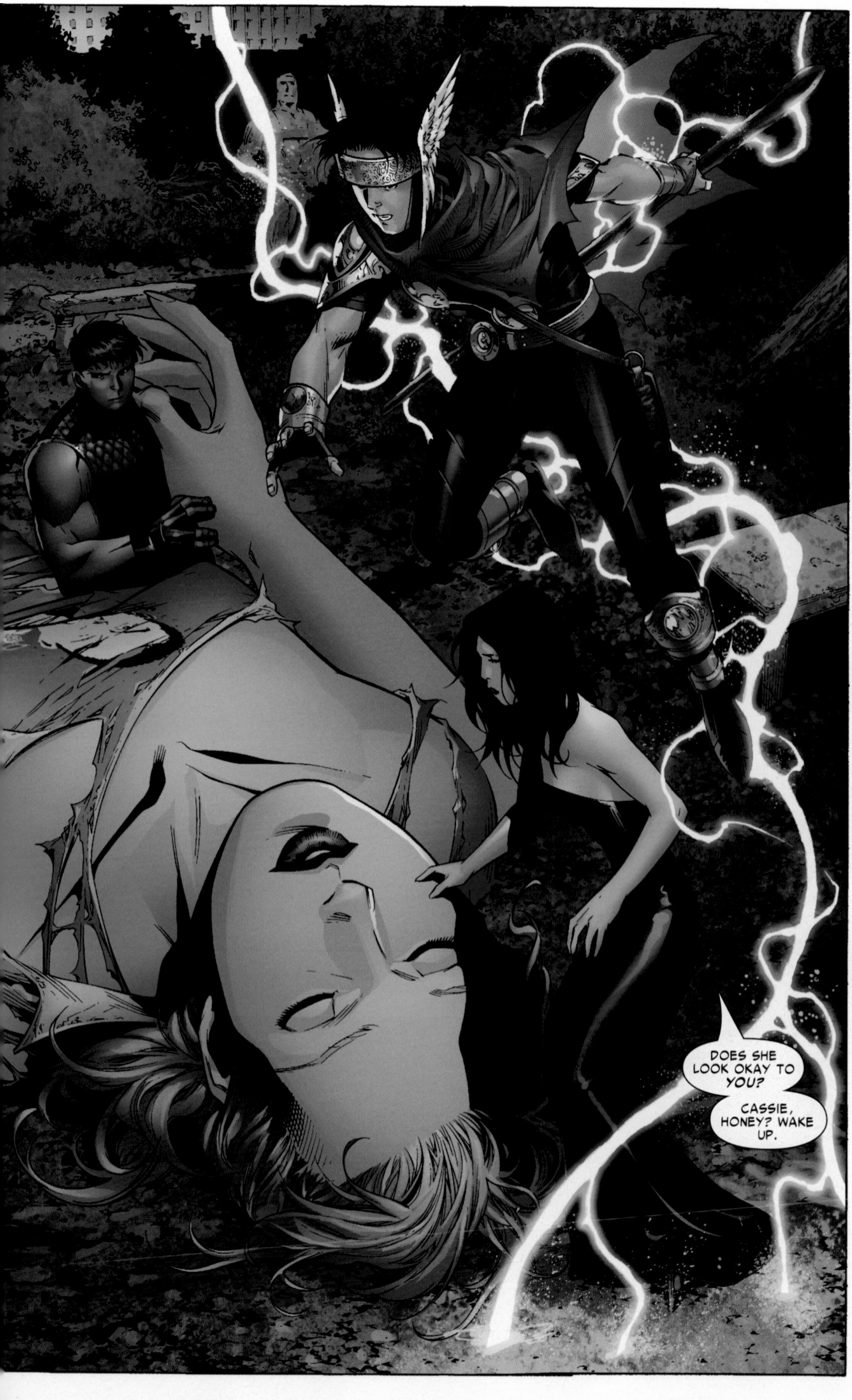
DOES SHE LOOK OKAY TO YOU?
CASSIE, HONEY? WAKE UP.

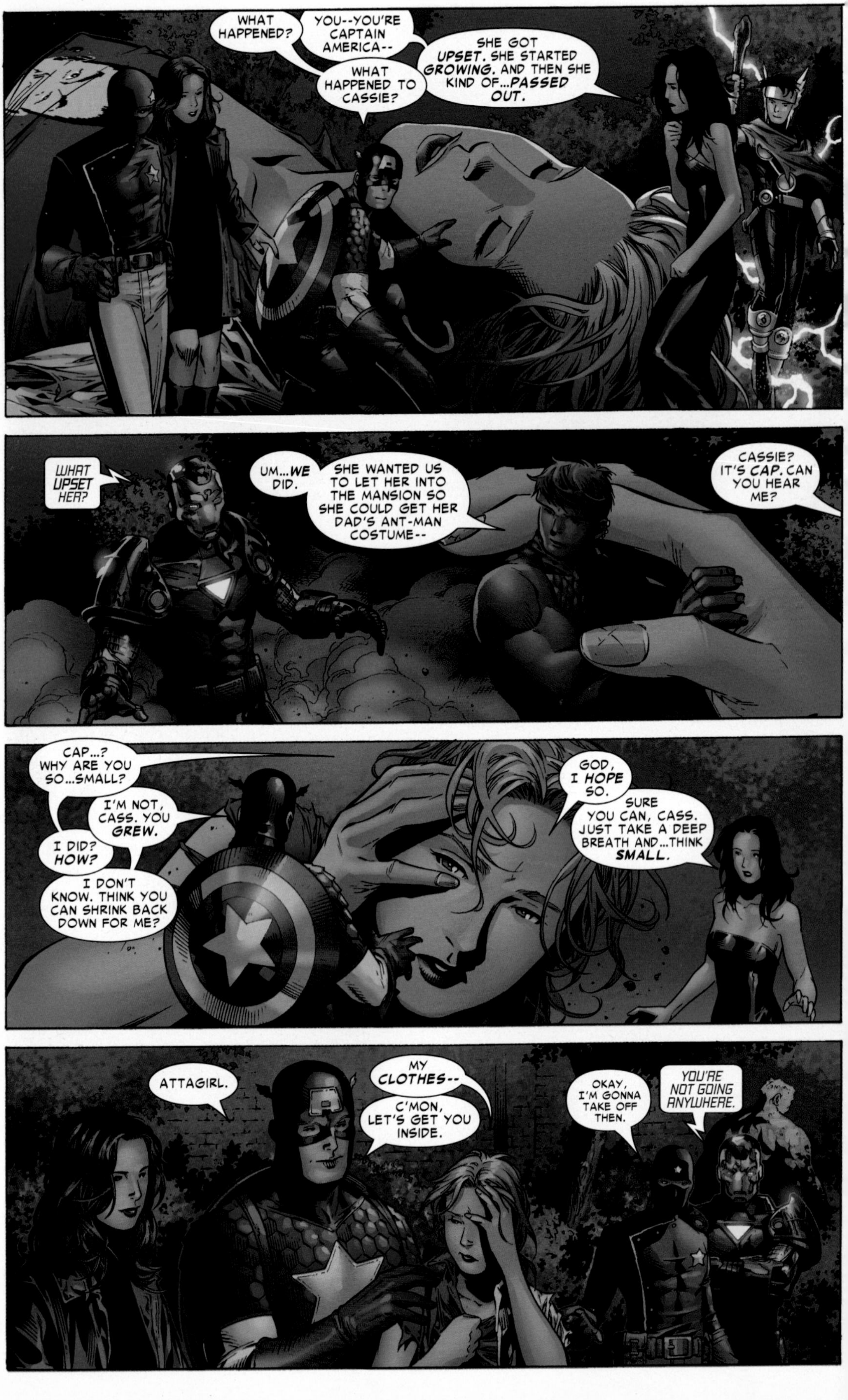
WHAT HAPPENED?
YOU--YOU'RE CAPTAIN AMERICA--
WHAT HAPPENED TO CASSIE?
SHE GOT UPSET. SHE STARTED GROWING. AND THEN SHE KIND OF...PASSED OUT.
WHAT UPSET HER?
UM...WE DID.
SHE WANTED US TO LET HER INTO THE MANSION SO SHE COULD GET HER DAD'S ANT-MAN COSTUME--
CASSIE? IT'S CAP. CAN YOU HEAR ME?
CAP...? WHY ARE YOU SO...SMALL?
I'M NOT, CASS. YOU GREW.
I DID? HOW?
I DON'T KNOW. THINK YOU CAN SHRINK BACK DOWN FOR ME?
GOD, I HOPE SO.
SURE YOU CAN, CASS. JUST TAKE A DEEP BREATH AND...THINK SMALL.
ATTAGIRL.
MY CLOTHES--
C'MON, LET'S GET YOU INSIDE.
OKAY, I'M GONNA TAKE OFF THEN.
YOU'RE NOT GOING ANYWHERE.

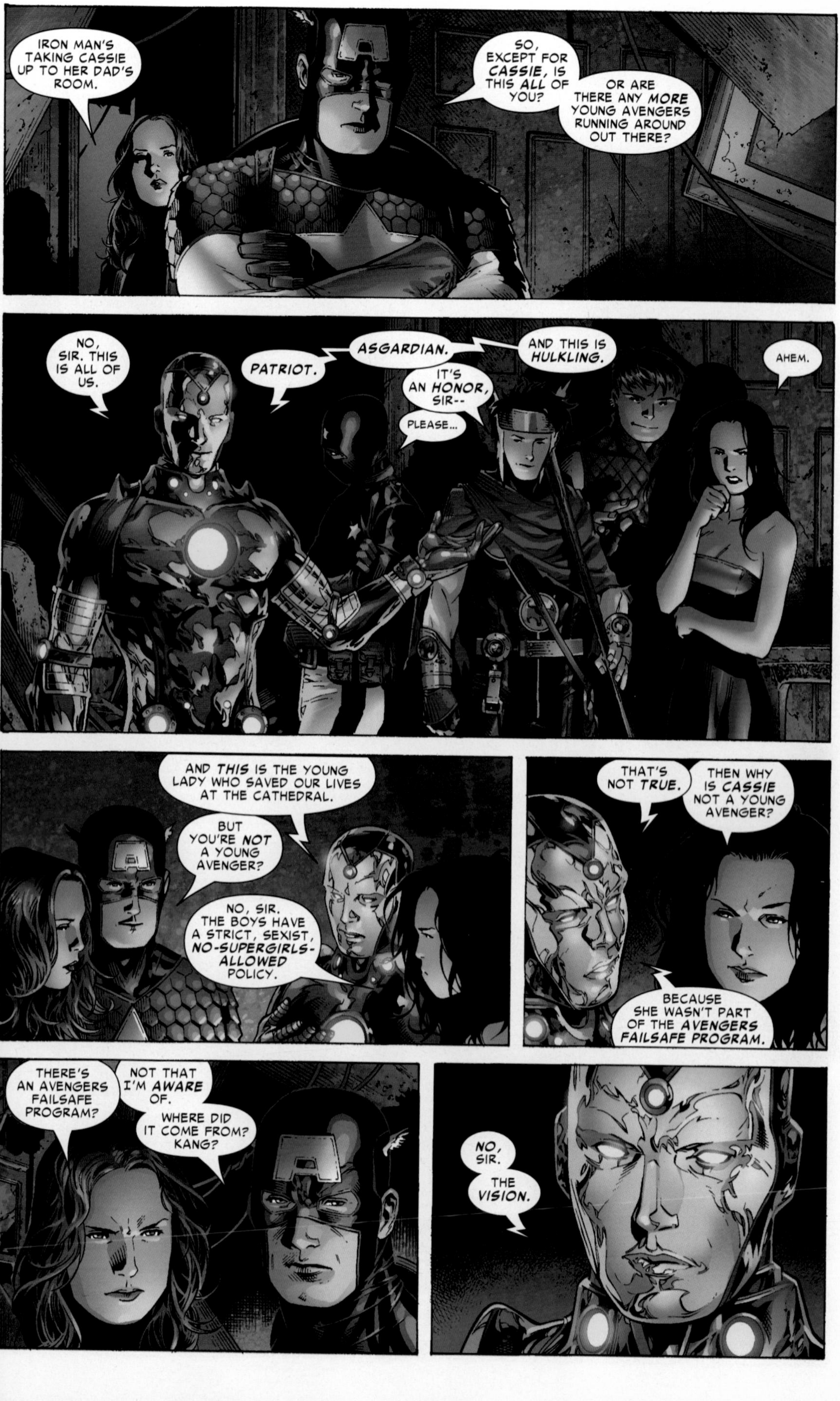
IRON MAN'S TAKING CASSIE UP TO HER DAD'S ROOM.
SO, EXCEPT FOR CASSIE, IS THIS ALL OF YOU?
OR ARE THERE ANY MORE YOUNG AVENGERS RUNNING AROUND OUT THERE?
NO, SIR. THIS IS ALL OF US.
PATRIOT.
ASGARDIAN.
AND THIS IS HULKLING.
IT'S AN HONOR, SIR--
PLEASE...
AHEM.
AND THIS IS THE YOUNG LADY WHO SAVED OUR LIVES AT THE CATHEDRAL.
BUT YOU'RE NOT A YOUNG AVENGER?
NO, SIR. THE BOYS HAVE A STRICT, SEXIST, NO-SUPERGIRLS-ALLOWED POLICY.
THAT'S NOT TRUE.
THEN WHY IS CASSIE NOT A YOUNG AVENGER?
BECAUSE SHE WASN'T PART OF THE AVENGERS FAILSAFE PROGRAM.
THERE'S AN AVENGERS FAILSAFE PROGRAM?
NOT THAT I'M AWARE OF.
WHERE DID IT COME FROM? KANG?
NO, SIR.
THE VISION.

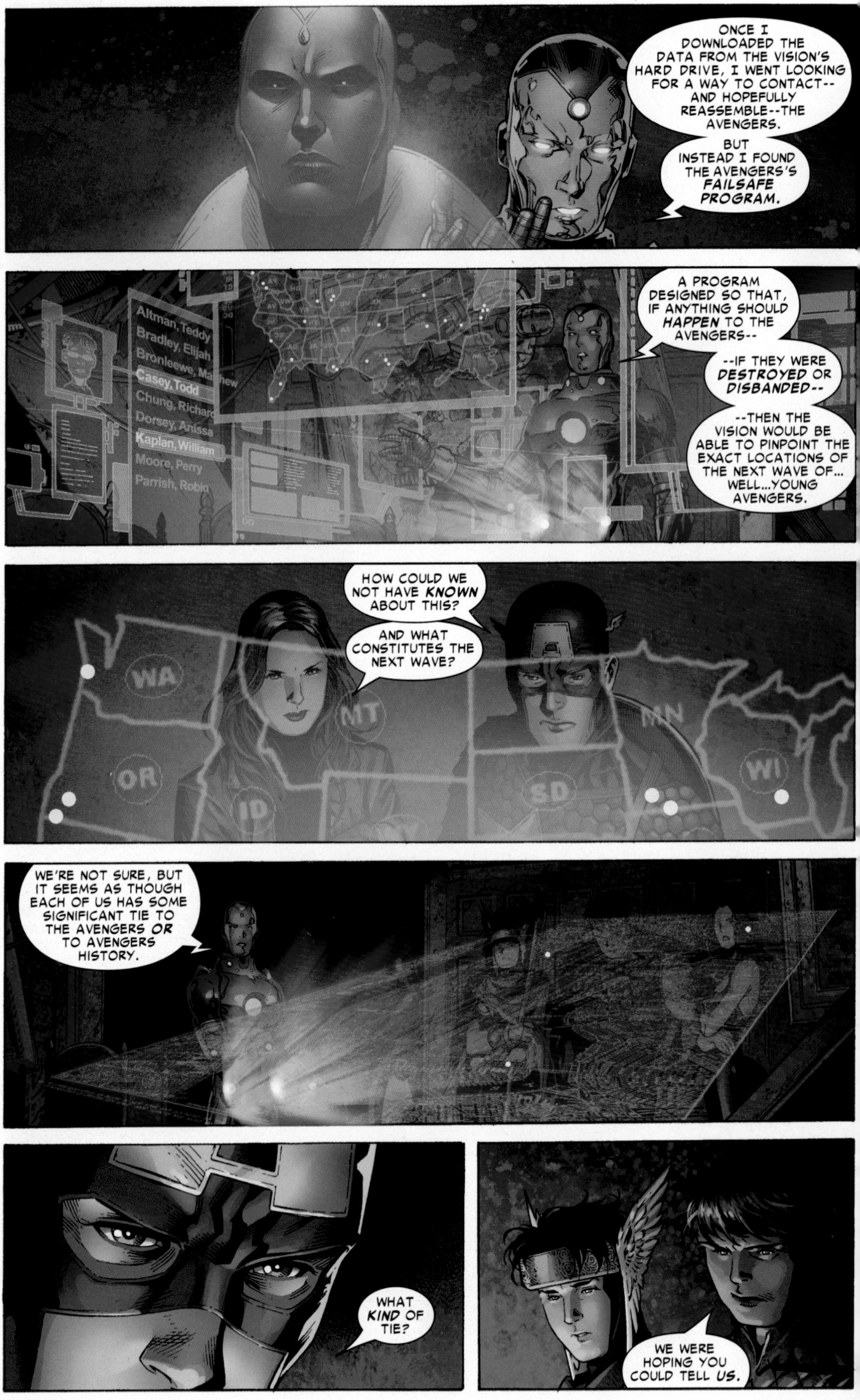
ONCE I DOWNLOADED THE DATA FROM THE VISION'S HARD DRIVE, I WENT LOOKING FOR A WAY TO CONTACT-- AND HOPEFULLY REASSEMBLE--THE AVENGERS.
BUT INSTEAD I FOUND THE AVENGERS'S FAILSAFE PROGRAM.
Altman, Teddy
Bradley, Elijah
Casey, Todd
Dorsey, Anissa
Kaplan, William
Moore, Perry
Parrish, Robin
A PROGRAM DESIGNED SO THAT, IF ANYTHING SHOULD HAPPEN TO THE AVENGERS--
--IF THEY WERE DESTROYED OR DISBANDED--
--THEN THE VISION WOULD BE ABLE TO PINPOINT THE EXACT LOCATIONS OF THE NEXT WAVE OF... WELL...YOUNG AVENGERS.
HOW COULD WE NOT HAVE KNOWN ABOUT THIS?
AND WHAT CONSTITUTES THE NEXT WAVE?
WA
MT
MN
OR
ID
SD
WI
WE'RE NOT SURE, BUT IT SEEMS AS THOUGH EACH OF US HAS SOME SIGNIFICANT TIE TO THE AVENGERS OR TO AVENGERS HISTORY.
WHAT KIND OF TIE?
WE WERE HOPING YOU COULD TELL US.

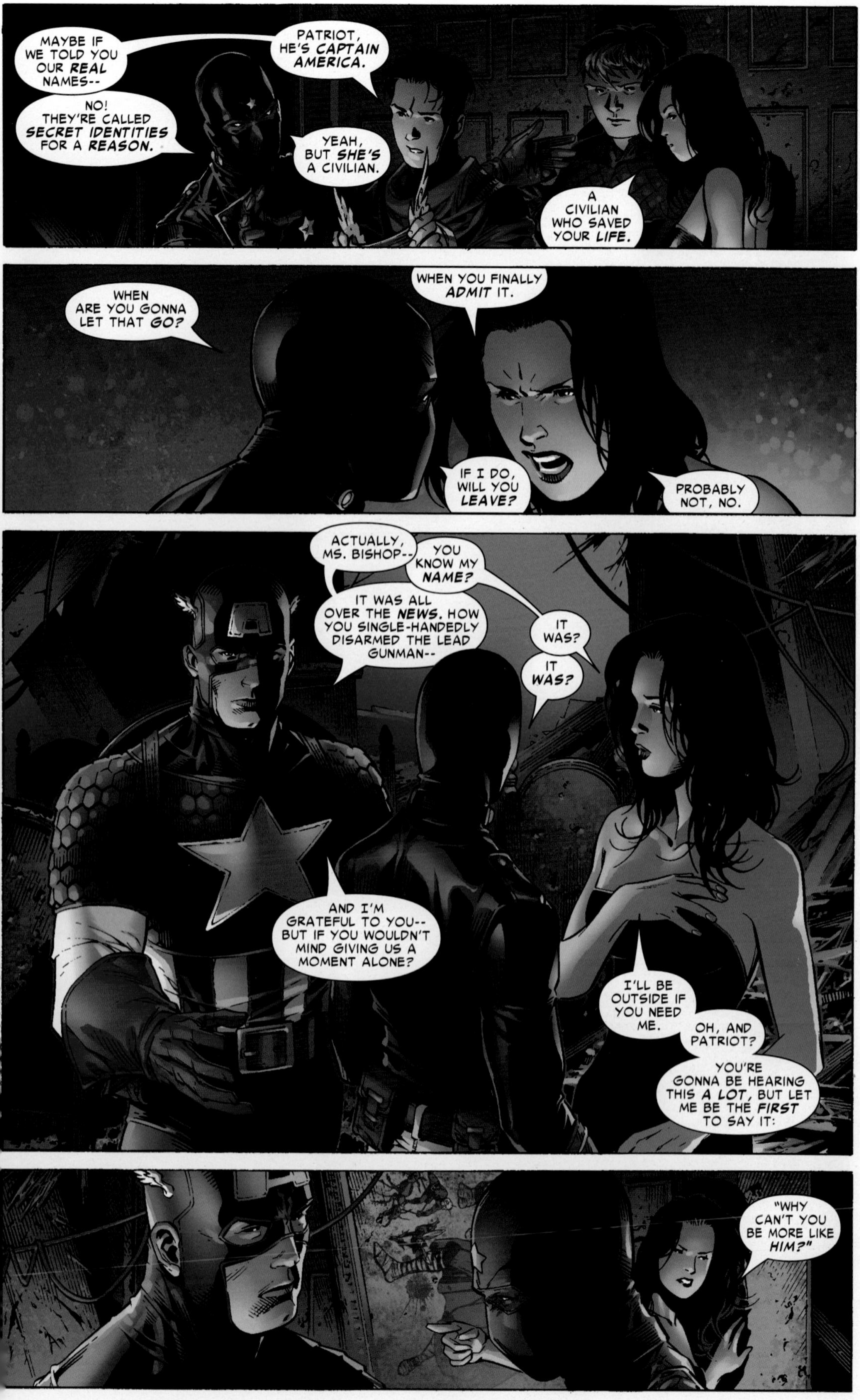
MAYBE IF WE TOLD YOU OUR REAL NAMES--
PATRIOT, HE'S CAPTAIN AMERICA.
NO! THEY'RE CALLED SECRET IDENTITIES FOR A REASON.
YEAH, BUT SHE'S A CIVILIAN.
A CIVILIAN WHO SAVED YOUR LIFE.
WHEN ARE YOU GONNA LET THAT GO?
WHEN YOU FINALLY ADMIT IT.
IF I DO, WILL YOU LEAVE?
PROBABLY NOT, NO.
ACTUALLY, MS. BISHOP--
YOU KNOW MY NAME?
IT WAS ALL OVER THE NEWS. HOW YOU SINGLE-HANDEDLY DISARMED THE LEAD GUNMAN--
IT WAS?
IT WAS?
AND I'M GRATEFUL TO YOU--BUT IF YOU WOULDN'T MIND GIVING US A MOMENT ALONE?
I'LL BE OUTSIDE IF YOU NEED ME.
OH, AND PATRIOT?
YOU'RE GONNA BE HEARING THIS A LOT, BUT LET ME BE THE FIRST TO SAY IT:
"WHY CAN'T YOU BE MORE LIKE HIM?"

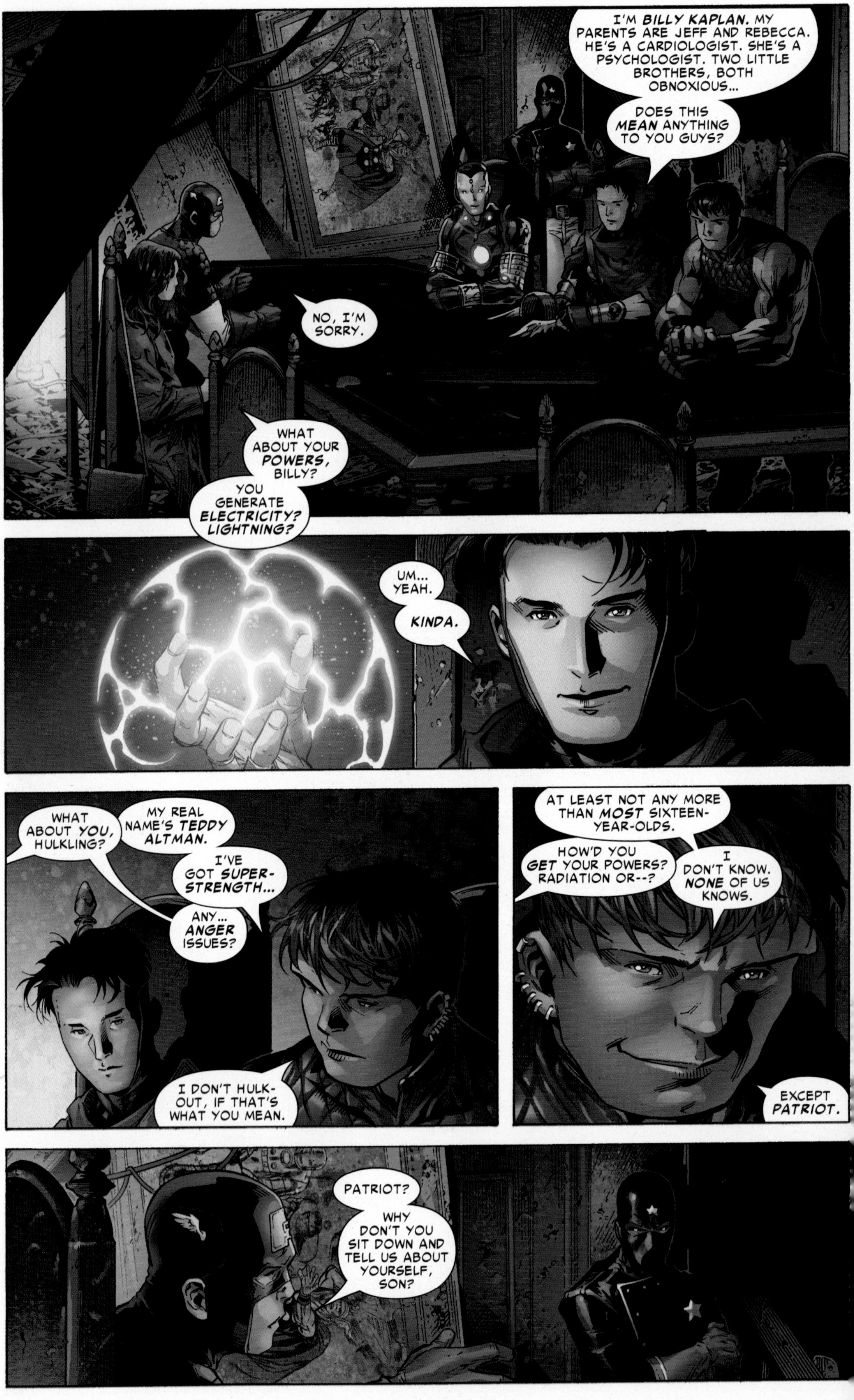

I'M BILLY KAPLAN. MY PARENTS ARE JEFF AND REBECCA. HE'S A CARDIOLOGIST. SHE'S A PSYCHOLOGIST. TWO LITTLE BROTHERS, BOTH OBNOXIOUS...
DOES THIS MEAN ANYTHING TO YOU GUYS?
NO, I'M SORRY.
WHAT ABOUT YOUR POWERS, BILLY?
YOU GENERATE ELECTRICITY? LIGHTNING?
UM... YEAH.
KINDA.
WHAT ABOUT YOU, HULKLING?
MY REAL NAME'S TEDDY ALTMAN.
I'VE GOT SUPER-STRENGTH...
ANY... ANGER ISSUES?
I DON'T HULK-OUT, IF THAT'S WHAT YOU MEAN.
AT LEAST NOT ANY MORE THAN MOST SIXTEEN-YEAR-OLDS.
HOW'D YOU GET YOUR POWERS? RADIATION OR--?
I DON'T KNOW. NONE OF US KNOWS.
EXCEPT PATRIOT.
PATRIOT?
WHY DON'T YOU SIT DOWN AND TELL US ABOUT YOURSELF, SON?

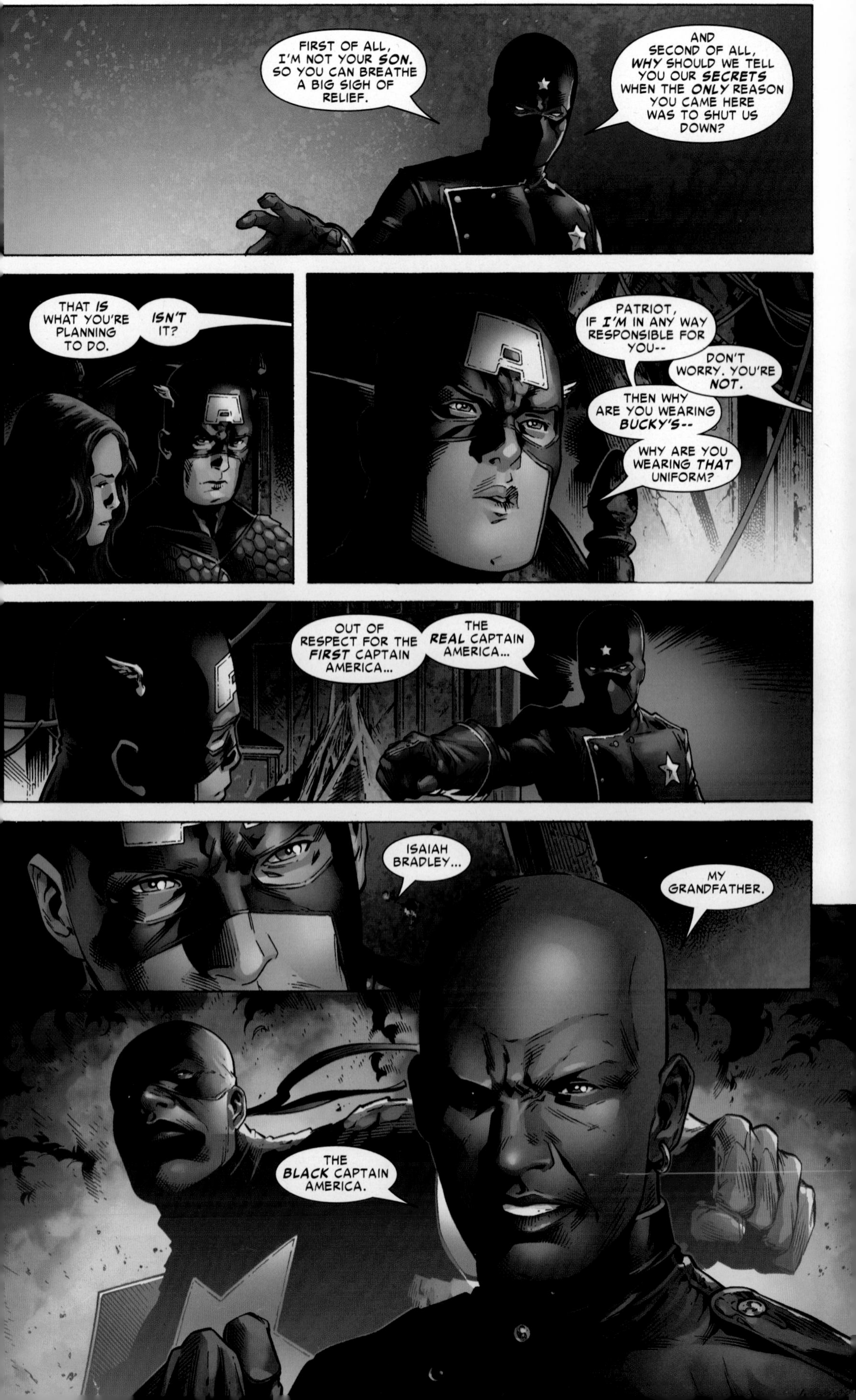
FIRST OF ALL, I'M NOT YOUR SON. SO YOU CAN BREATHE A BIG SIGH OF RELIEF.
AND SECOND OF ALL, WHY SHOULD WE TELL YOU OUR SECRETS WHEN THE ONLY REASON YOU CAME HERE WAS TO SHUT US DOWN?
THAT IS WHAT YOU'RE PLANNING TO DO.
ISN'T IT?
PATRIOT, IF I'M IN ANY WAY RESPONSIBLE FOR YOU--
DON'T WORRY. YOU'RE NOT.
THEN WHY ARE YOU WEARING BUCKY'S--
WHY ARE YOU WEARING THAT UNIFORM?
OUT OF RESPECT FOR THE FIRST CAPTAIN AMERICA...
THE REAL CAPTAIN AMERICA...
ISAIAH BRADLEY...
MY GRANDFATHER.
THE BLACK CAPTAIN AMERICA.

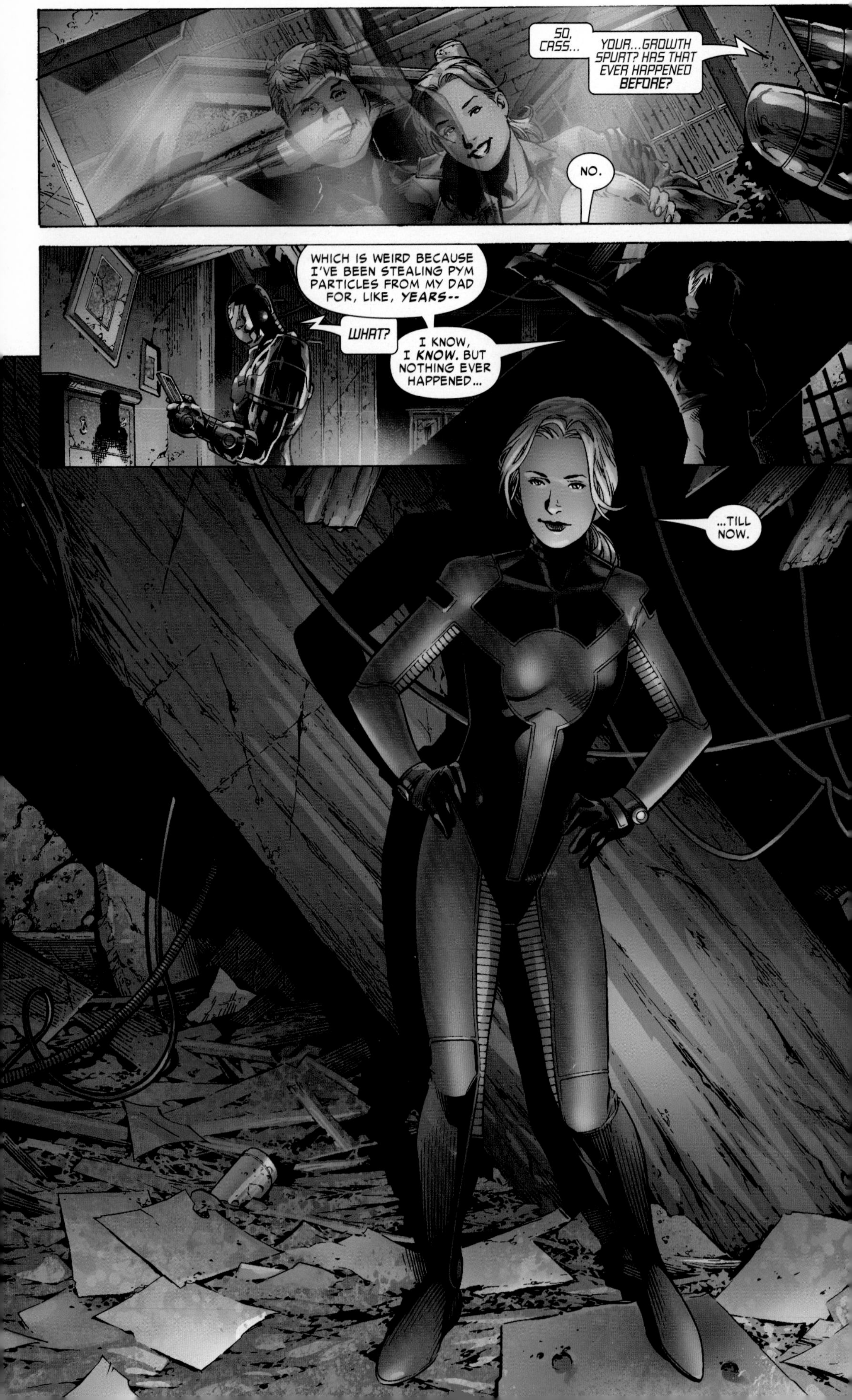
SO, CASS...
YOUR...GROWTH SPURT? HAS THAT EVER HAPPENED BEFORE?
NO.
WHICH IS WEIRD BECAUSE I'VE BEEN STEALING PYM PARTICLES FROM MY DAD FOR, LIKE, YEARS--
WHAT?
I KNOW, I KNOW. BUT NOTHING EVER HAPPENED...
...TILL NOW.

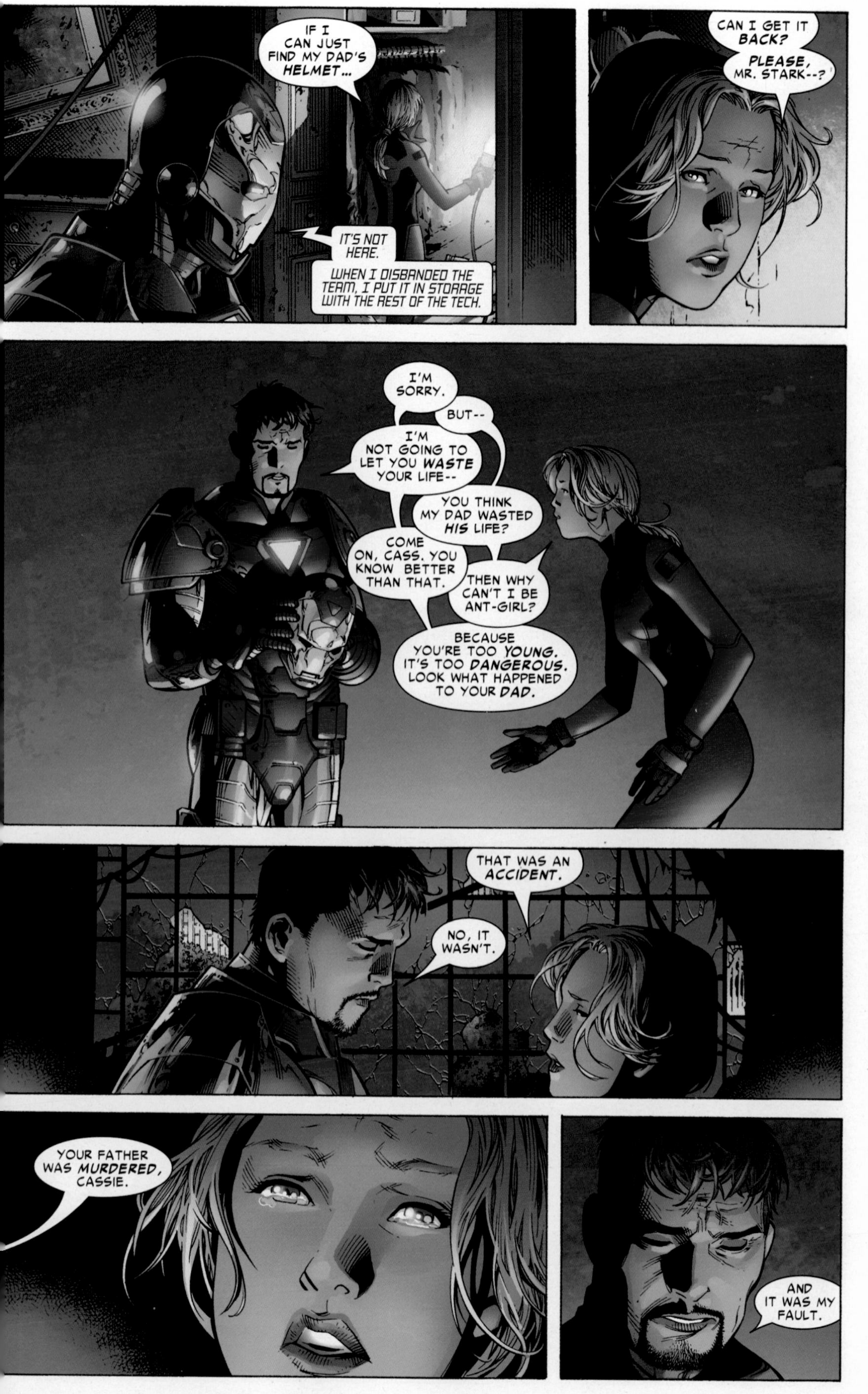
IF I CAN JUST FIND MY DAD'S HELMET...
IT'S NOT HERE.
WHEN I DISBANDED THE TEAM, I PUT IT IN STORAGE WITH THE REST OF THE TECH.
CAN I GET IT BACK?
PLEASE, MR. STARK--?
I'M SORRY.
BUT--
I'M NOT GOING TO LET YOU WASTE YOUR LIFE--
YOU THINK MY DAD WASTED HIS LIFE?
COME ON, CASS. YOU KNOW BETTER THAN THAT.
THEN WHY CAN'T I BE ANT-GIRL?
BECAUSE YOU'RE TOO YOUNG. IT'S TOO DANGEROUS. LOOK WHAT HAPPENED TO YOUR DAD.
THAT WAS AN ACCIDENT.
NO, IT WASN'T.
YOUR FATHER WAS MURDERED, CASSIE.
AND IT WAS MY FAULT.

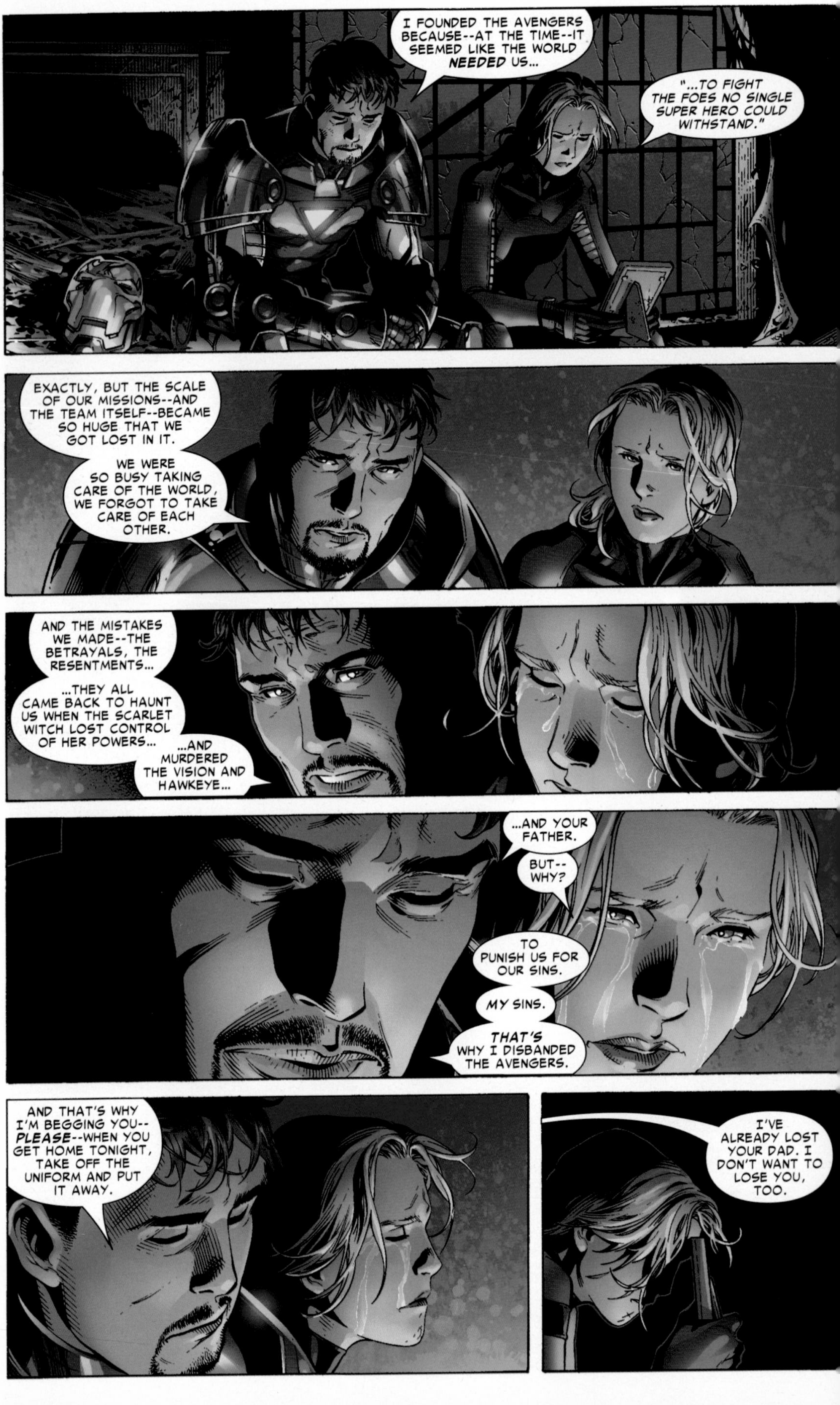
I FOUNDED THE AVENGERS BECAUSE--AT THE TIME--IT SEEMED LIKE THE WORLD *NEEDED* US...
"...TO FIGHT THE FOES NO SINGLE SUPER HERO COULD WITHSTAND."
EXACTLY, BUT THE SCALE OF OUR MISSIONS--AND THE TEAM ITSELF--BECAME SO HUGE THAT WE GOT LOST IN IT.
WE WERE SO BUSY TAKING CARE OF THE WORLD, WE FORGOT TO TAKE CARE OF EACH OTHER.
AND THE MISTAKES WE MADE--THE BETRAYALS, THE RESENTMENTS...
...THEY ALL CAME BACK TO HAUNT US WHEN THE SCARLET WITCH LOST CONTROL OF HER POWERS...
...AND MURDERED THE VISION AND HAWKEYE...
...AND YOUR FATHER.
BUT-- WHY?
TO PUNISH US FOR OUR SINS.
MY SINS.
THAT'S WHY I DISBANDED THE AVENGERS.
AND THAT'S WHY I'M BEGGING YOU-- *PLEASE*--WHEN YOU GET HOME TONIGHT, TAKE OFF THE UNIFORM AND PUT IT AWAY.
I'VE ALREADY LOST YOUR DAD. I DON'T WANT TO LOSE YOU, TOO.

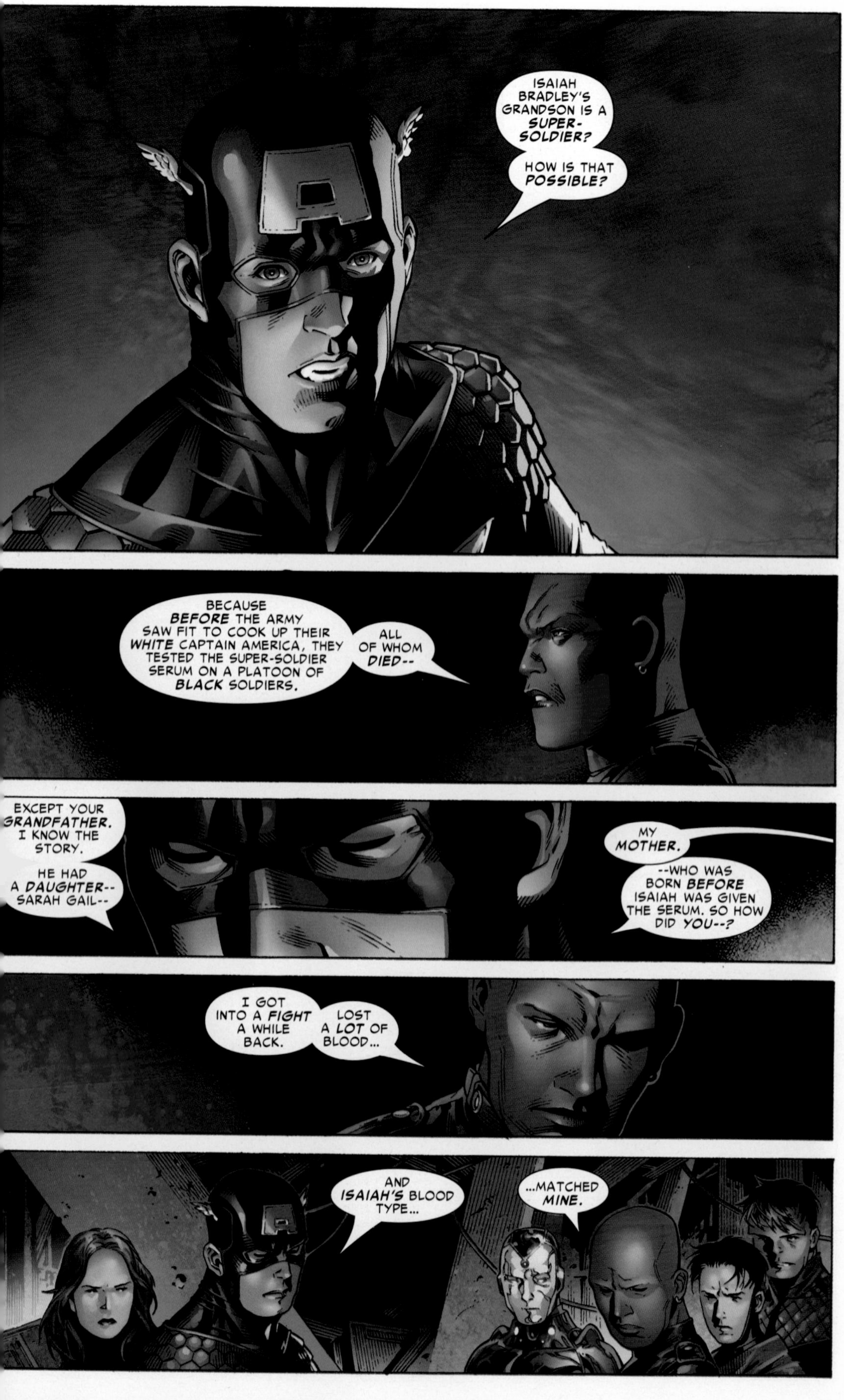
ISAIAH BRADLEY'S GRANDSON IS A SUPER-SOLDIER?
HOW IS THAT POSSIBLE?
BECAUSE BEFORE THE ARMY SAW FIT TO COOK UP THEIR WHITE CAPTAIN AMERICA, THEY TESTED THE SUPER-SOLDIER SERUM ON A PLATOON OF BLACK SOLDIERS.
ALL OF WHOM DIED--
EXCEPT YOUR GRANDFATHER. I KNOW THE STORY.
HE HAD A DAUGHTER-- SARAH GAIL--
MY MOTHER.
--WHO WAS BORN BEFORE ISAIAH WAS GIVEN THE SERUM. SO HOW DID YOU--?
I GOT INTO A FIGHT A WHILE BACK.
LOST A LOT OF BLOOD...
AND ISAIAH'S BLOOD TYPE...
...MATCHED MINE.

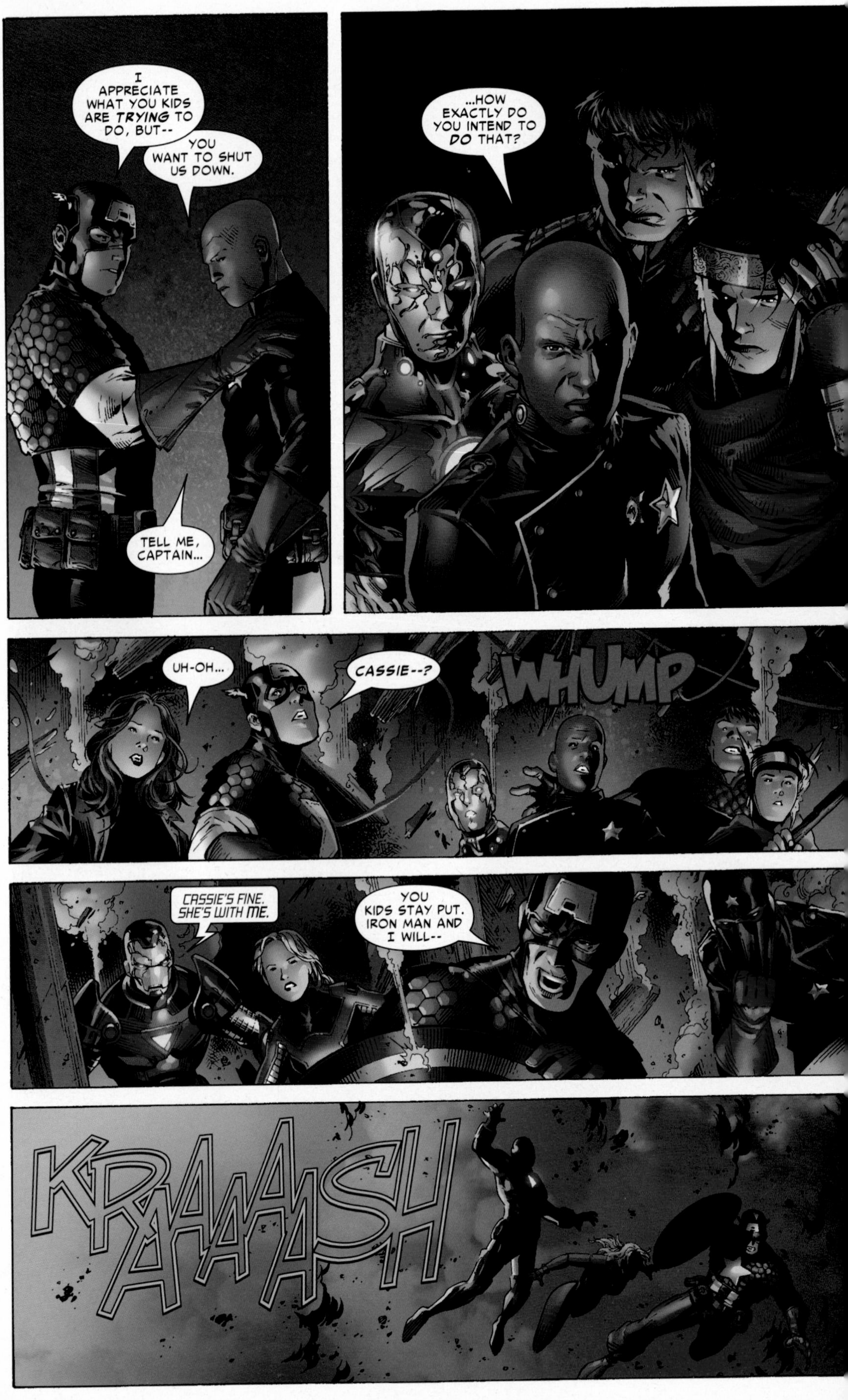
I APPRECIATE WHAT YOU KIDS ARE TRYING TO DO, BUT--
YOU WANT TO SHUT US DOWN.
TELL ME, CAPTAIN...
...HOW EXACTLY DO YOU INTEND TO DO THAT?
UH-OH...
CASSIE--?
WHUMP
CASSIE'S FINE. SHE'S WITH ME.
YOU KIDS STAY PUT. IRON MAN AND I WILL--
KRAAAASH
AAAAH

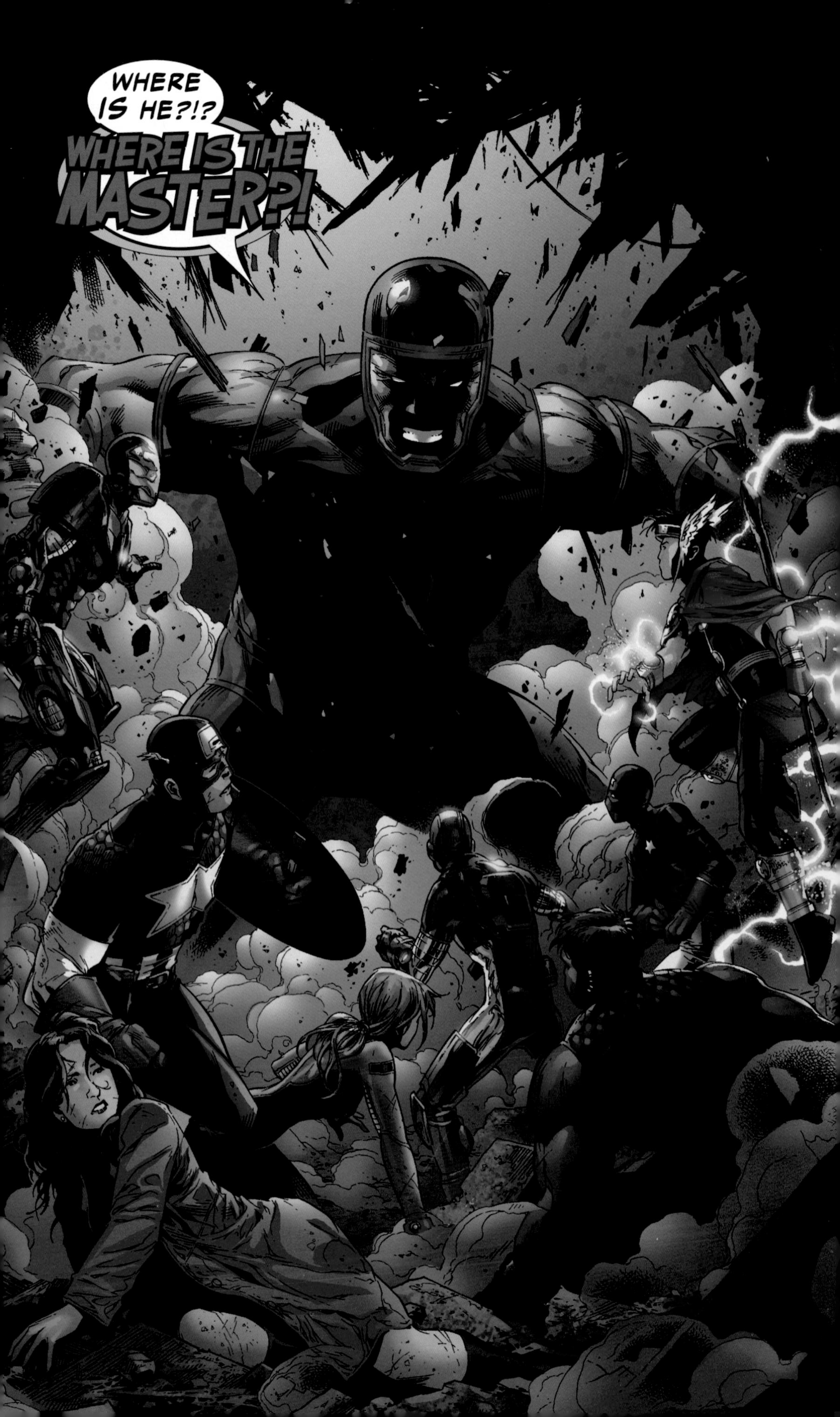
WHERE IS HE?!?
WHERE IS THE MASTER?!

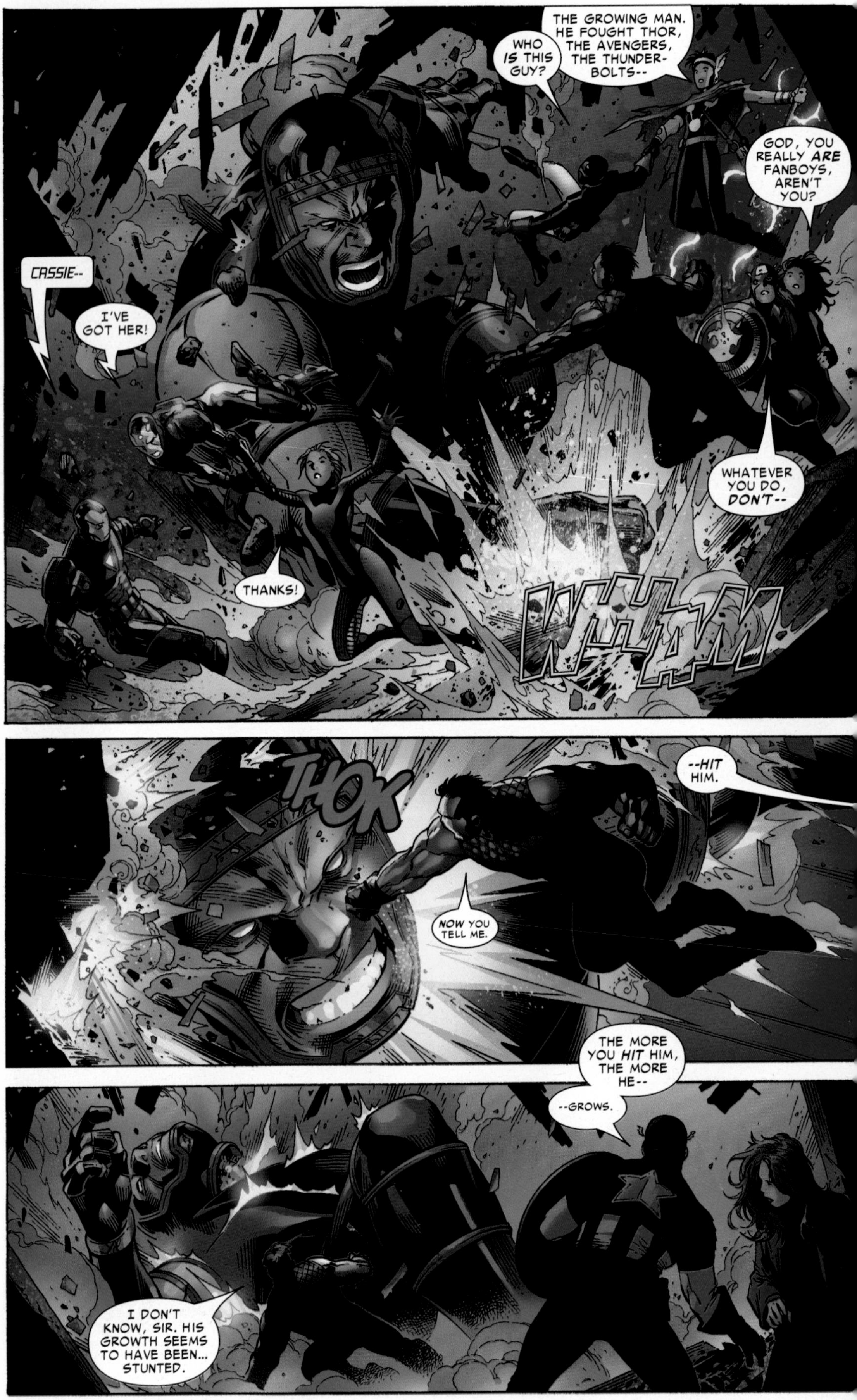
WHO IS THIS GUY?
THE GROWING MAN. HE FOUGHT THOR, THE AVENGERS, THE THUNDER-BOLTS--
GOD, YOU REALLY ARE FANBOYS, AREN'T YOU?
CASSIE--
I'VE GOT HER!
THANKS!
WHATEVER YOU DO, DON'T--
WHAM
THOK
--HIT HIM.
NOW YOU TELL ME.
THE MORE YOU HIT HIM, THE MORE HE--
--GROWS.
I DON'T KNOW, SIR. HIS GROWTH SEEMS TO HAVE BEEN... STUNTED.

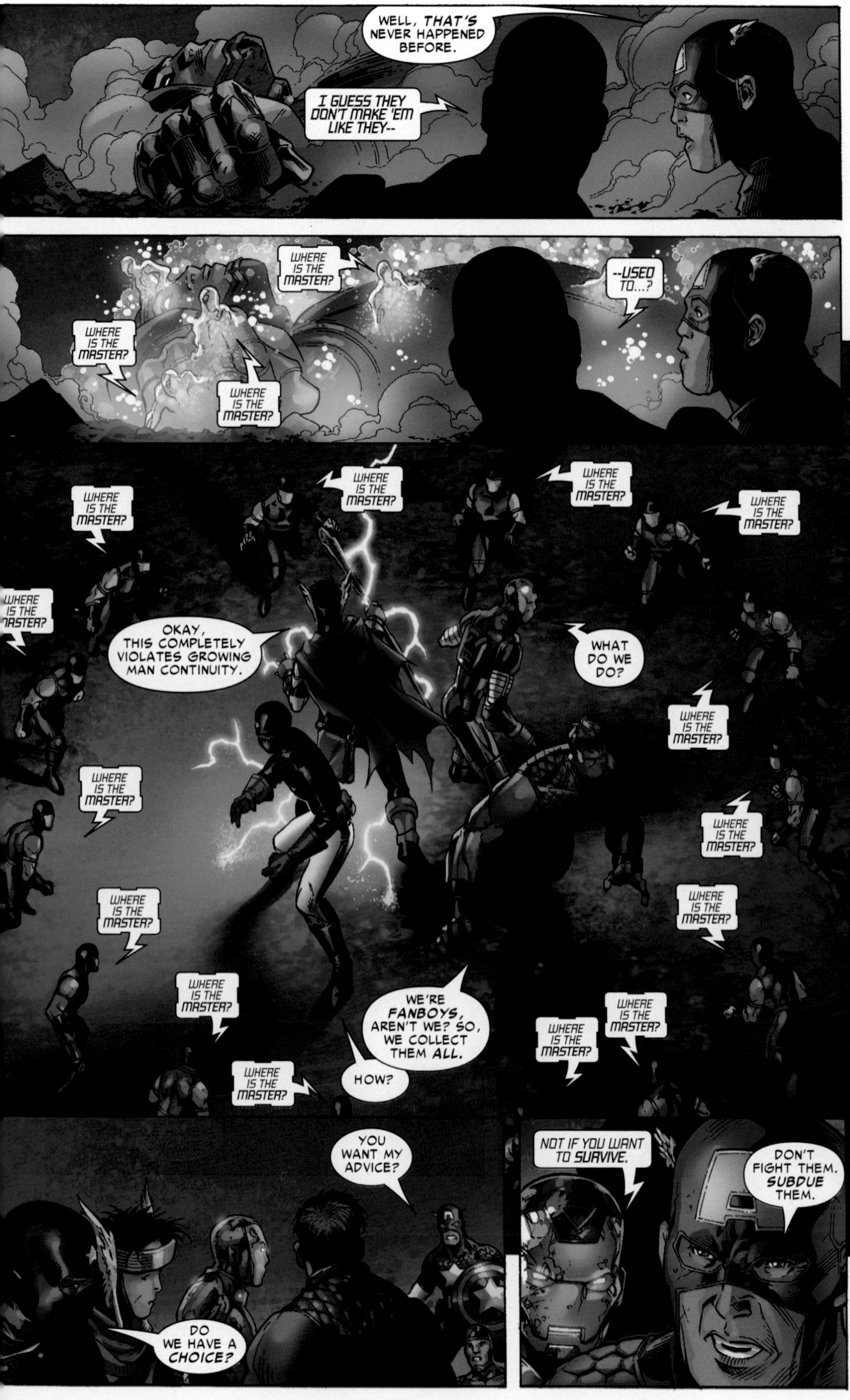
WELL, THAT'S NEVER HAPPENED BEFORE.
I GUESS THEY DON'T MAKE 'EM LIKE THEY--
WHERE IS THE MASTER?
--USED TO...?
WHERE IS THE MASTER?
WHERE IS THE MASTER?
WHERE IS THE MASTER?
WHERE IS THE MASTER?
WHERE IS THE MASTER?
WHERE IS THE MASTER?
OKAY, THIS COMPLETELY VIOLATES GROWING MAN CONTINUITY.
WHAT DO WE DO?
WHERE IS THE MASTER?
WHERE IS THE MASTER?
WHERE IS THE MASTER?
WHERE IS THE MASTER?
WHERE IS THE MASTER?
WHERE IS THE MASTER?
WE'RE FANBOYS, AREN'T WE? SO, WE COLLECT THEM ALL.
HOW?
WHERE IS THE MASTER?
WHERE IS THE MASTER?
WHERE IS THE MASTER?
YOU WANT MY ADVICE?
DO WE HAVE A CHOICE?
NOT IF YOU WANT TO SURVIVE.
DON'T FIGHT THEM. SUBDUE THEM.

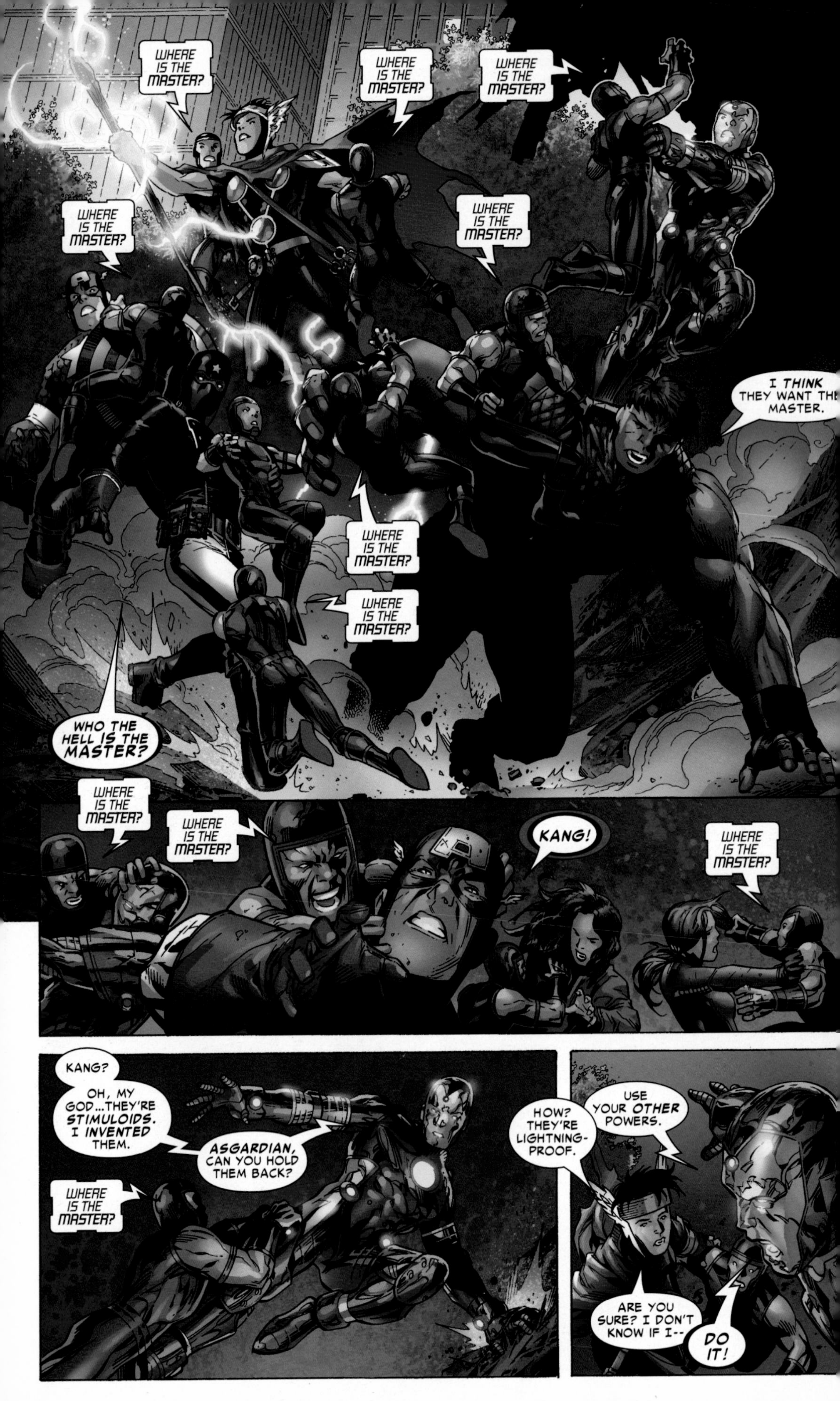
WHERE IS THE MASTER?
WHERE IS THE MASTER?
WHERE IS THE MASTER?
WHERE IS THE MASTER?
WHERE IS THE MASTER?
I THINK THEY WANT THE MASTER.
WHERE IS THE MASTER?
WHERE IS THE MASTER?
WHO THE HELL IS THE MASTER?
WHERE IS THE MASTER?
WHERE IS THE MASTER?
KANG!
WHERE IS THE MASTER?
KANG?
OH, MY GOD...THEY'RE STIMULOIDS. I INVENTED THEM.
ASGARDIAN, CAN YOU HOLD THEM BACK?
WHERE IS THE MASTER?
HOW? THEY'RE LIGHTNING-PROOF.
USE YOUR OTHER POWERS.
ARE YOU SURE? I DON'T KNOW IF I--
DO IT!

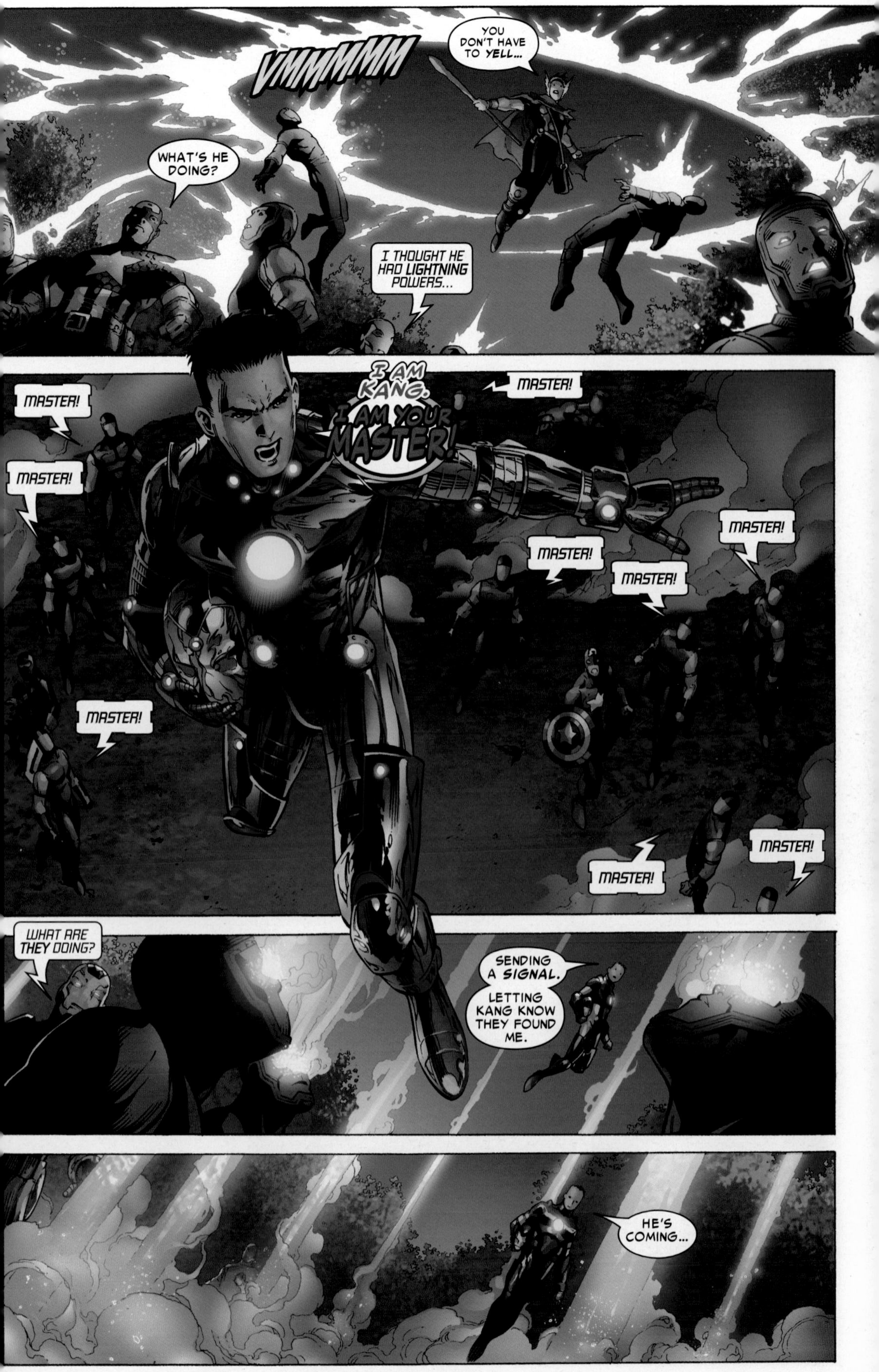
VMMMMM
YOU DON'T HAVE TO YELL...
WHAT'S HE DOING?
I THOUGHT HE HAD LIGHTNING POWERS...
I AM KANG. I AM YOUR MASTER!
MASTER!
MASTER!
MASTER!
MASTER!
MASTER!
MASTER!
MASTER!
MASTER!
MASTER!
WHAT ARE THEY DOING?
SENDING A SIGNAL.
LETTING KANG KNOW THEY FOUND ME.
HE'S COMING...

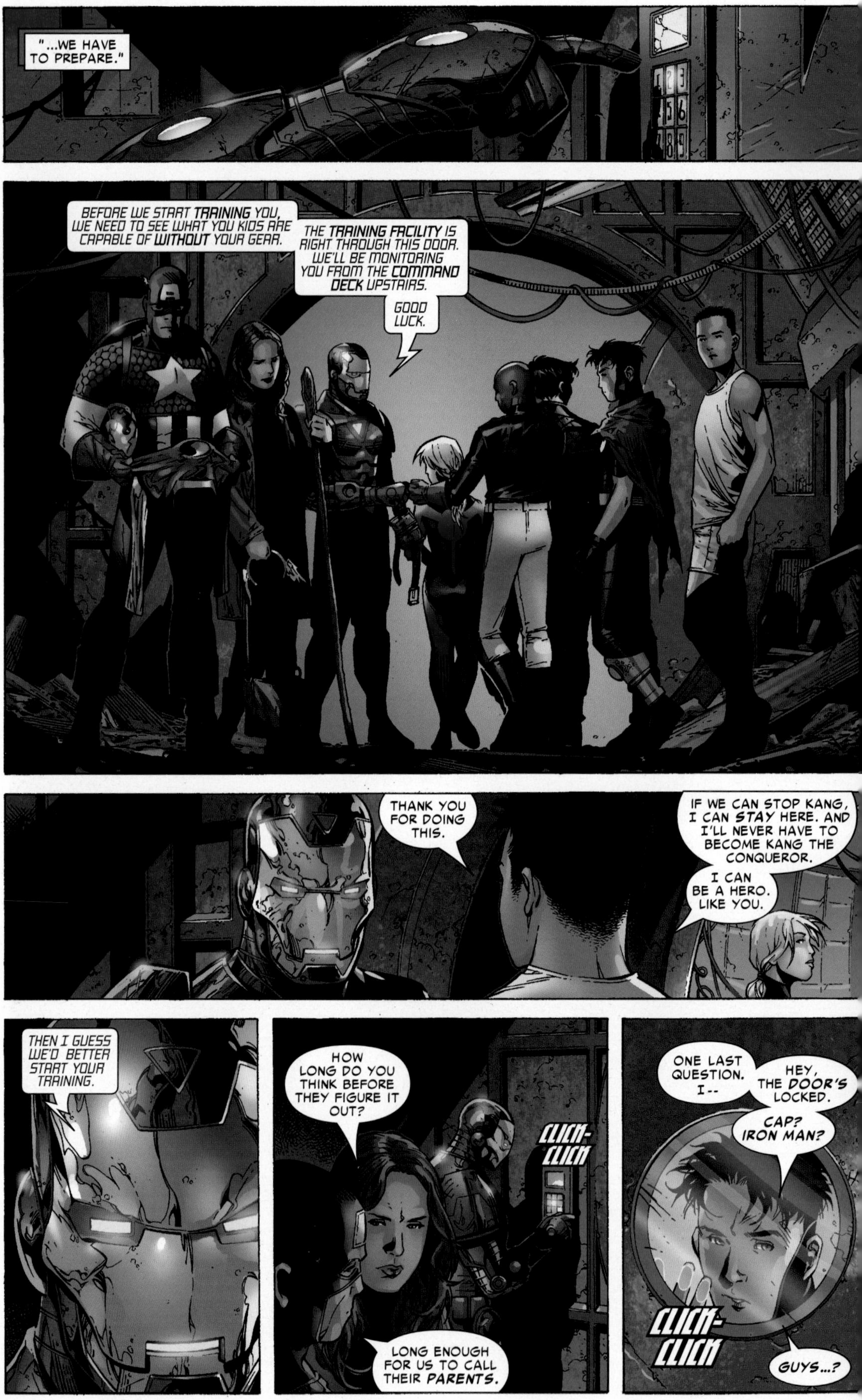
"...WE HAVE TO PREPARE."
BEFORE WE START TRAINING YOU, WE NEED TO SEE WHAT YOU KIDS ARE CAPABLE OF WITHOUT YOUR GEAR.
THE TRAINING FACILITY IS RIGHT THROUGH THIS DOOR. WE'LL BE MONITORING YOU FROM THE COMMAND DECK UPSTAIRS.
GOOD LUCK.
THANK YOU FOR DOING THIS.
IF WE CAN STOP KANG, I CAN STAY HERE. AND I'LL NEVER HAVE TO BECOME KANG THE CONQUEROR.
I CAN BE A HERO. LIKE YOU.
THEN I GUESS WE'D BETTER START YOUR TRAINING.
HOW LONG DO YOU THINK BEFORE THEY FIGURE IT OUT?
CLICK-CLICK
LONG ENOUGH FOR US TO CALL THEIR PARENTS.
ONE LAST QUESTION. I--
HEY, THE DOOR'S LOCKED.
CAP? IRON MAN?
CLICK-CLICK
GUYS...?

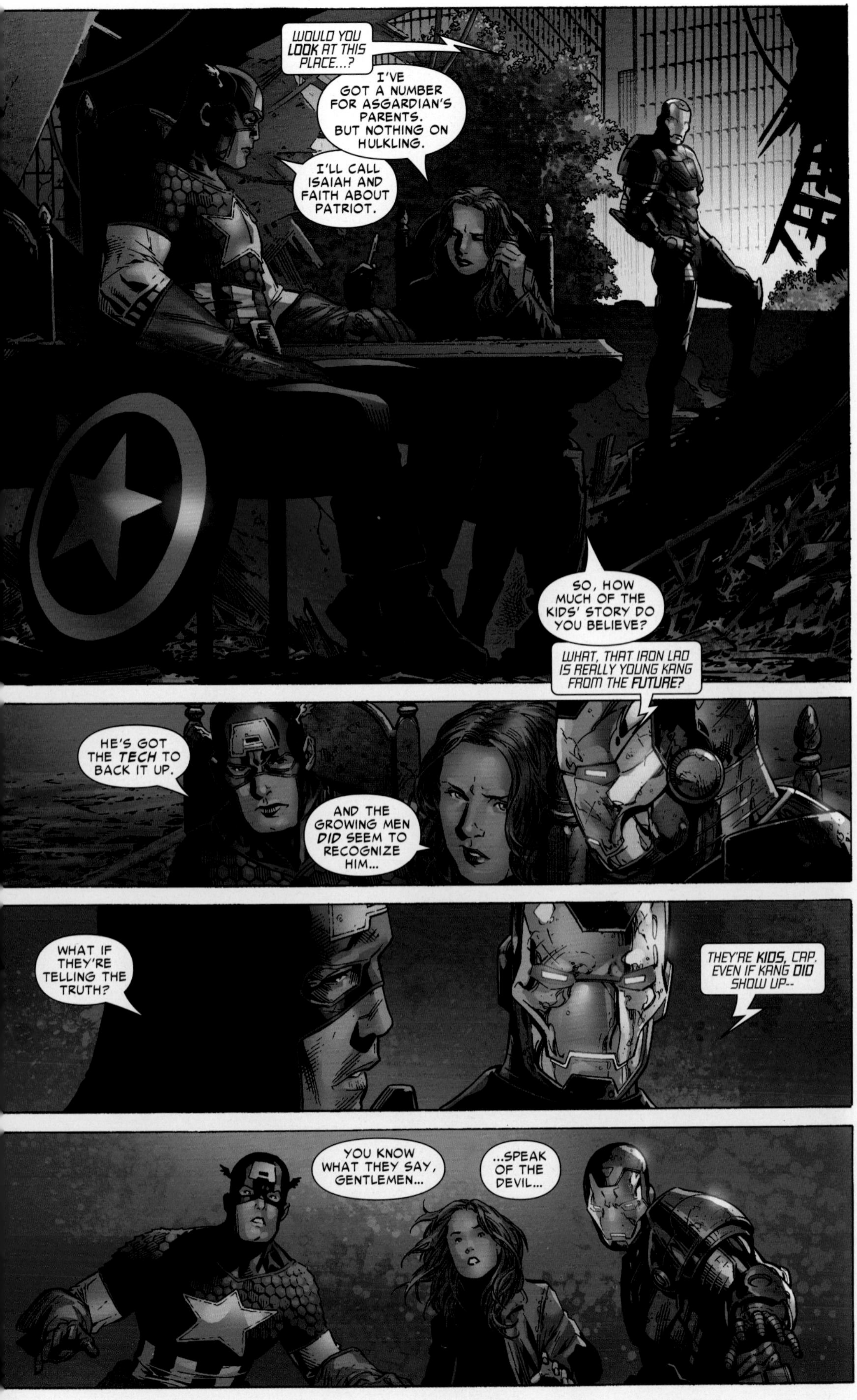
WOULD YOU LOOK AT THIS PLACE...?
I'VE GOT A NUMBER FOR ASGARDIAN'S PARENTS. BUT NOTHING ON HULKLING.
I'LL CALL ISAIAH AND FAITH ABOUT PATRIOT.
SO, HOW MUCH OF THE KIDS' STORY DO YOU BELIEVE?
WHAT, THAT IRON LAD IS REALLY YOUNG KANG FROM THE FUTURE?
HE'S GOT THE TECH TO BACK IT UP.
AND THE GROWING MEN DID SEEM TO RECOGNIZE HIM...
WHAT IF THEY'RE TELLING THE TRUTH?
THEY'RE KIDS, CAP. EVEN IF KANG DID SHOW UP--
YOU KNOW WHAT THEY SAY, GENTLEMEN...
...SPEAK OF THE DEVIL...

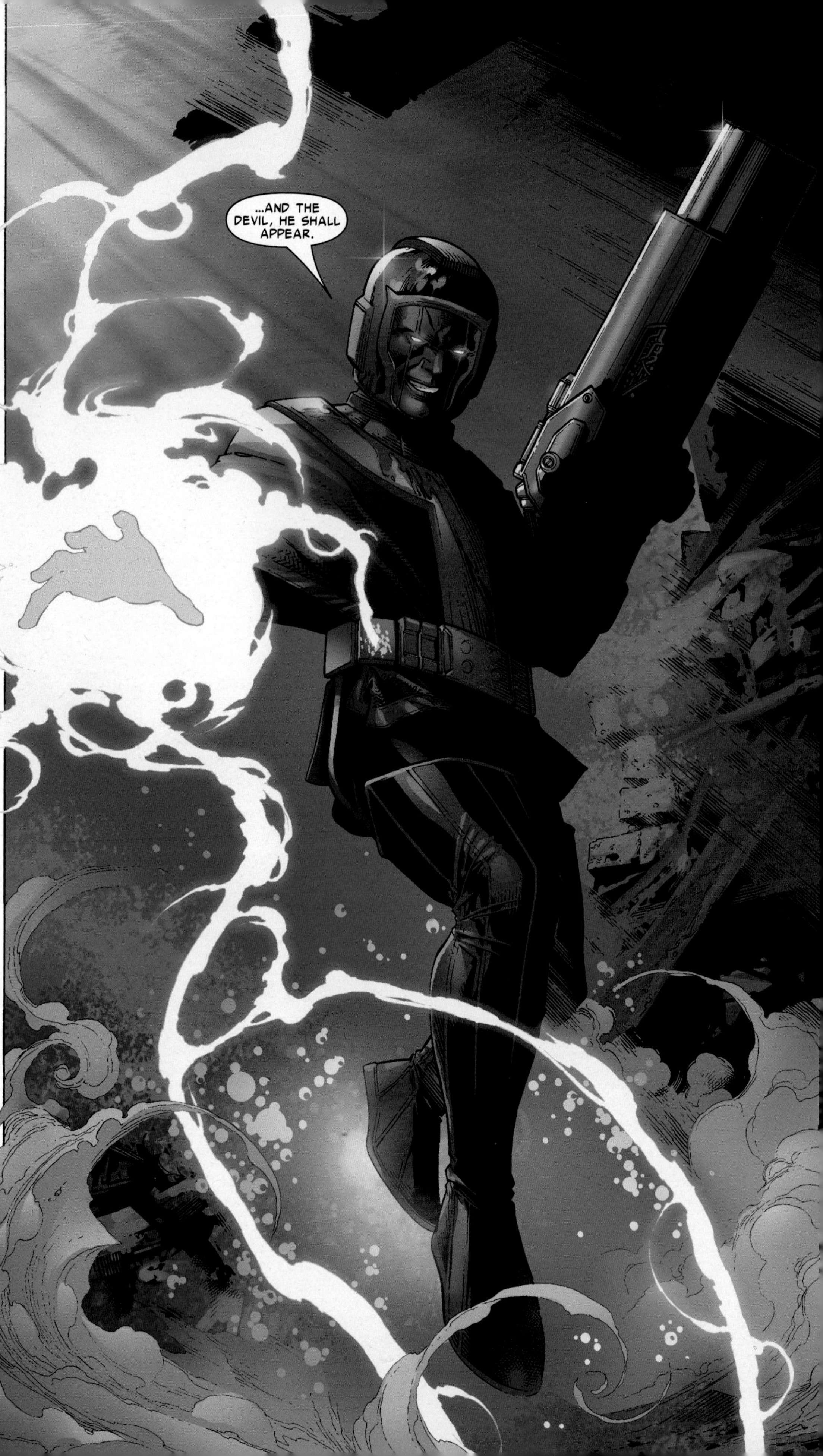
...AND THE DEVIL, HE SHALL APPEAR.

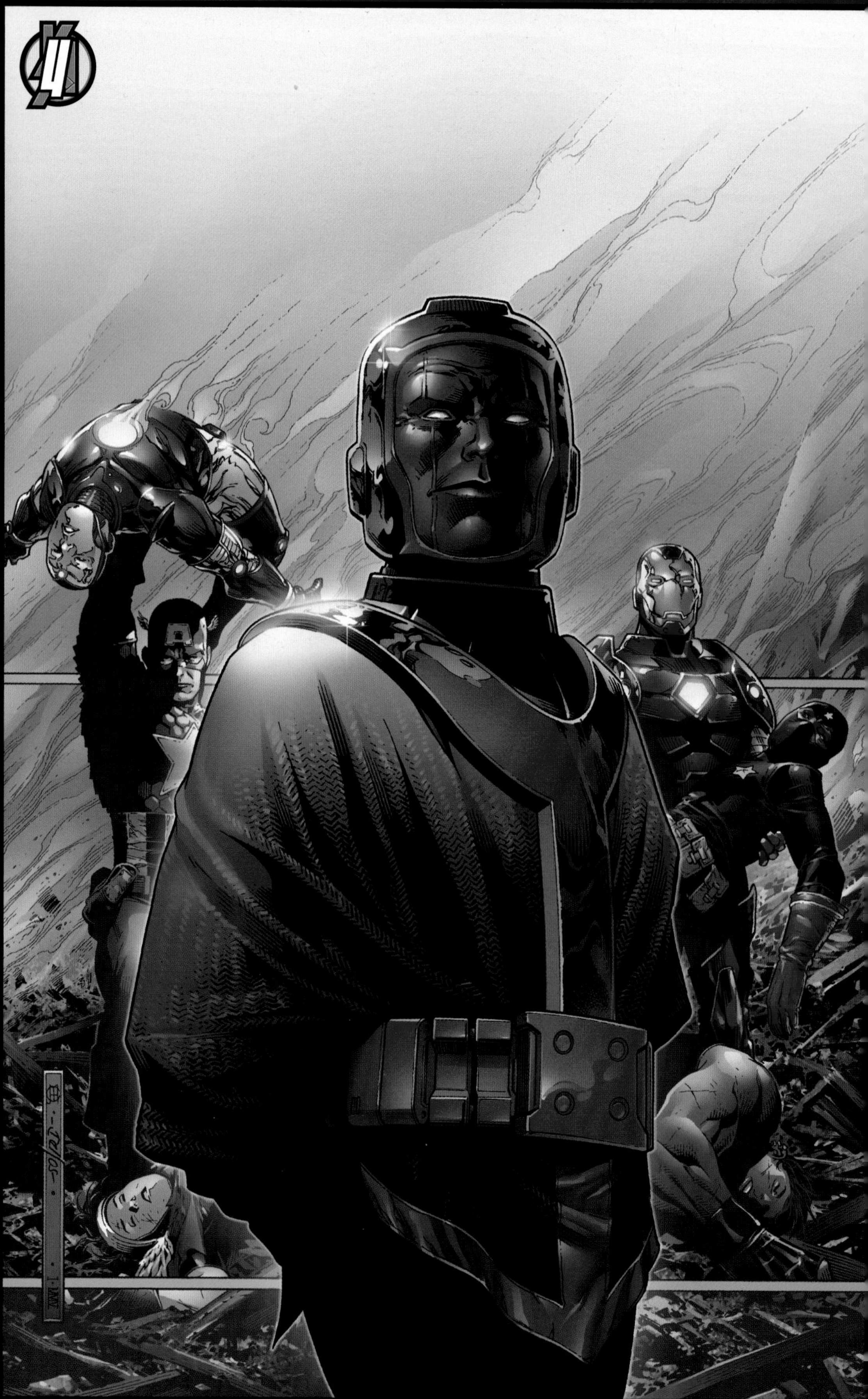

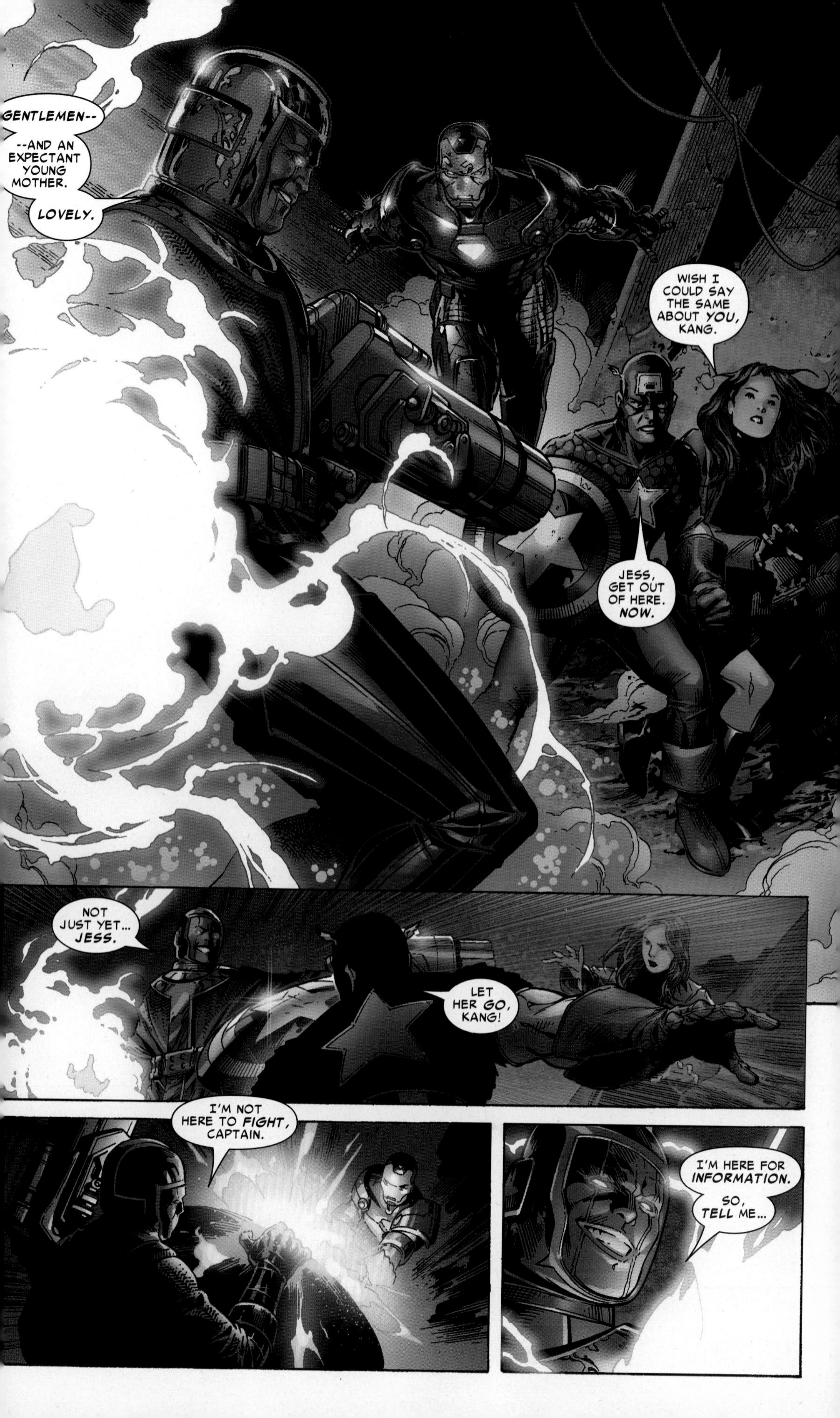
GENTLEMEN--
--AND AN EXPECTANT YOUNG MOTHER.
LOVELY.
WISH I COULD SAY THE SAME ABOUT YOU, KANG.
JESS, GET OUT OF HERE. NOW.
NOT JUST YET... JESS.
LET HER GO, KANG!
I'M NOT HERE TO FIGHT, CAPTAIN.
I'M HERE FOR INFORMATION.
SO, TELL ME...

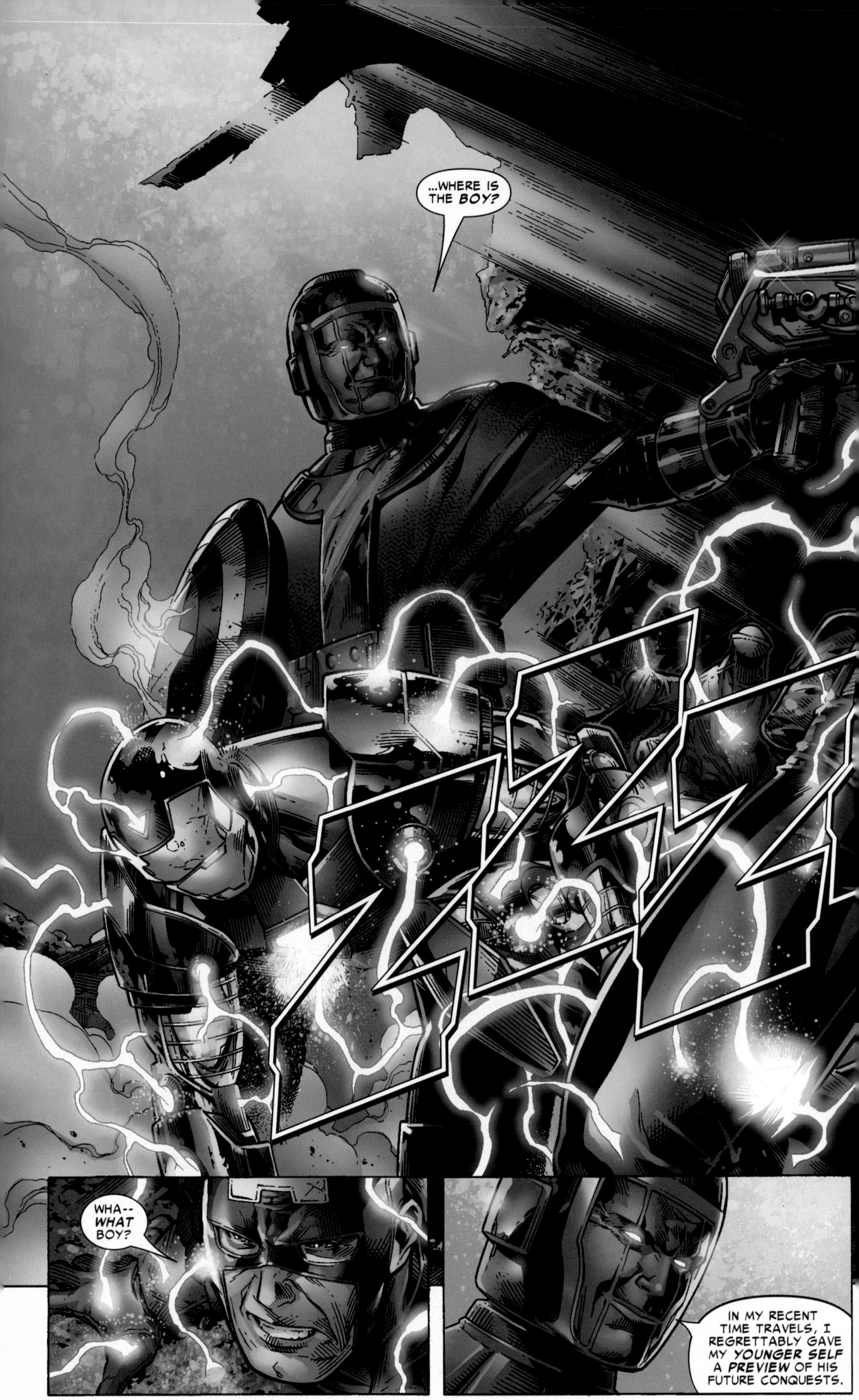
...WHERE IS THE BOY?
WHA-- WHAT BOY?
IN MY RECENT TIME TRAVELS, I REGRETTABLY GAVE MY YOUNGER SELF A PREVIEW OF HIS FUTURE CONQUESTS.

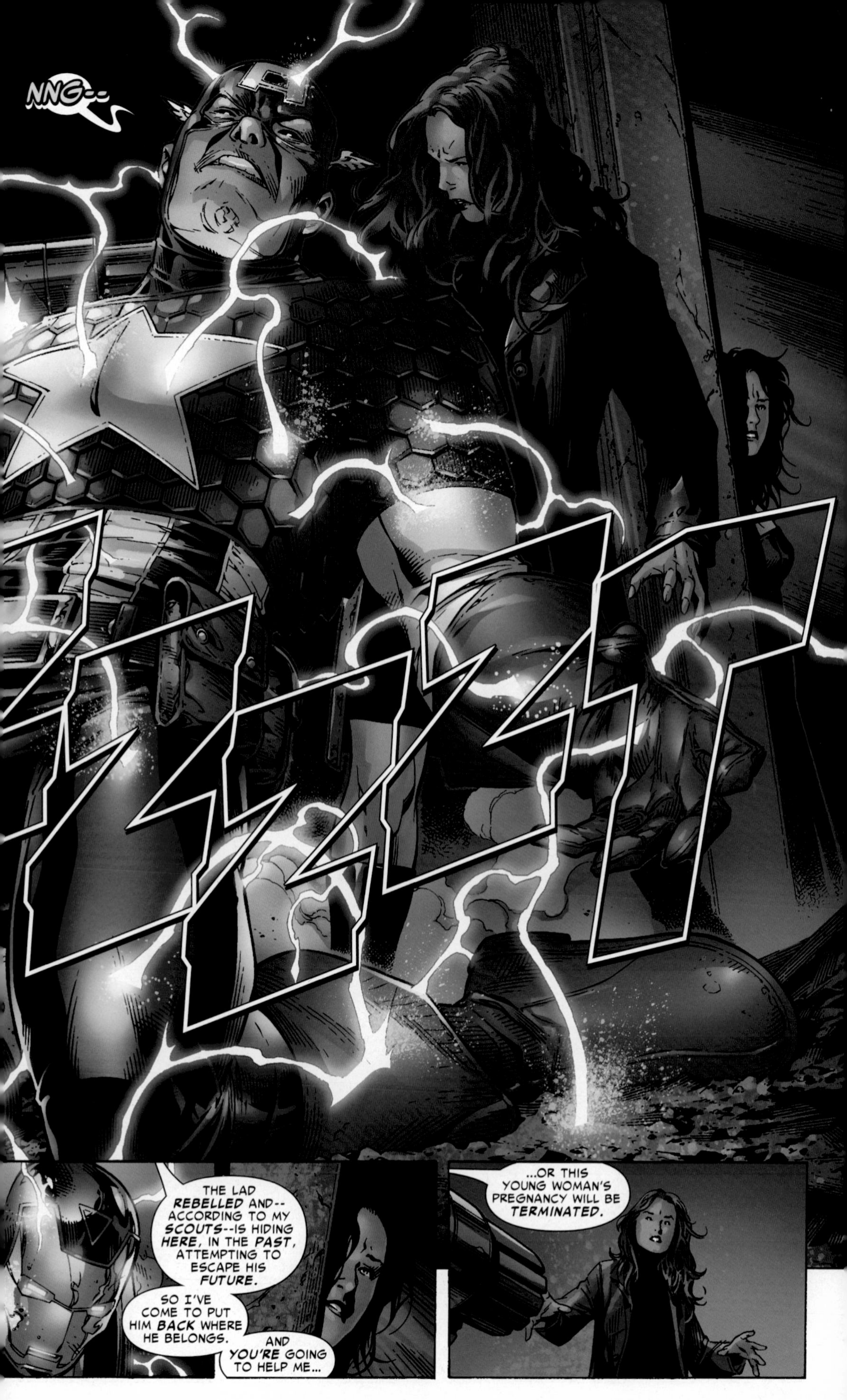
NNG--
ZZZT
THE LAD REBELLED AND-- ACCORDING TO MY SCOUTS--IS HIDING HERE, IN THE PAST, ATTEMPTING TO ESCAPE HIS FUTURE.
SO I'VE COME TO PUT HIM BACK WHERE HE BELONGS.
AND YOU'RE GOING TO HELP ME...
...OR THIS YOUNG WOMAN'S PREGNANCY WILL BE TERMINATED.

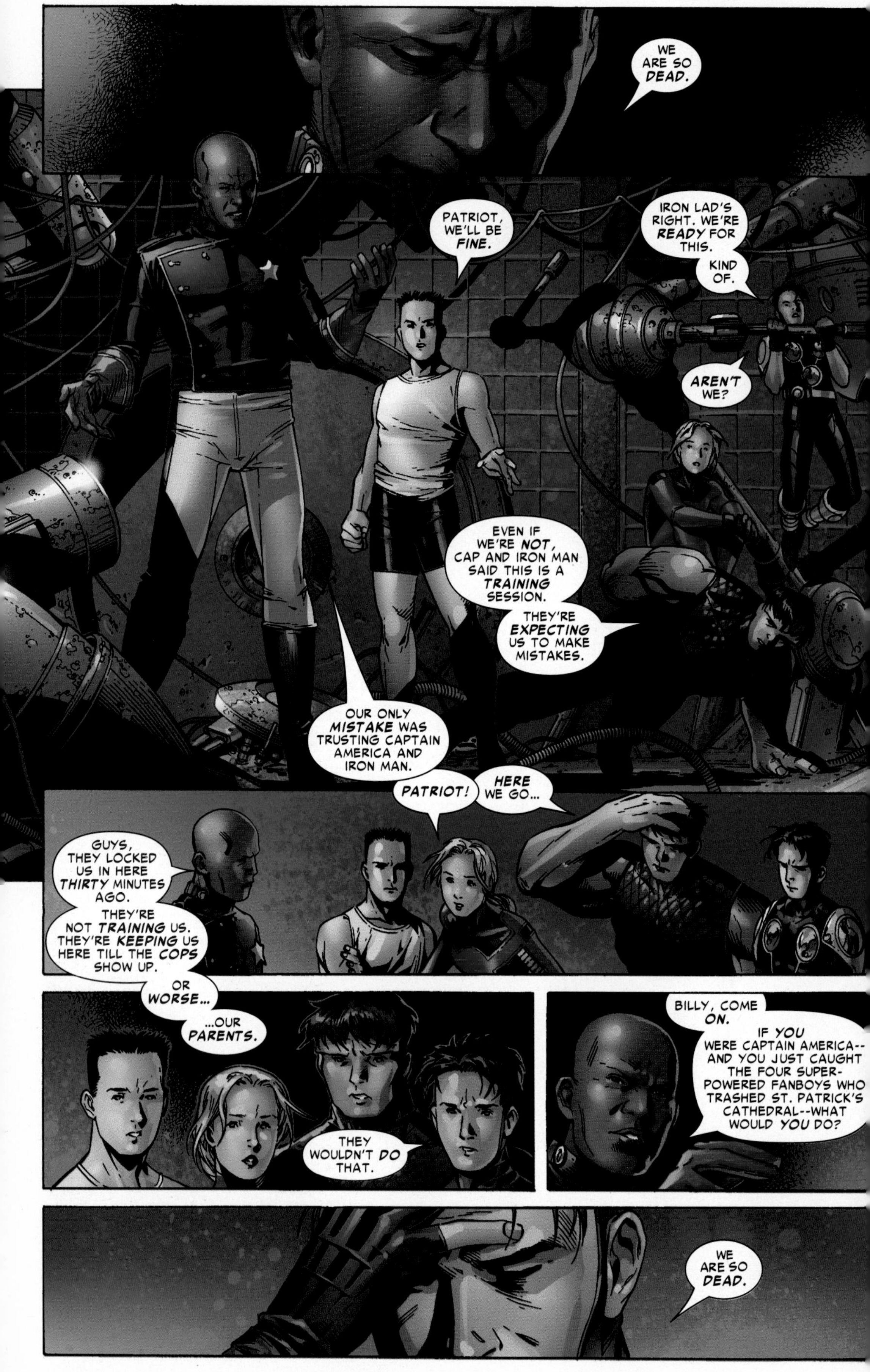
WE ARE SO DEAD.
PATRIOT, WE'LL BE FINE.
IRON LAD'S RIGHT. WE'RE READY FOR THIS.
KIND OF.
AREN'T WE?
EVEN IF WE'RE NOT, CAP AND IRON MAN SAID THIS IS A TRAINING SESSION.
THEY'RE EXPECTING US TO MAKE MISTAKES.
OUR ONLY MISTAKE WAS TRUSTING CAPTAIN AMERICA AND IRON MAN.
PATRIOT!
HERE WE GO...
GUYS, THEY LOCKED US IN HERE THIRTY MINUTES AGO.
THEY'RE NOT TRAINING US. THEY'RE KEEPING US HERE TILL THE COPS SHOW UP.
OR WORSE...
...OUR PARENTS.
THEY WOULDN'T DO THAT.
BILLY, COME ON.
IF YOU WERE CAPTAIN AMERICA-- AND YOU JUST CAUGHT THE FOUR SUPER-POWERED FANBOYS WHO TRASHED ST. PATRICK'S CATHEDRAL--WHAT WOULD YOU DO?
WE ARE SO DEAD.

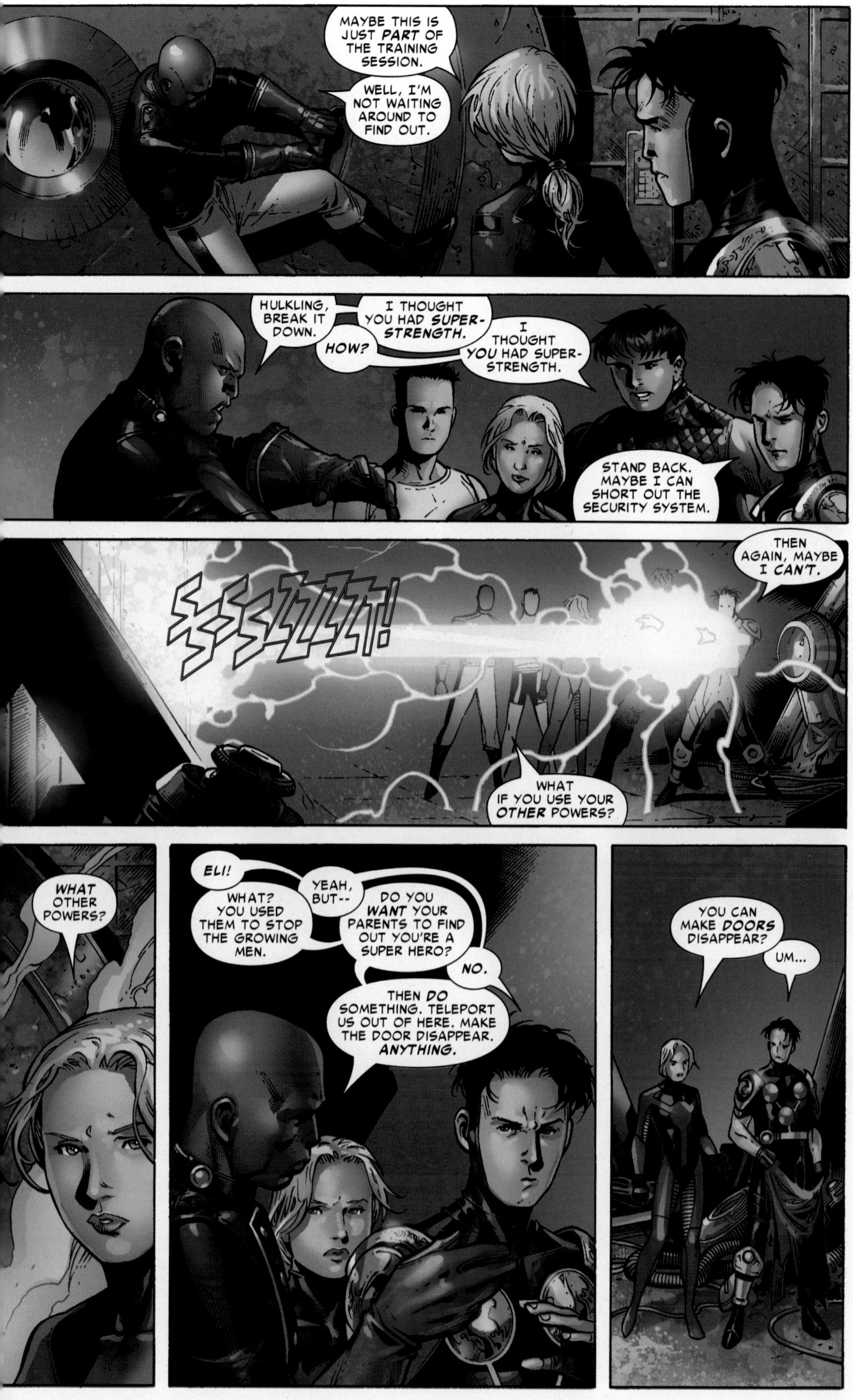
MAYBE THIS IS JUST PART OF THE TRAINING SESSION.
WELL, I'M NOT WAITING AROUND TO FIND OUT.
HULKLING, BREAK IT DOWN.
HOW?
I THOUGHT YOU HAD SUPER-STRENGTH.
I THOUGHT YOU HAD SUPER-STRENGTH.
STAND BACK. MAYBE I CAN SHORT OUT THE SECURITY SYSTEM.
SSSZZZT!
THEN AGAIN, MAYBE I CAN'T.
WHAT IF YOU USE YOUR OTHER POWERS?
WHAT OTHER POWERS?
ELI!
WHAT? YOU USED THEM TO STOP THE GROWING MEN.
YEAH, BUT--
DO YOU WANT YOUR PARENTS TO FIND OUT YOU'RE A SUPER HERO?
NO.
THEN DO SOMETHING. TELEPORT US OUT OF HERE. MAKE THE DOOR DISAPPEAR. ANYTHING.
YOU CAN MAKE DOORS DISAPPEAR?
UM...

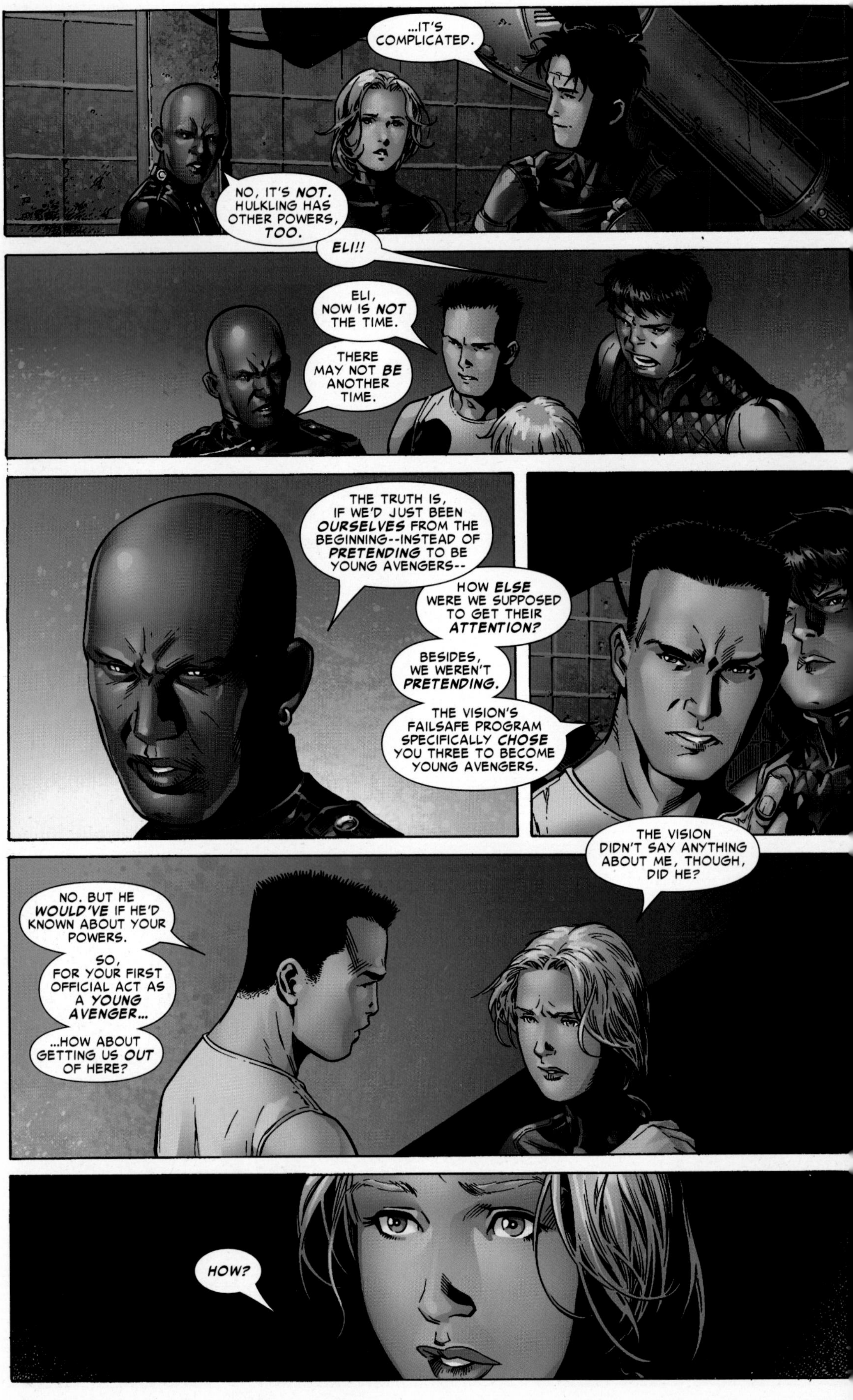
...IT'S COMPLICATED.
NO, IT'S NOT. HULKLING HAS OTHER POWERS, TOO.
ELI!!
ELI, NOW IS NOT THE TIME.
THERE MAY NOT BE ANOTHER TIME.
THE TRUTH IS, IF WE'D JUST BEEN OURSELVES FROM THE BEGINNING--INSTEAD OF PRETENDING TO BE YOUNG AVENGERS--
HOW ELSE WERE WE SUPPOSED TO GET THEIR ATTENTION?
BESIDES, WE WEREN'T PRETENDING.
THE VISION'S FAILSAFE PROGRAM SPECIFICALLY CHOSE YOU THREE TO BECOME YOUNG AVENGERS.
THE VISION DIDN'T SAY ANYTHING ABOUT ME, THOUGH, DID HE?
NO. BUT HE WOULD'VE IF HE'D KNOWN ABOUT YOUR POWERS.
SO, FOR YOUR FIRST OFFICIAL ACT AS A YOUNG AVENGER...
...HOW ABOUT GETTING US OUT OF HERE?
HOW?

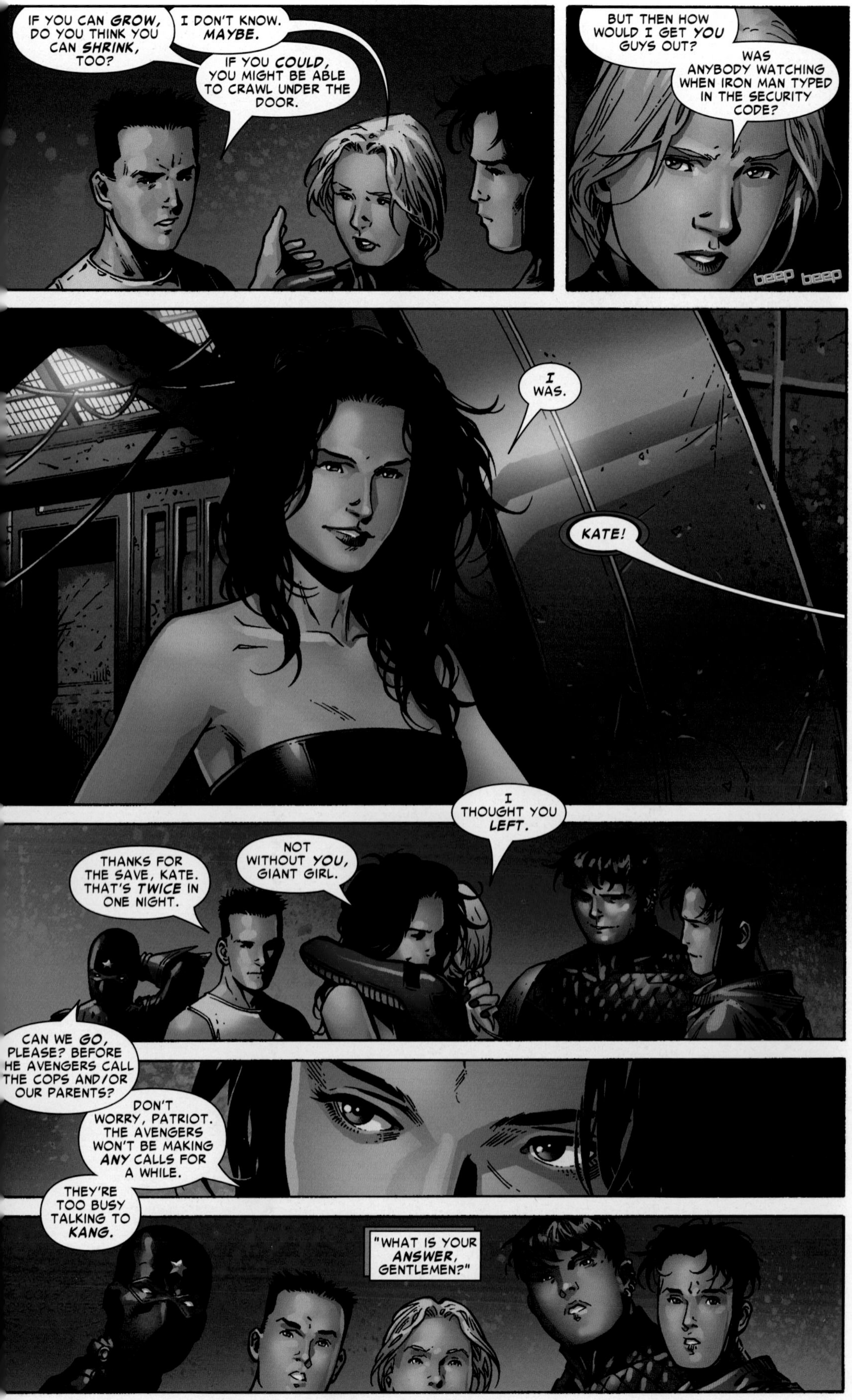
IF YOU CAN GROW, DO YOU THINK YOU CAN SHRINK, TOO?
I DON'T KNOW. MAYBE.
IF YOU COULD, YOU MIGHT BE ABLE TO CRAWL UNDER THE DOOR.
BUT THEN HOW WOULD I GET YOU GUYS OUT?
WAS ANYBODY WATCHING WHEN IRON MAN TYPED IN THE SECURITY CODE?
beep beep
I WAS.
KATE!
THANKS FOR THE SAVE, KATE. THAT'S TWICE IN ONE NIGHT.
NOT WITHOUT YOU, GIANT GIRL.
I THOUGHT YOU LEFT.
CAN WE GO, PLEASE? BEFORE HE AVENGERS CALL THE COPS AND/OR OUR PARENTS?
DON'T WORRY, PATRIOT. THE AVENGERS WON'T BE MAKING ANY CALLS FOR A WHILE.
THEY'RE TOO BUSY TALKING TO KANG.
"WHAT IS YOUR ANSWER, GENTLEMEN?"

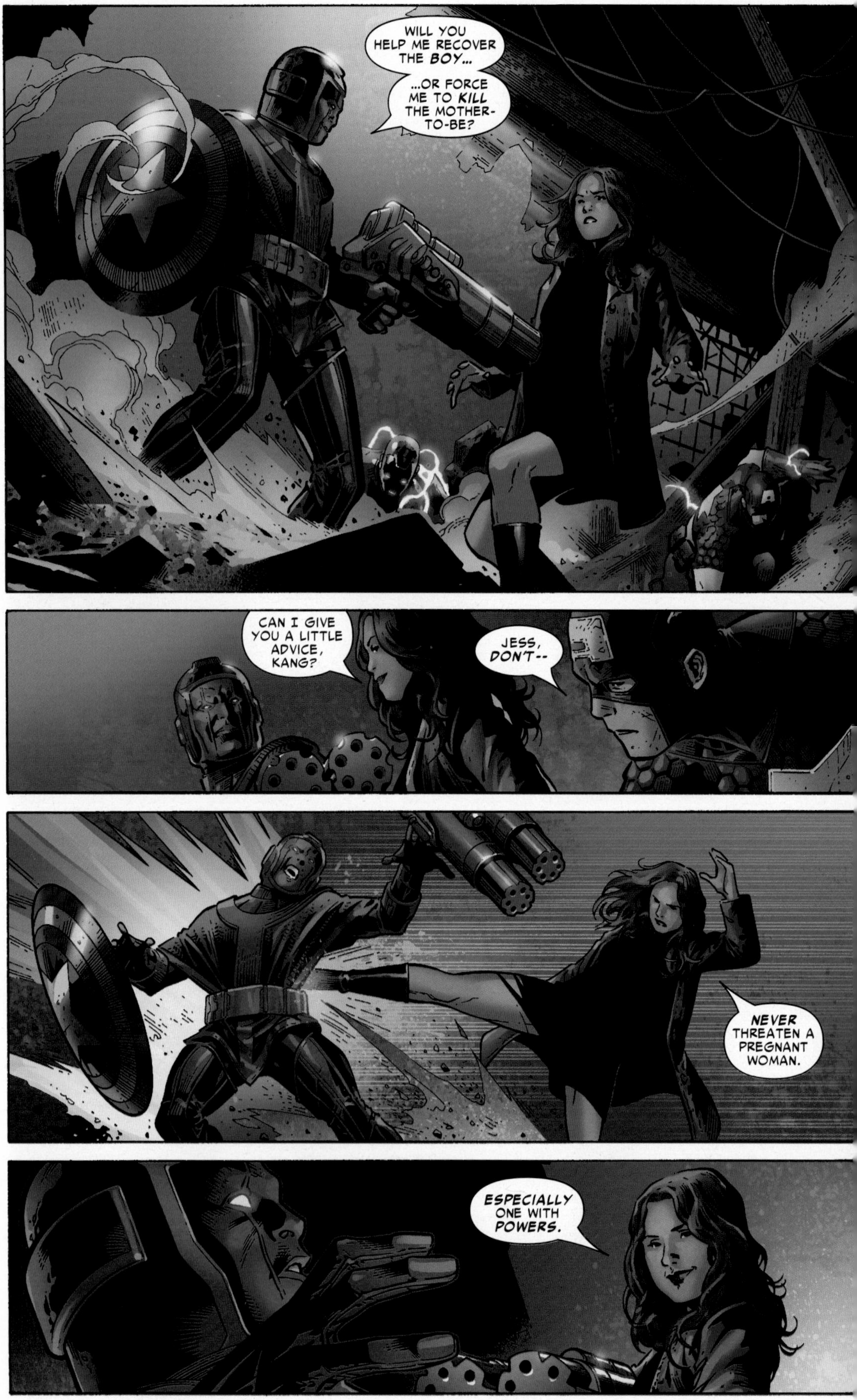
WILL YOU HELP ME RECOVER THE BOY...
...OR FORCE ME TO KILL THE MOTHER-TO-BE?
CAN I GIVE YOU A LITTLE ADVICE, KANG?
JESS, DON'T--
NEVER THREATEN A PREGNANT WOMAN.
ESPECIALLY ONE WITH POWERS.

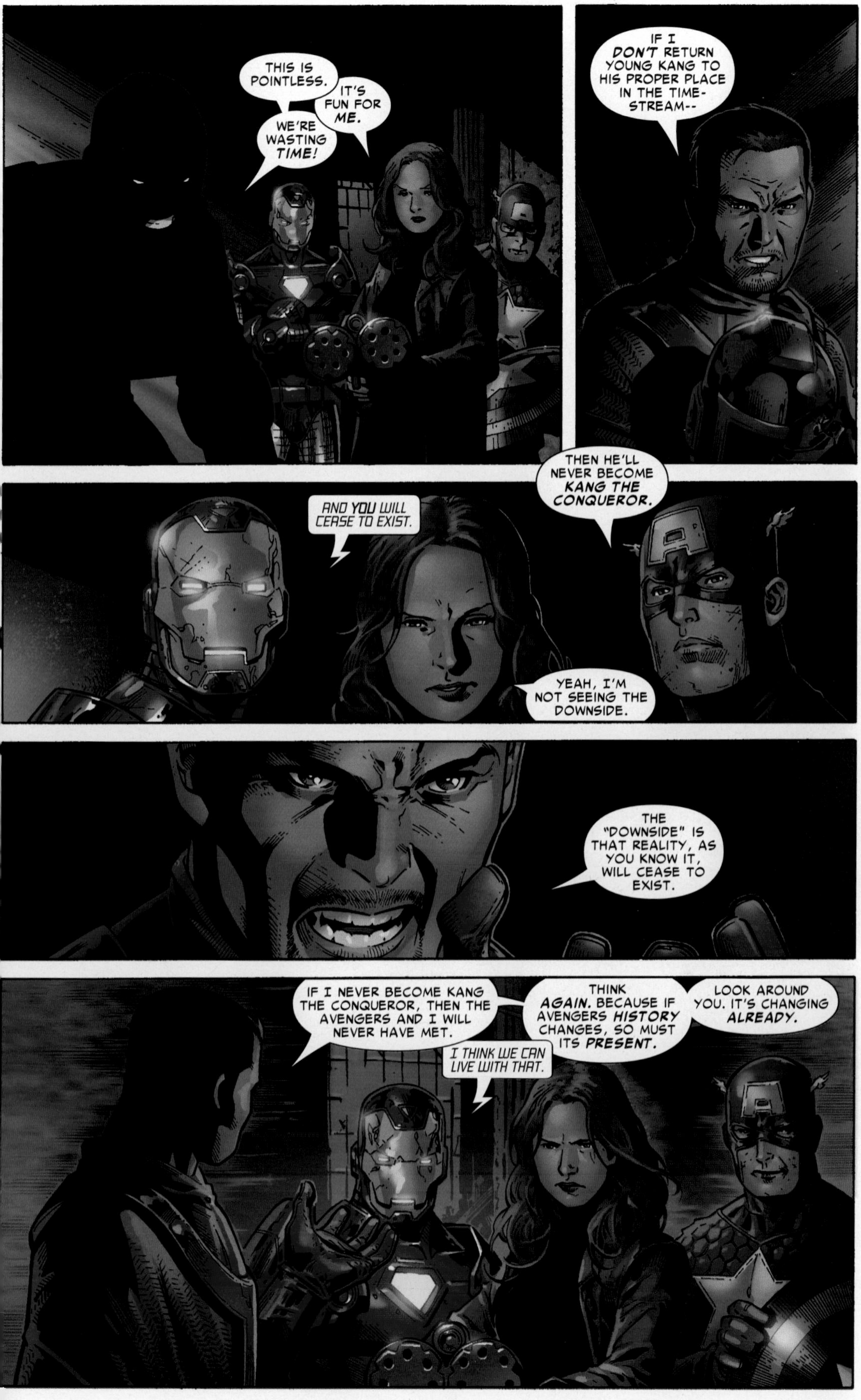

THIS IS POINTLESS.
WE'RE WASTING *TIME!*
IT'S FUN FOR *ME.*
IF I *DON'T* RETURN YOUNG KANG TO HIS PROPER PLACE IN THE TIME-STREAM--
THEN HE'LL NEVER BECOME *KANG THE CONQUEROR.*
AND *YOU* WILL CEASE TO EXIST.
YEAH, I'M NOT SEEING THE DOWNSIDE.
THE "DOWNSIDE" IS THAT REALITY, AS YOU KNOW IT, WILL CEASE TO EXIST.
IF I NEVER BECOME KANG THE CONQUEROR, THEN THE AVENGERS AND I WILL NEVER HAVE MET.
I THINK WE CAN LIVE WITH THAT.
THINK *AGAIN.* BECAUSE IF AVENGERS *HISTORY* CHANGES, SO MUST ITS *PRESENT.*
LOOK AROUND YOU. IT'S CHANGING *ALREADY.*

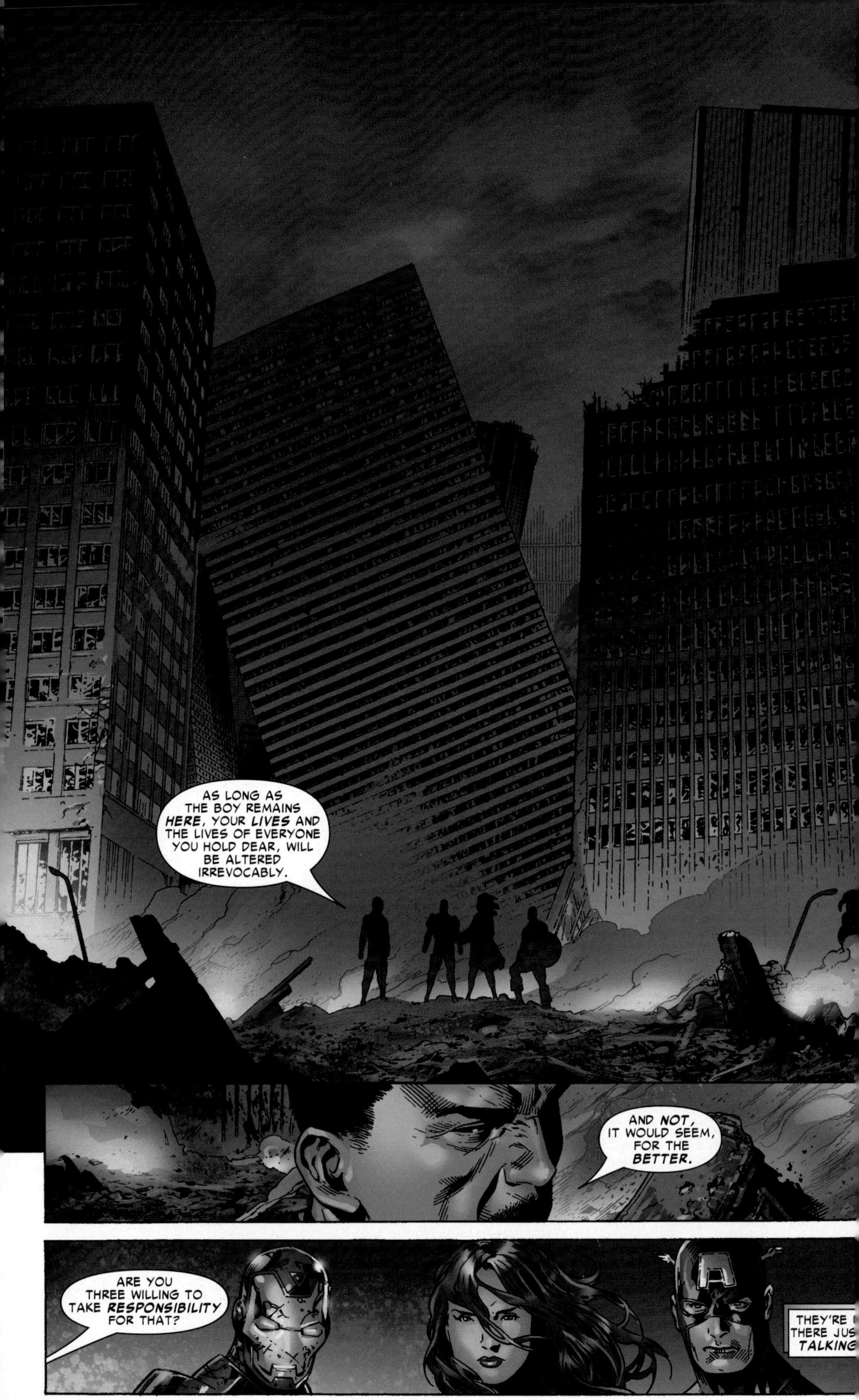
AS LONG AS THE BOY REMAINS HERE, YOUR LIVES AND THE LIVES OF EVERYONE YOU HOLD DEAR, WILL BE ALTERED IRREVOCABLY.
AND NOT, IT WOULD SEEM, FOR THE BETTER.
ARE YOU THREE WILLING TO TAKE RESPONSIBILITY FOR THAT?
THEY'RE
THERE JUS
TALKING

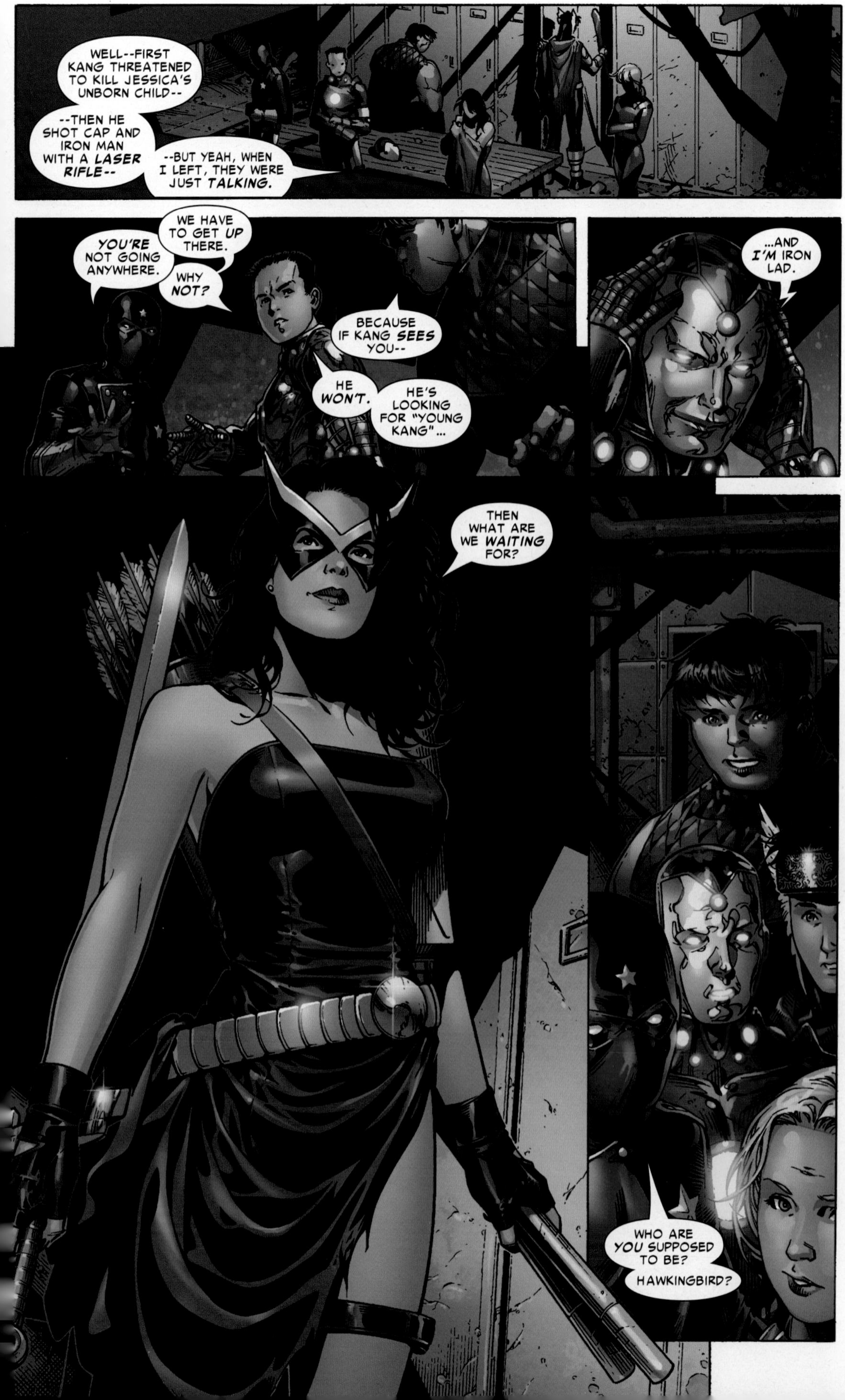
WELL--FIRST KANG THREATENED TO KILL JESSICA'S UNBORN CHILD--
--THEN HE SHOT CAP AND IRON MAN WITH A LASER RIFLE--
--BUT YEAH, WHEN I LEFT, THEY WERE JUST TALKING.
WE HAVE TO GET UP THERE.
YOU'RE NOT GOING ANYWHERE.
WHY NOT?
BECAUSE IF KANG SEES YOU--
HE WON'T.
HE'S LOOKING FOR "YOUNG KANG"...
...AND I'M IRON LAD.
THEN WHAT ARE WE WAITING FOR?
WHO ARE YOU SUPPOSED TO BE?
HAWKINGBIRD?

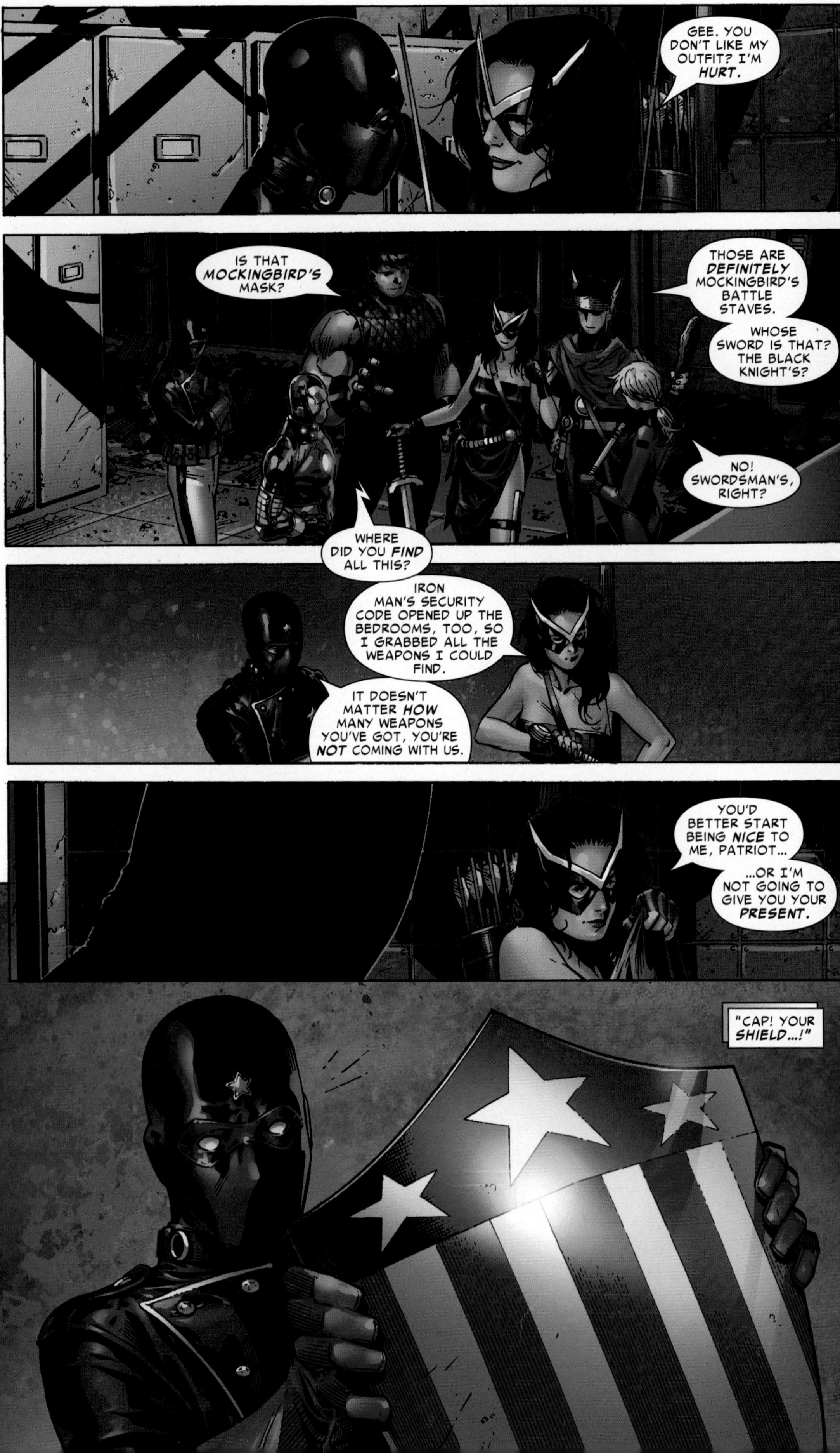
GEE. YOU DON'T LIKE MY OUTFIT? I'M HURT.
IS THAT MOCKINGBIRD'S MASK?
THOSE ARE DEFINITELY MOCKINGBIRD'S BATTLE STAVES.
WHOSE SWORD IS THAT? THE BLACK KNIGHT'S?
NO! SWORDSMAN'S, RIGHT?
WHERE DID YOU FIND ALL THIS?
IRON MAN'S SECURITY CODE OPENED UP THE BEDROOMS, TOO, SO I GRABBED ALL THE WEAPONS I COULD FIND.
IT DOESN'T MATTER HOW MANY WEAPONS YOU'VE GOT, YOU'RE NOT COMING WITH US.
YOU'D BETTER START BEING NICE TO ME, PATRIOT...
...OR I'M NOT GOING TO GIVE YOU YOUR PRESENT.
"CAP! YOUR SHIELD...!"

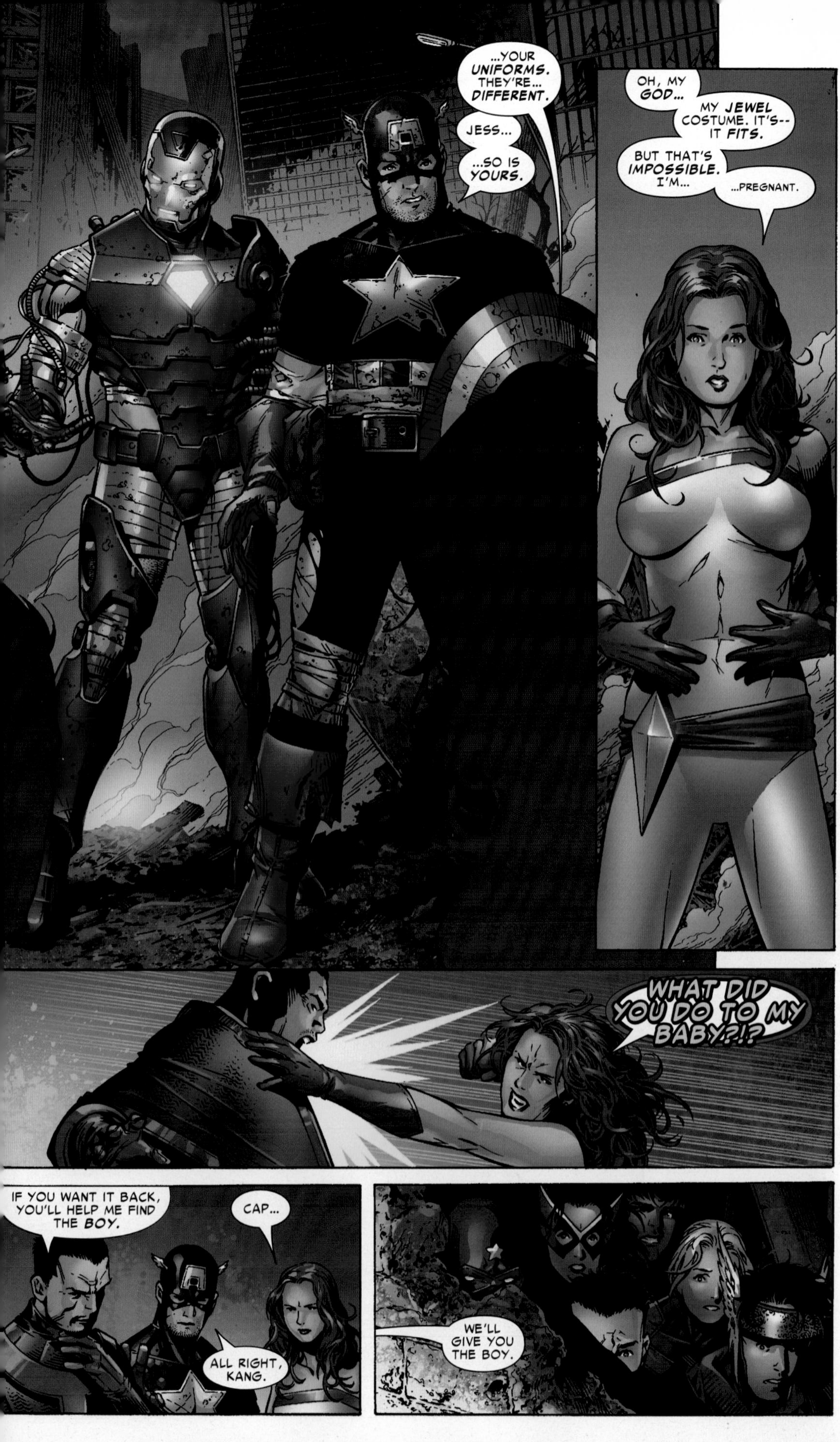
...YOUR UNIFORMS. THEY'RE... DIFFERENT.
JESS...
...SO IS YOURS.
OH, MY GOD...
MY JEWEL COSTUME. IT'S-- IT FITS.
BUT THAT'S IMPOSSIBLE. I'M...
...PREGNANT.
WHAT DID YOU DO TO MY BABY?!?
IF YOU WANT IT BACK, YOU'LL HELP ME FIND THE BOY.
CAP...
ALL RIGHT, KANG.
WE'LL GIVE YOU THE BOY.

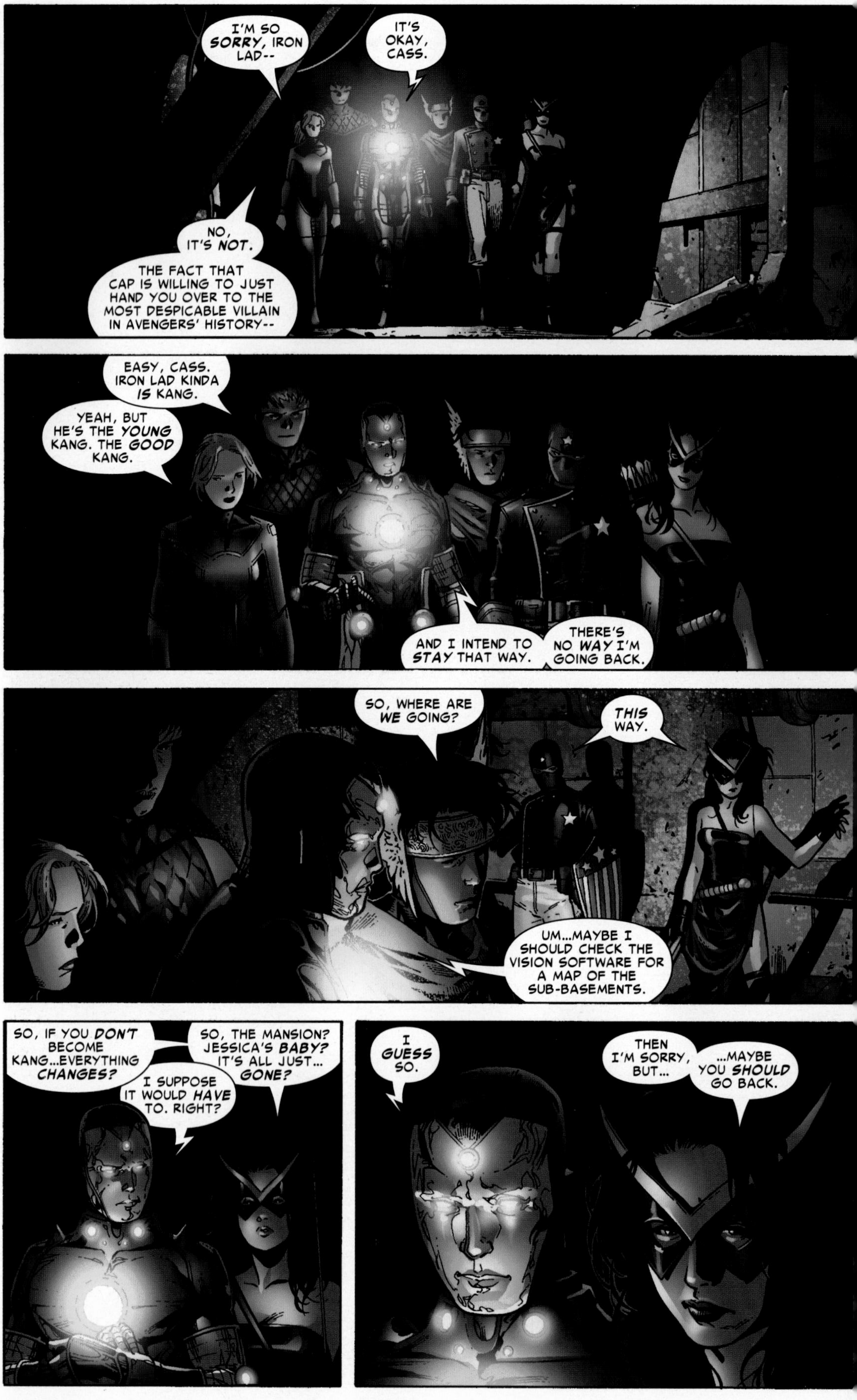

I'M SO SORRY, IRON LAD--
IT'S OKAY, CASS.
NO, IT'S NOT.
THE FACT THAT CAP IS WILLING TO JUST HAND YOU OVER TO THE MOST DESPICABLE VILLAIN IN AVENGERS' HISTORY--
EASY, CASS. IRON LAD KINDA IS KANG.
YEAH, BUT HE'S THE YOUNG KANG. THE GOOD KANG.
AND I INTEND TO STAY THAT WAY.
THERE'S NO WAY I'M GOING BACK.
SO, WHERE ARE WE GOING?
THIS WAY.
UM...MAYBE I SHOULD CHECK THE VISION SOFTWARE FOR A MAP OF THE SUB-BASEMENTS.
SO, IF YOU DON'T BECOME KANG...EVERYTHING CHANGES?
SO, THE MANSION? JESSICA'S BABY? IT'S ALL JUST... GONE?
I SUPPOSE IT WOULD HAVE TO. RIGHT?
I GUESS SO.
THEN I'M SORRY, BUT...
...MAYBE YOU SHOULD GO BACK.

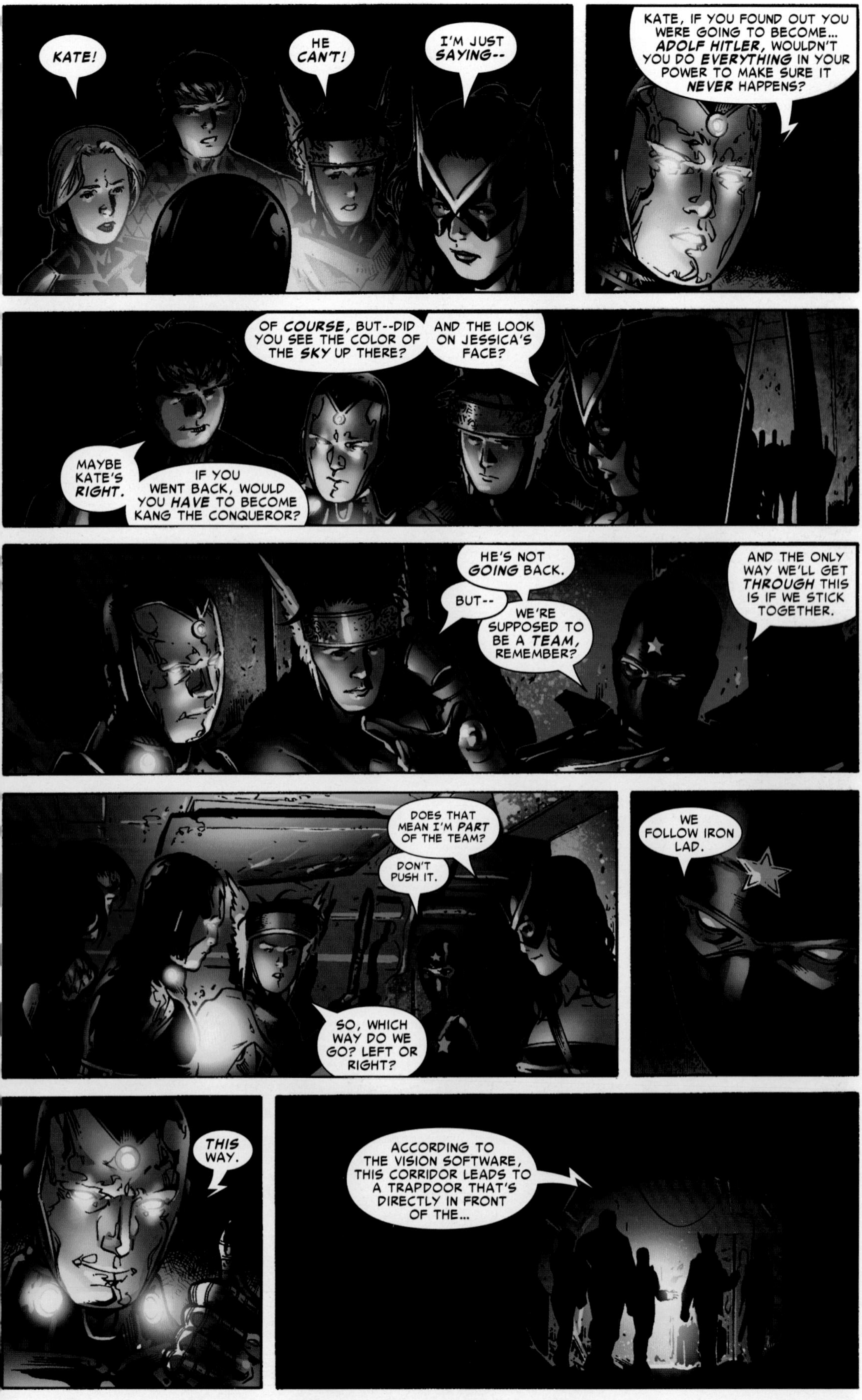

KATE!
HE CAN'T!
I'M JUST SAYING--
KATE, IF YOU FOUND OUT YOU WERE GOING TO BECOME... ADOLF HITLER, WOULDN'T YOU DO EVERYTHING IN YOUR POWER TO MAKE SURE IT NEVER HAPPENS?
OF COURSE, BUT--DID YOU SEE THE COLOR OF THE SKY UP THERE?
AND THE LOOK ON JESSICA'S FACE?
MAYBE KATE'S RIGHT.
IF YOU WENT BACK, WOULD YOU HAVE TO BECOME KANG THE CONQUEROR?
HE'S NOT GOING BACK.
BUT--
WE'RE SUPPOSED TO BE A TEAM, REMEMBER?
AND THE ONLY WAY WE'LL GET THROUGH THIS IS IF WE STICK TOGETHER.
DOES THAT MEAN I'M PART OF THE TEAM?
DON'T PUSH IT.
SO, WHICH WAY DO WE GO? LEFT OR RIGHT?
WE FOLLOW IRON LAD.
THIS WAY.
ACCORDING TO THE VISION SOFTWARE, THIS CORRIDOR LEADS TO A TRAPDOOR THAT'S DIRECTLY IN FRONT OF THE...

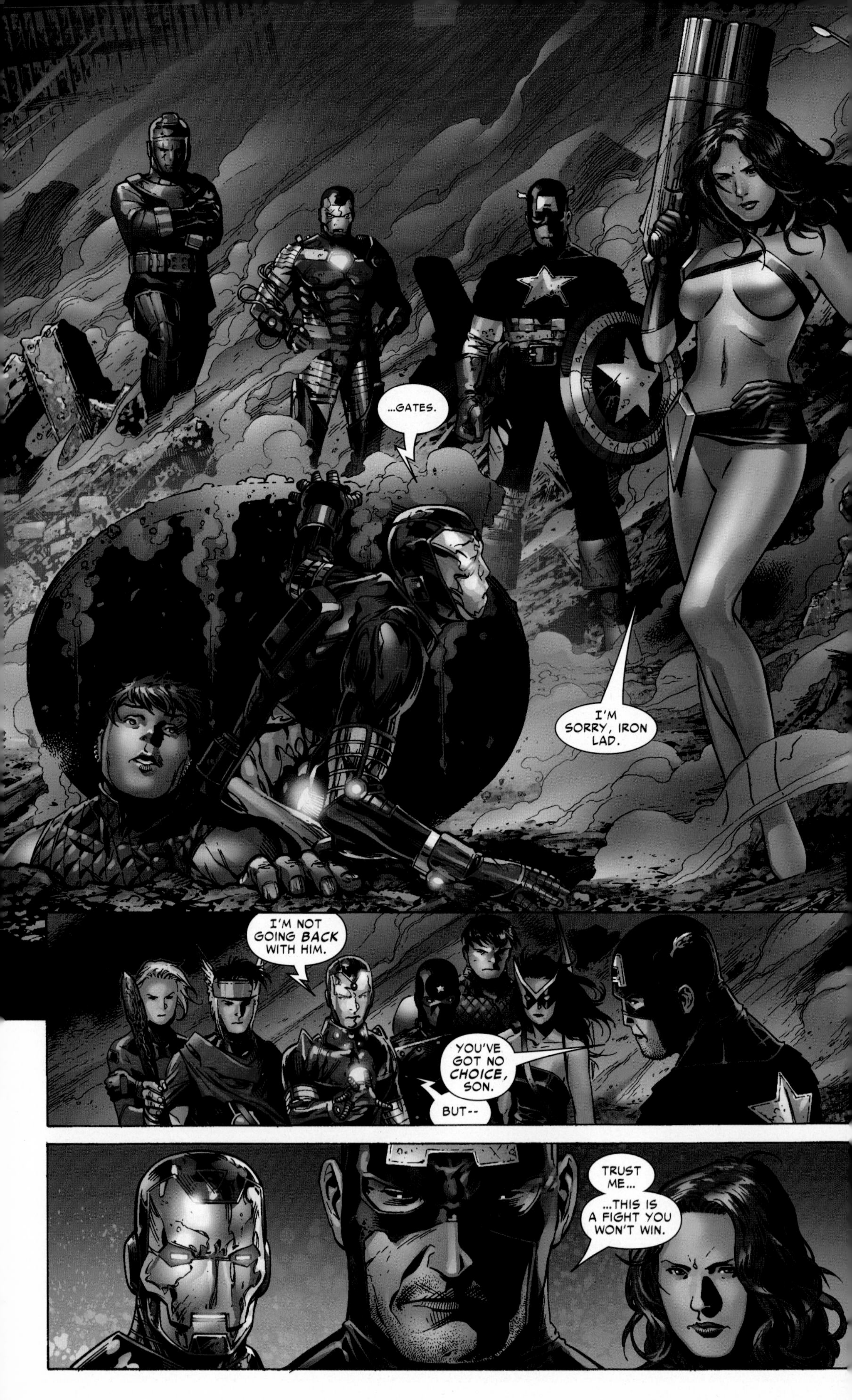
...GATES.
I'M SORRY, IRON LAD.
I'M NOT GOING BACK WITH HIM.
YOU'VE GOT NO CHOICE, SON.
BUT--
TRUST ME...
...THIS IS A FIGHT YOU WON'T WIN.

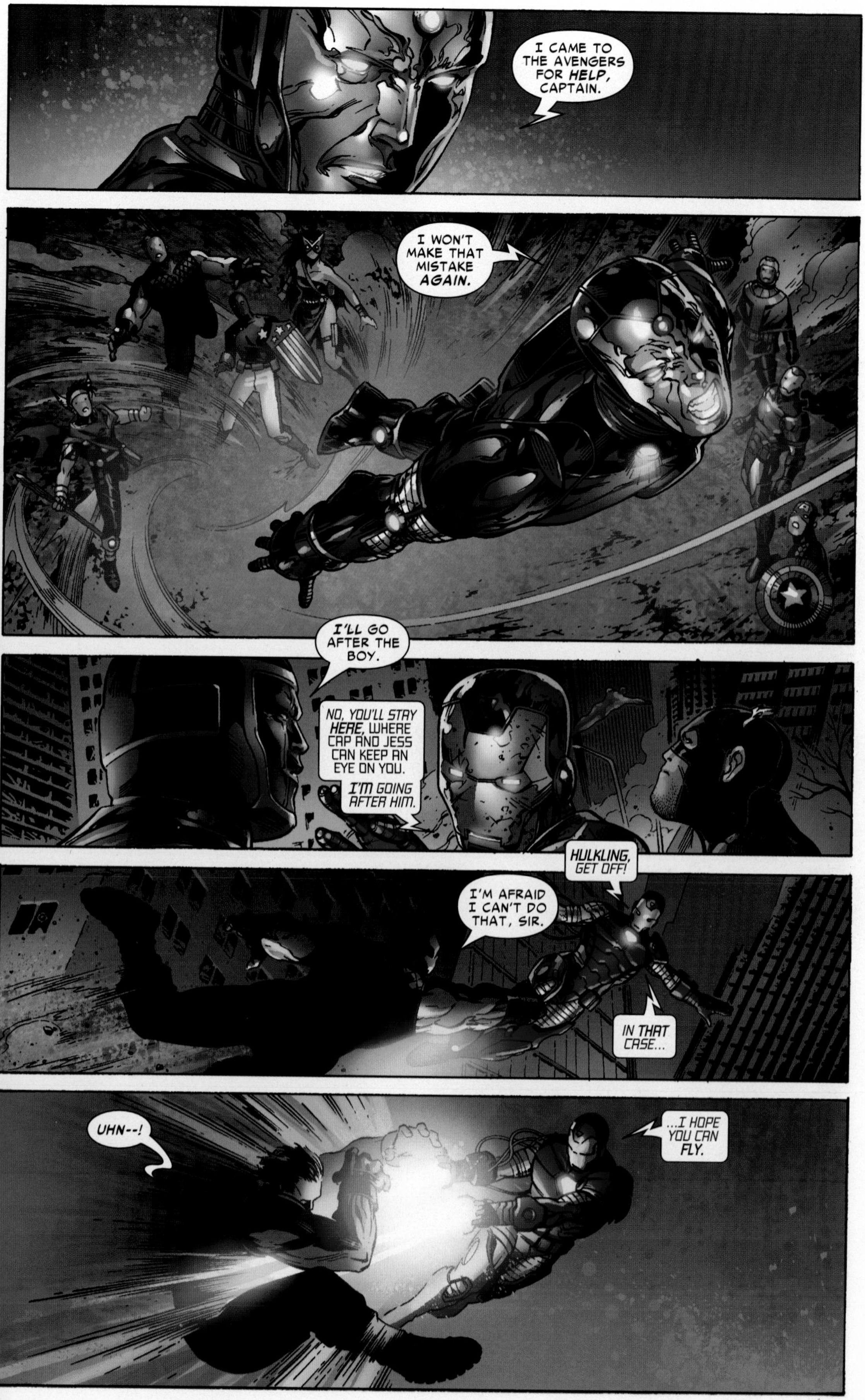
I CAME TO THE AVENGERS FOR HELP, CAPTAIN.
I WON'T MAKE THAT MISTAKE AGAIN.
I'LL GO AFTER THE BOY.
NO, YOU'LL STAY HERE, WHERE CAP AND JESS CAN KEEP AN EYE ON YOU.
I'M GOING AFTER HIM.
HULKLING, GET OFF!
I'M AFRAID I CAN'T DO THAT, SIR.
IN THAT CASE...
UHN--!
...I HOPE YOU CAN FLY.

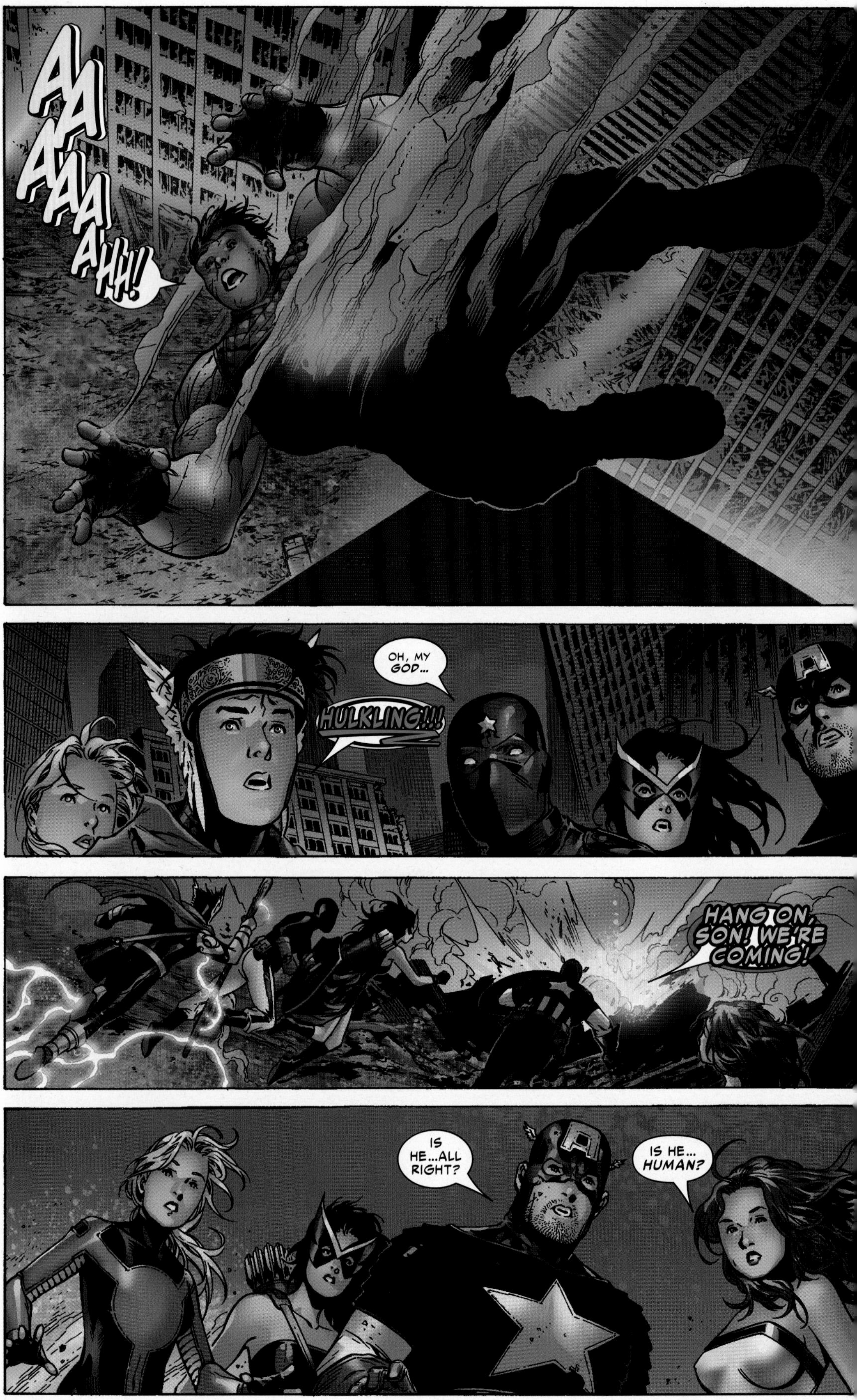
AAAAAAAHH!
OH, MY GOD...
HULKLING!!!
HANG ON, SON! WE'RE COMING!
IS HE...ALL RIGHT?
IS HE... HUMAN?

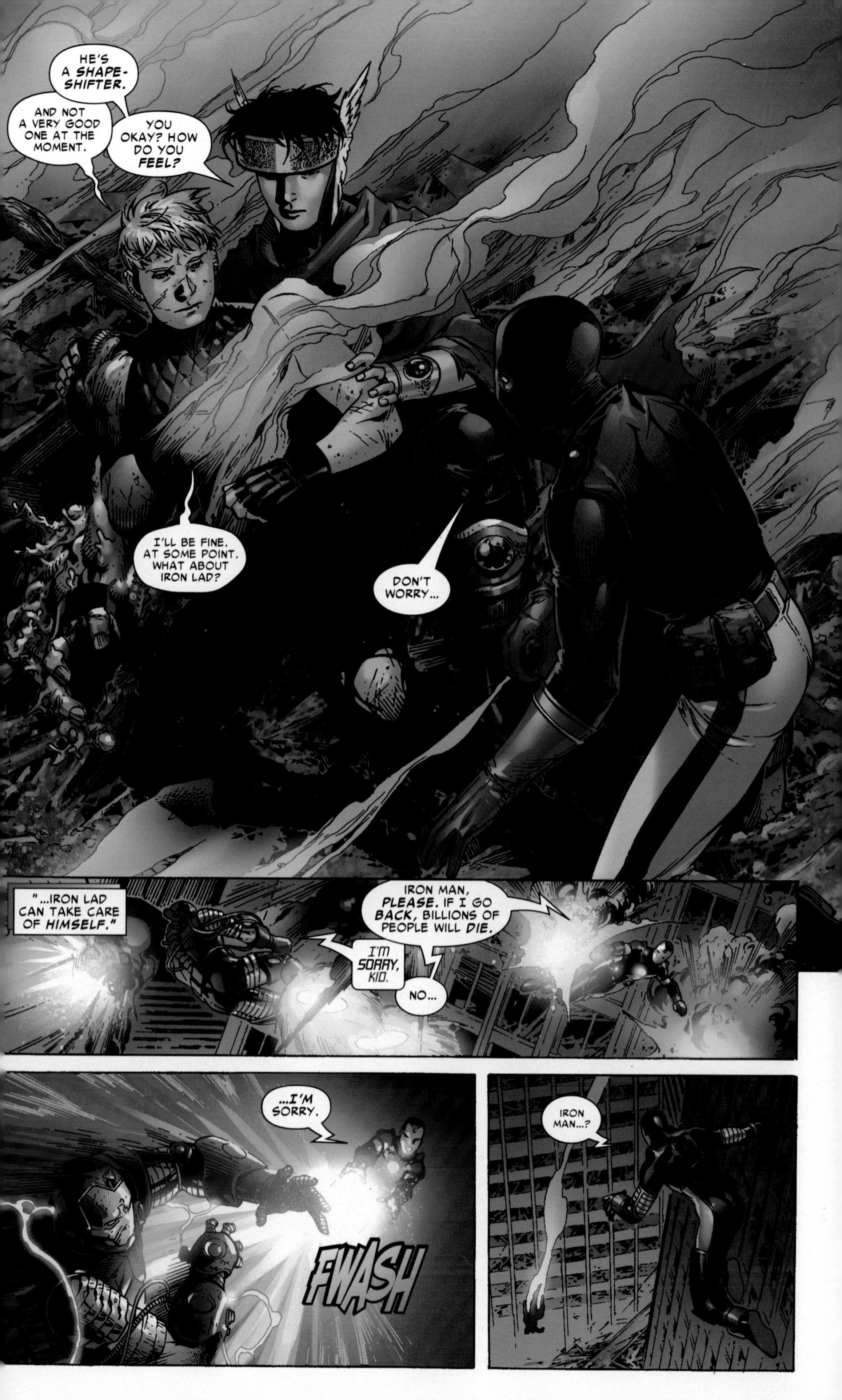
HE'S A SHAPE-SHIFTER.
AND NOT A VERY GOOD ONE AT THE MOMENT.
YOU OKAY? HOW DO YOU FEEL?
I'LL BE FINE. AT SOME POINT. WHAT ABOUT IRON LAD?
DON'T WORRY...
"...IRON LAD CAN TAKE CARE OF HIMSELF."
IRON MAN, PLEASE. IF I GO BACK, BILLIONS OF PEOPLE WILL DIE.
I'M SORRY, KID.
NO...
...I'M SORRY.
FWASH
IRON MAN...?

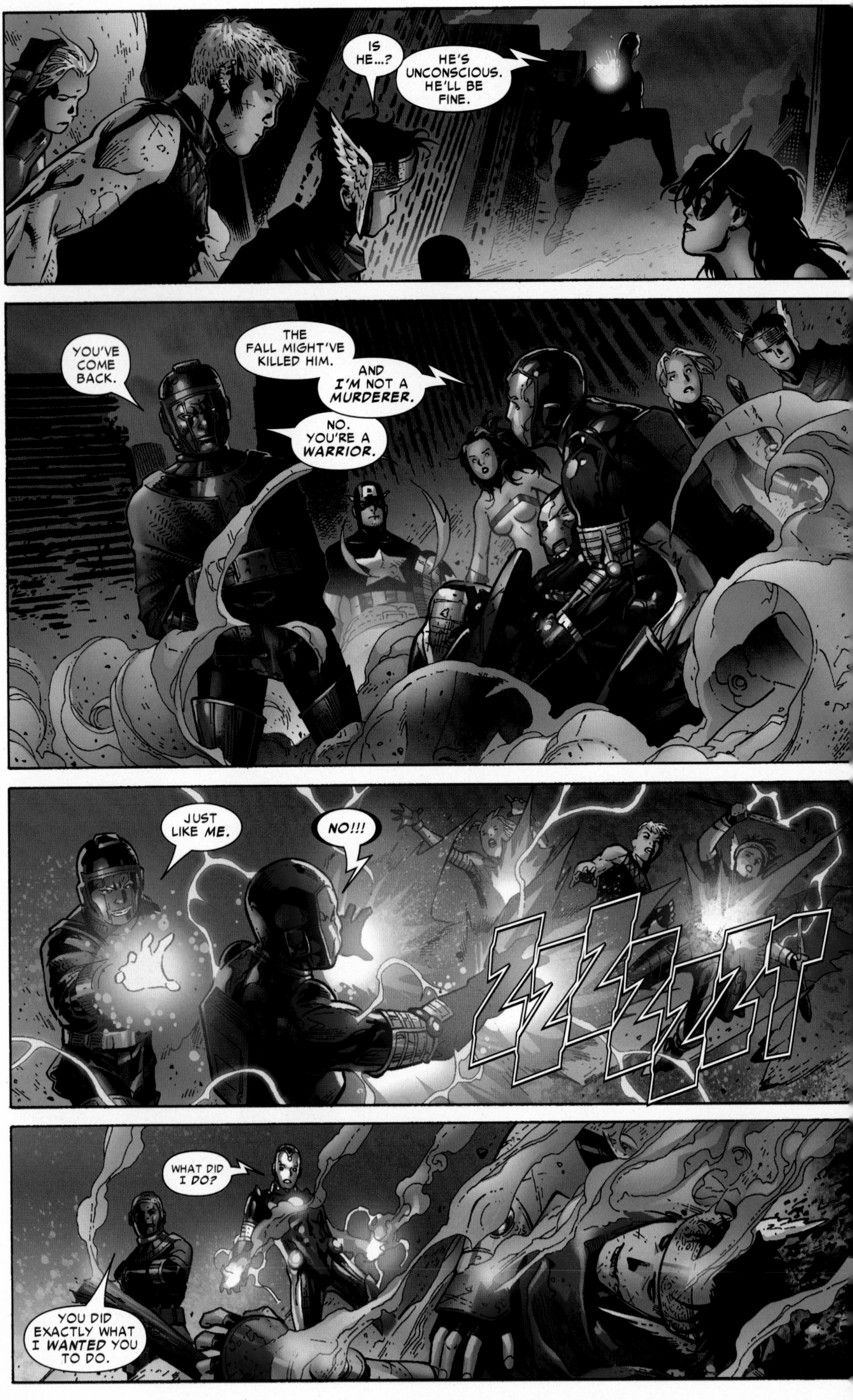
IS HE...?
HE'S UNCONSCIOUS. HE'LL BE FINE.
YOU'VE COME BACK.
THE FALL MIGHT'VE KILLED HIM.
AND I'M NOT A MURDERER.
NO. YOU'RE A WARRIOR.
JUST LIKE ME.
NO!!!
ZZZZZZT
WHAT DID I DO?
YOU DID EXACTLY WHAT I WANTED YOU TO DO.

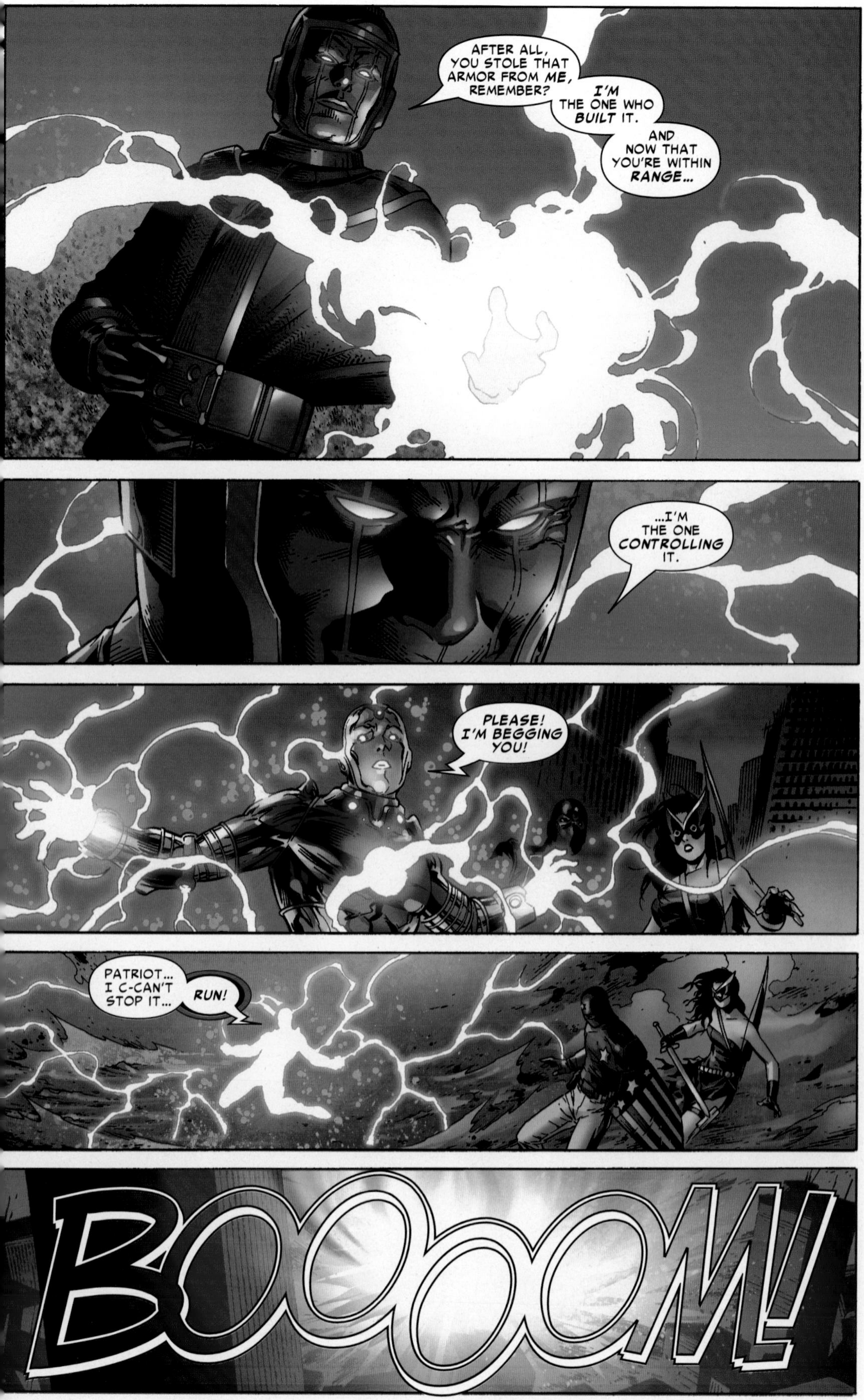
AFTER ALL, YOU STOLE THAT ARMOR FROM *ME*, REMEMBER?
I'M THE ONE WHO *BUILT* IT.
AND NOW THAT YOU'RE WITHIN *RANGE*...
...I'M THE ONE *CONTROLLING* IT.
PLEASE! I'M BEGGING YOU!
PATRIOT... I C-CAN'T STOP IT...
RUN!
BOOOOM!

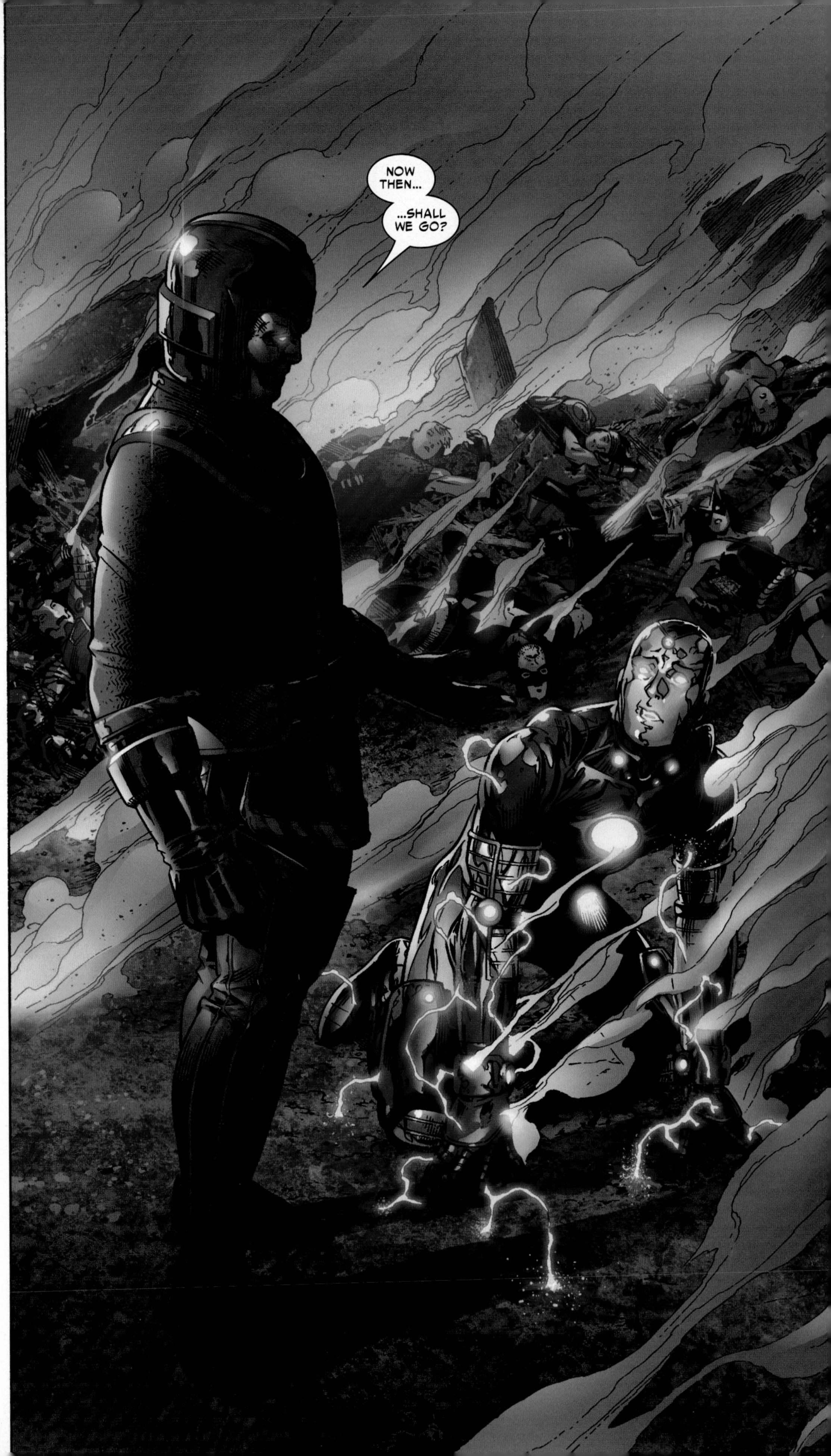
NOW THEN...
...SHALL WE GO?

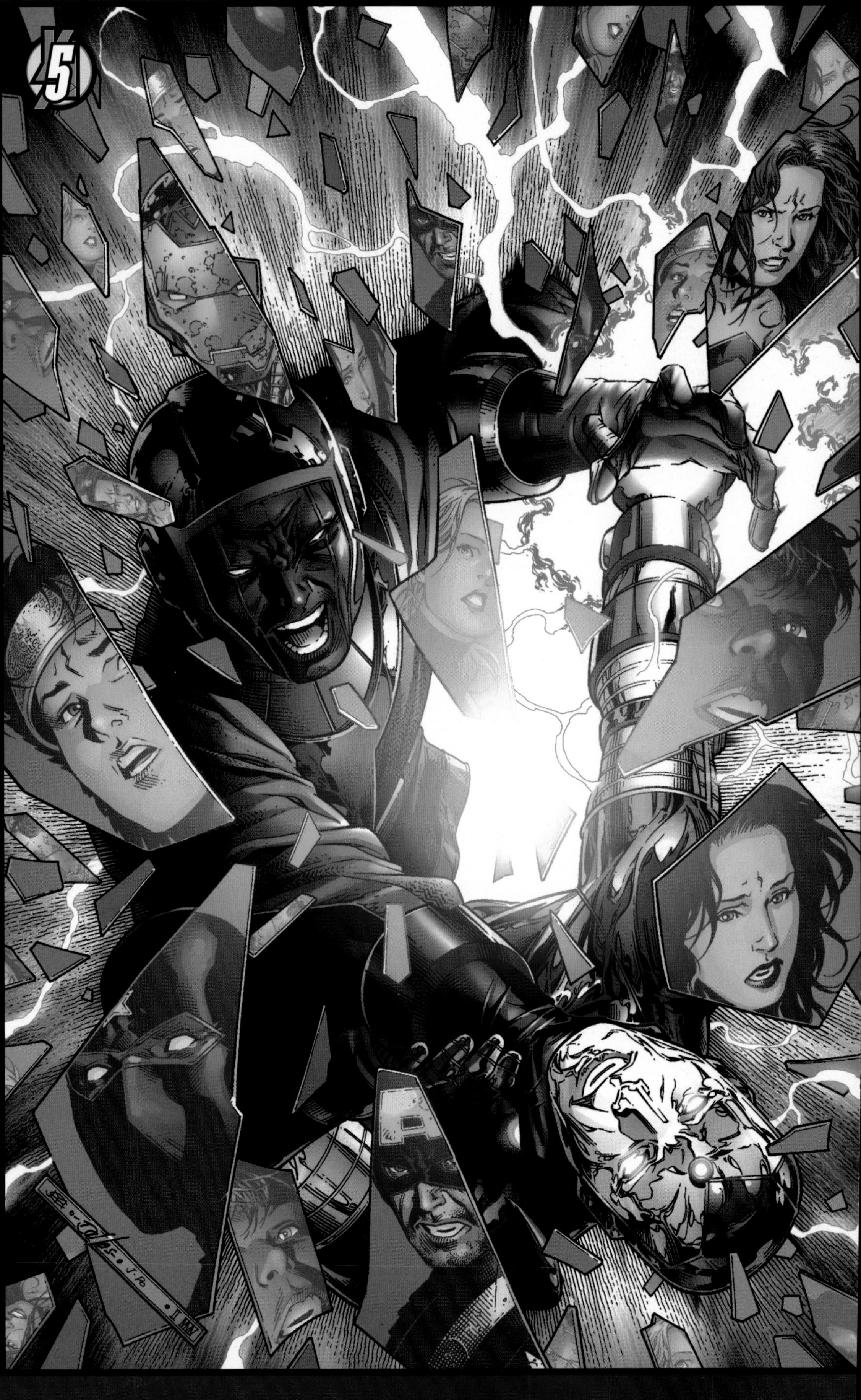

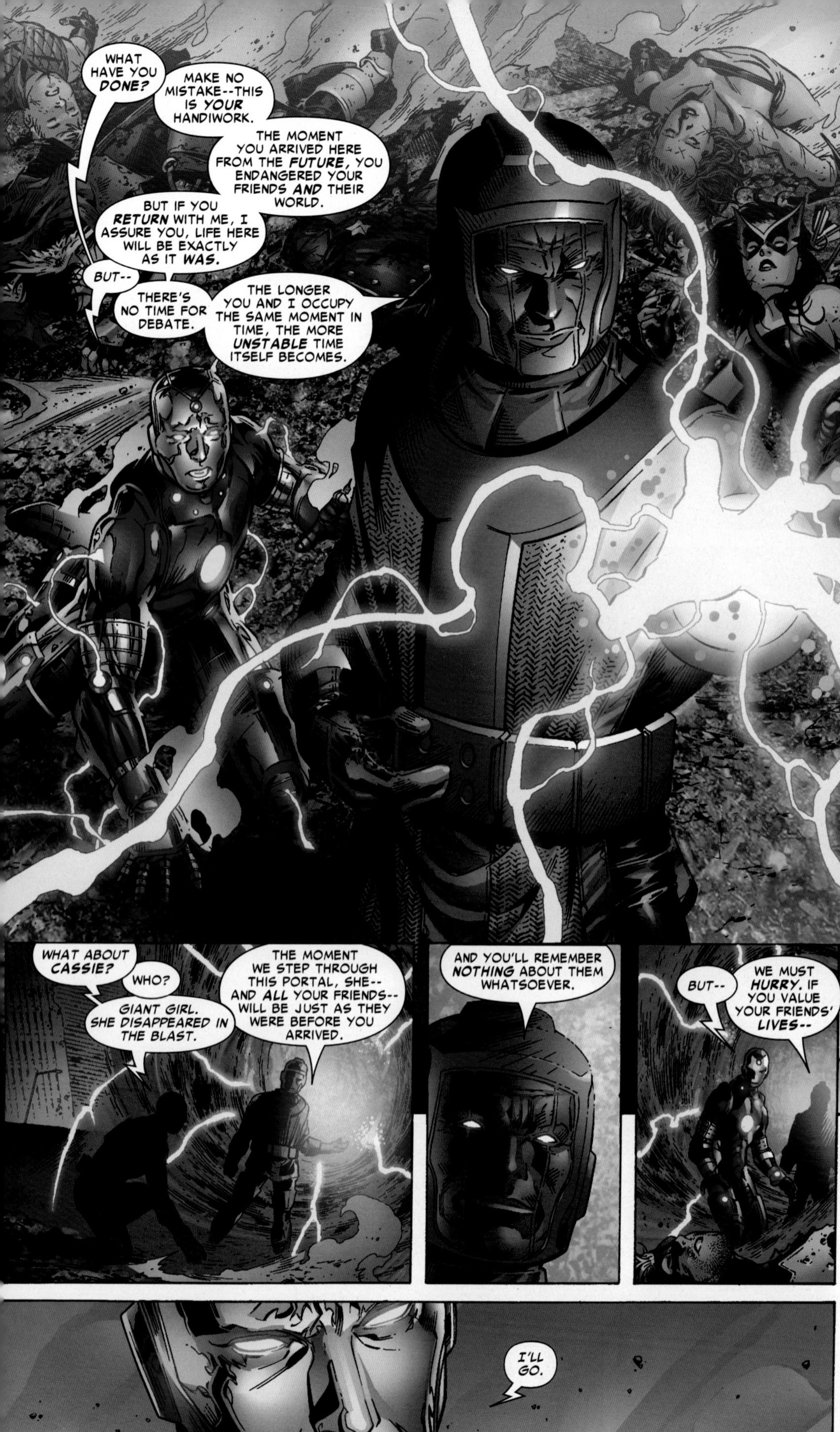
WHAT HAVE YOU DONE?
MAKE NO MISTAKE--THIS IS YOUR HANDIWORK.
THE MOMENT YOU ARRIVED HERE FROM THE FUTURE, YOU ENDANGERED YOUR FRIENDS AND THEIR WORLD.
BUT IF YOU RETURN WITH ME, I ASSURE YOU, LIFE HERE WILL BE EXACTLY AS IT WAS.
BUT--
THERE'S NO TIME FOR DEBATE.
THE LONGER YOU AND I OCCUPY THE SAME MOMENT IN TIME, THE MORE UNSTABLE TIME ITSELF BECOMES.
WHAT ABOUT CASSIE?
WHO?
GIANT GIRL. SHE DISAPPEARED IN THE BLAST.
THE MOMENT WE STEP THROUGH THIS PORTAL, SHE--AND ALL YOUR FRIENDS--WILL BE JUST AS THEY WERE BEFORE YOU ARRIVED.
AND YOU'LL REMEMBER NOTHING ABOUT THEM WHATSOEVER.
BUT--
WE MUST HURRY. IF YOU VALUE YOUR FRIENDS' LIVES--
I'LL GO.

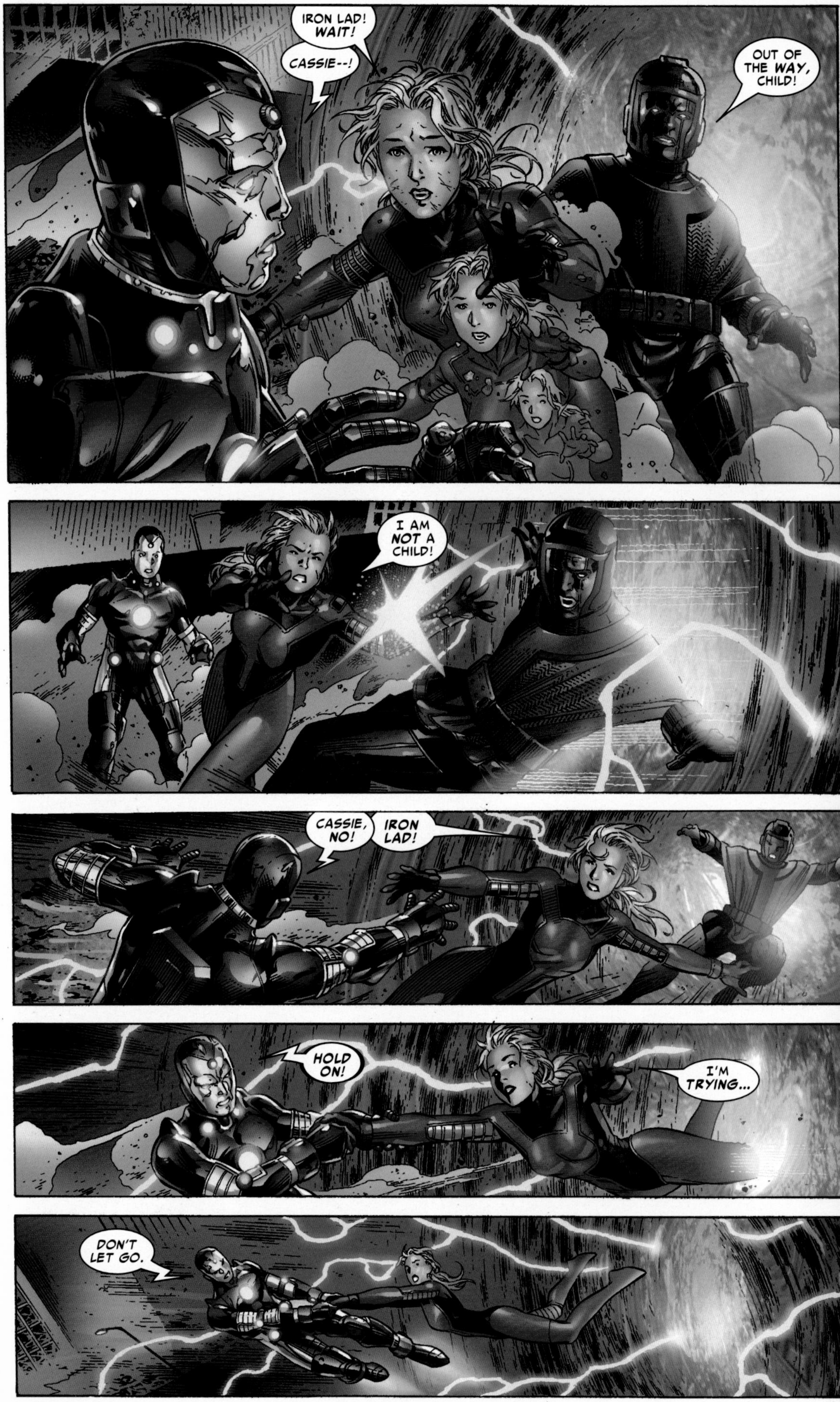
IRON LAD! WAIT!
CASSIE--!
OUT OF THE WAY, CHILD!
I AM NOT A CHILD!
CASSIE, NO!
IRON LAD!
HOLD ON!
I'M TRYING...
DON'T LET GO.

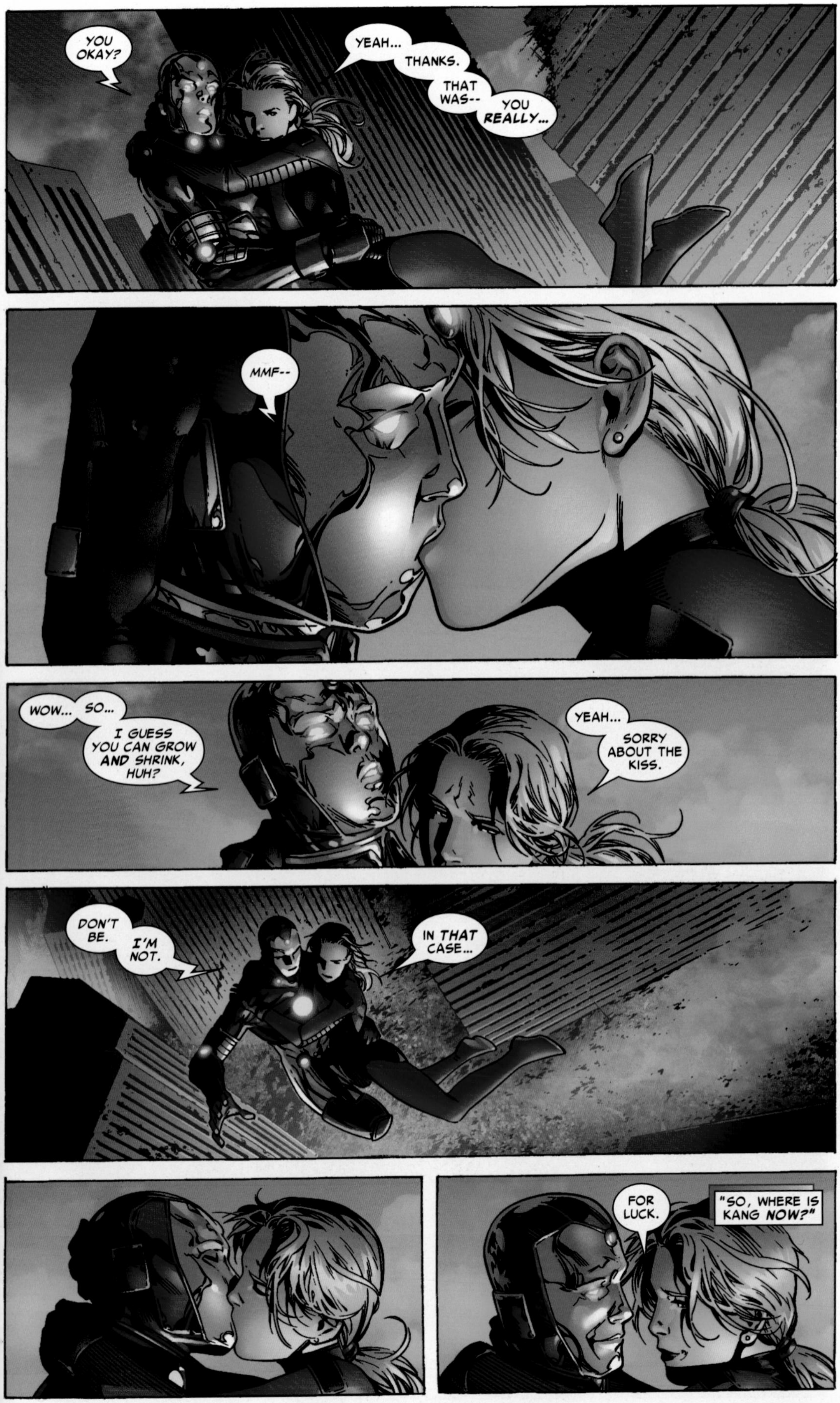
YOU OKAY?
YEAH...
THANKS.
THAT WAS--
YOU REALLY...
MMF--
WOW... SO...
I GUESS YOU CAN GROW AND SHRINK, HUH?
YEAH...
SORRY ABOUT THE KISS.
DON'T BE.
I'M NOT.
IN THAT CASE...
FOR LUCK.
"SO, WHERE IS KANG NOW?"

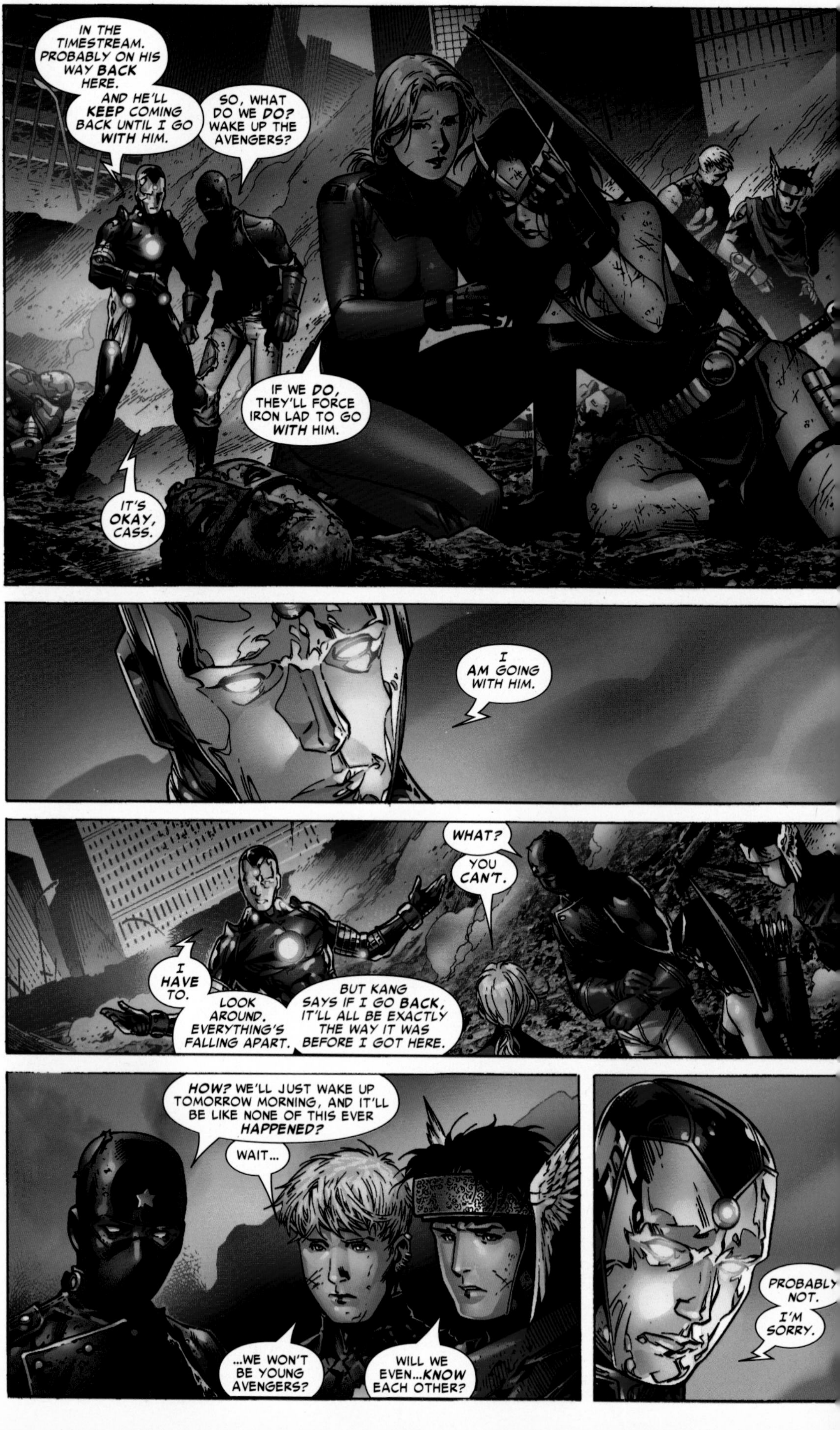
IN THE TIMESTREAM. PROBABLY ON HIS WAY BACK HERE.
AND HE'LL KEEP COMING BACK UNTIL I GO WITH HIM.
SO, WHAT DO WE DO? WAKE UP THE AVENGERS?
IF WE DO, THEY'LL FORCE IRON LAD TO GO WITH HIM.
IT'S OKAY, CASS.
I AM GOING WITH HIM.
WHAT?
YOU CAN'T.
I HAVE TO.
LOOK AROUND. EVERYTHING'S FALLING APART.
BUT KANG SAYS IF I GO BACK, IT'LL ALL BE EXACTLY THE WAY IT WAS BEFORE I GOT HERE.
HOW? WE'LL JUST WAKE UP TOMORROW MORNING, AND IT'LL BE LIKE NONE OF THIS EVER HAPPENED?
WAIT...
...WE WON'T BE YOUNG AVENGERS?
WILL WE EVEN...KNOW EACH OTHER?
PROBABLY NOT.
I'M SORRY.

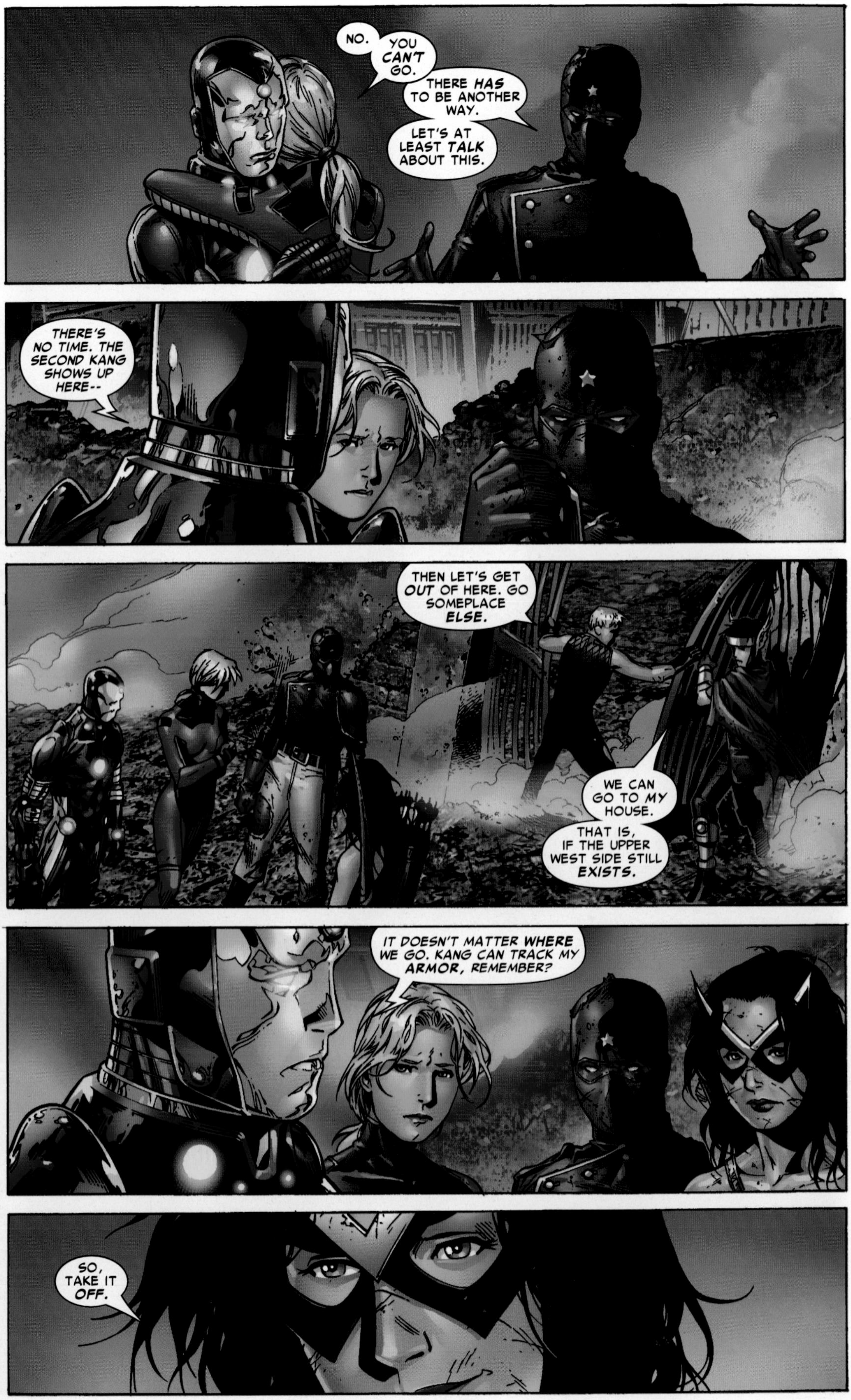
NO.
YOU CAN'T GO.
THERE HAS TO BE ANOTHER WAY.
LET'S AT LEAST TALK ABOUT THIS.
THERE'S NO TIME. THE SECOND KANG SHOWS UP HERE--
THEN LET'S GET OUT OF HERE. GO SOMEPLACE ELSE.
WE CAN GO TO MY HOUSE.
THAT IS, IF THE UPPER WEST SIDE STILL EXISTS.
IT DOESN'T MATTER WHERE WE GO. KANG CAN TRACK MY ARMOR, REMEMBER?
SO, TAKE IT OFF.

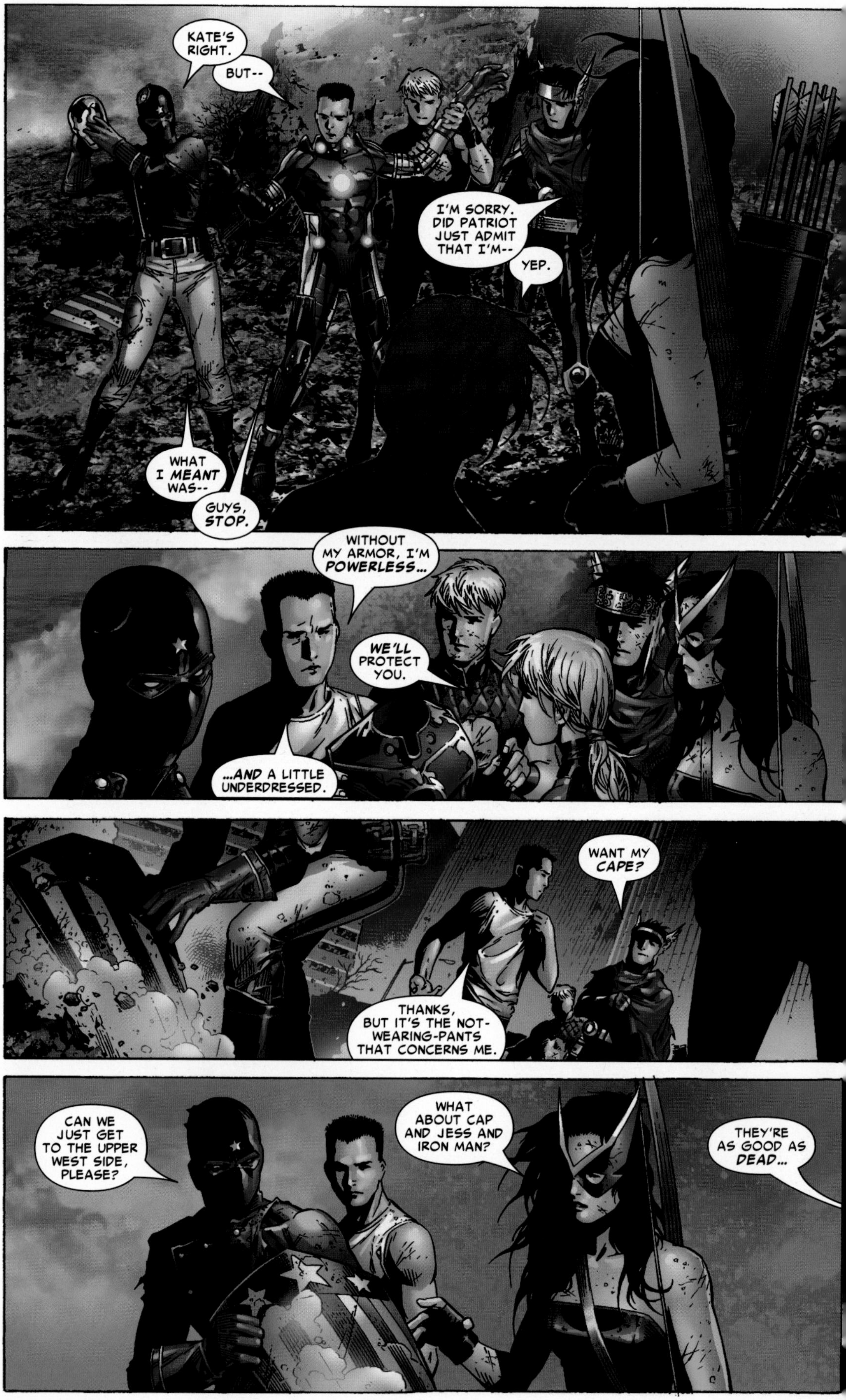
KATE'S RIGHT.
BUT--
I'M SORRY. DID PATRIOT JUST ADMIT THAT I'M--
YEP.
WHAT I MEANT WAS--
GUYS, STOP.
WITHOUT MY ARMOR, I'M POWERLESS...
WE'LL PROTECT YOU.
...AND A LITTLE UNDERDRESSED.
WANT MY CAPE?
THANKS, BUT IT'S THE NOT-WEARING-PANTS THAT CONCERNS ME.
CAN WE JUST GET TO THE UPPER WEST SIDE, PLEASE?
WHAT ABOUT CAP AND JESS AND IRON MAN?
THEY'RE AS GOOD AS DEAD...

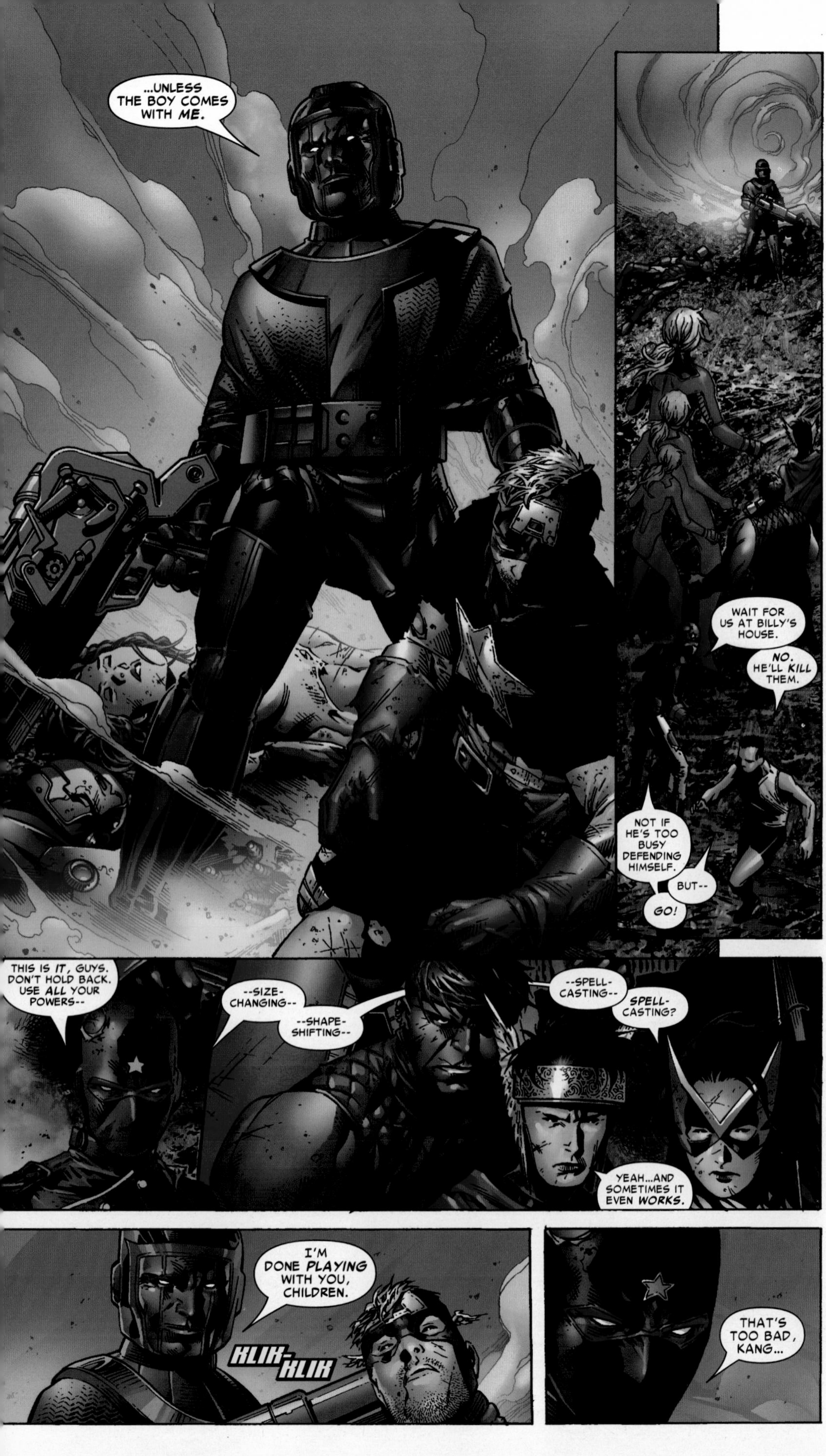
...UNLESS THE BOY COMES WITH ME.
WAIT FOR US AT BILLY'S HOUSE.
NO. HE'LL KILL THEM.
NOT IF HE'S TOO BUSY DEFENDING HIMSELF.
BUT--
GO!
THIS IS IT, GUYS. DON'T HOLD BACK. USE ALL YOUR POWERS--
--SIZE-CHANGING--
--SHAPE-SHIFTING--
--SPELL-CASTING--
SPELL-CASTING?
YEAH...AND SOMETIMES IT EVEN WORKS.
I'M DONE PLAYING WITH YOU, CHILDREN.
KLIK-KLIK
THAT'S TOO BAD, KANG...

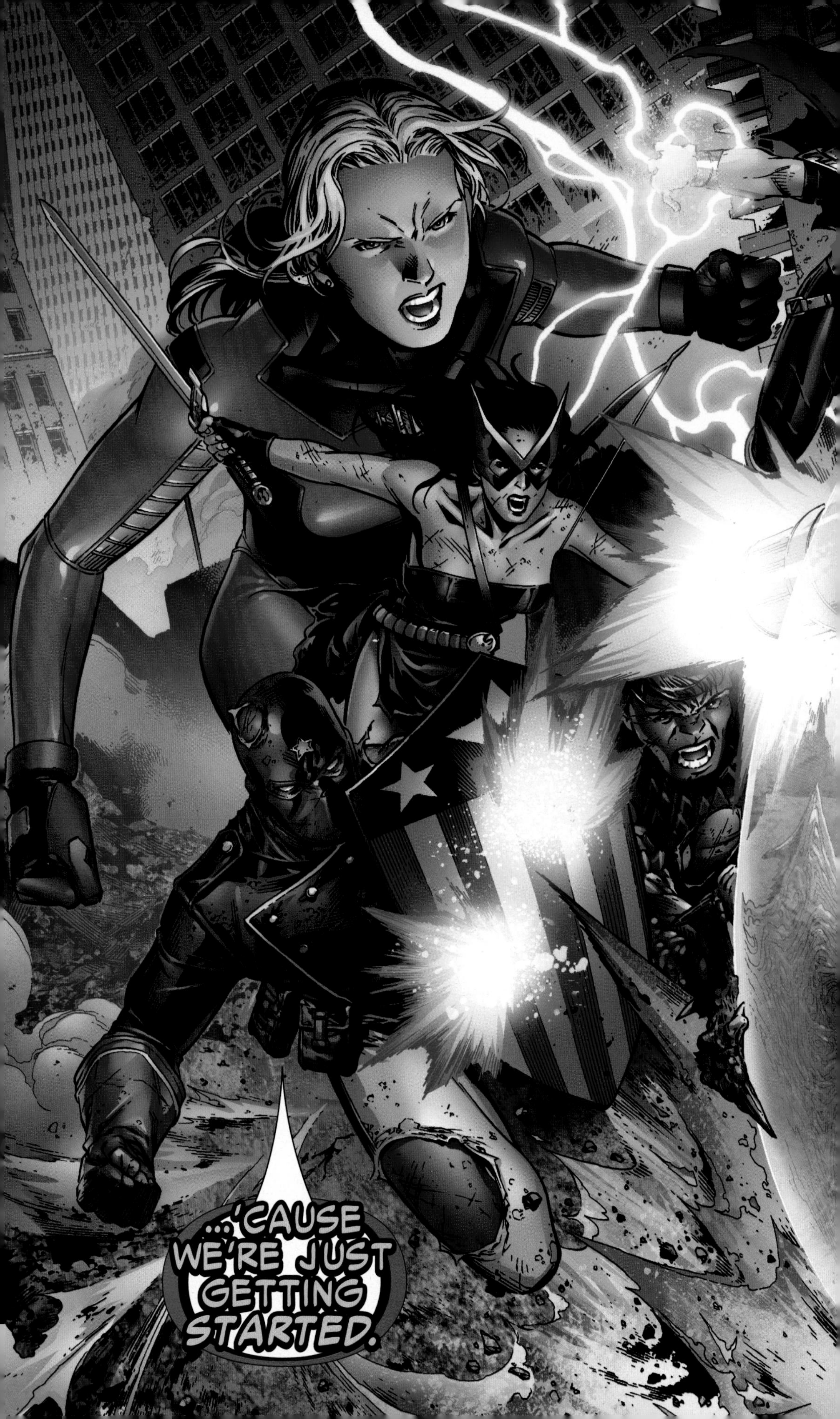
...'CAUSE WE'RE JUST GETTING STARTED.

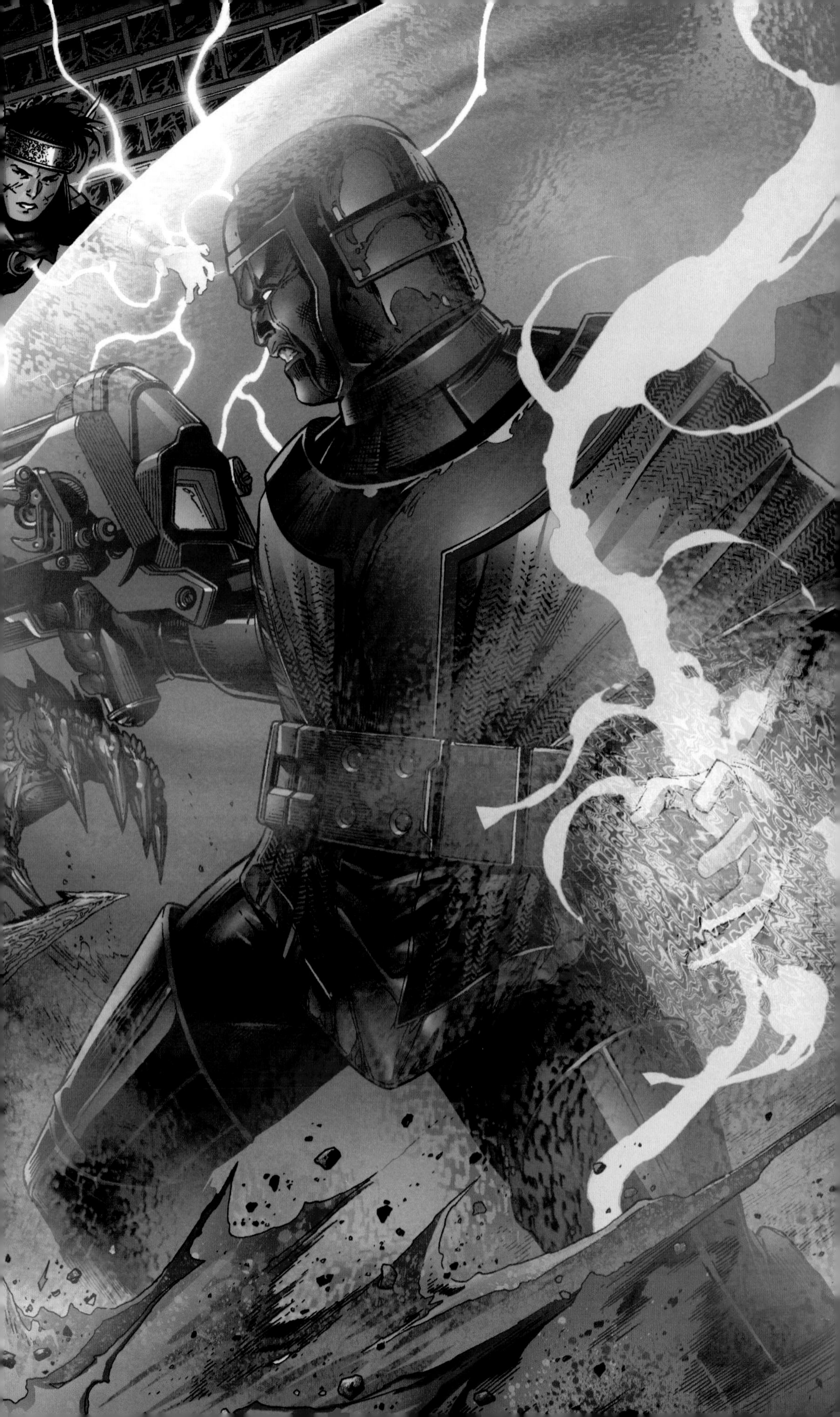

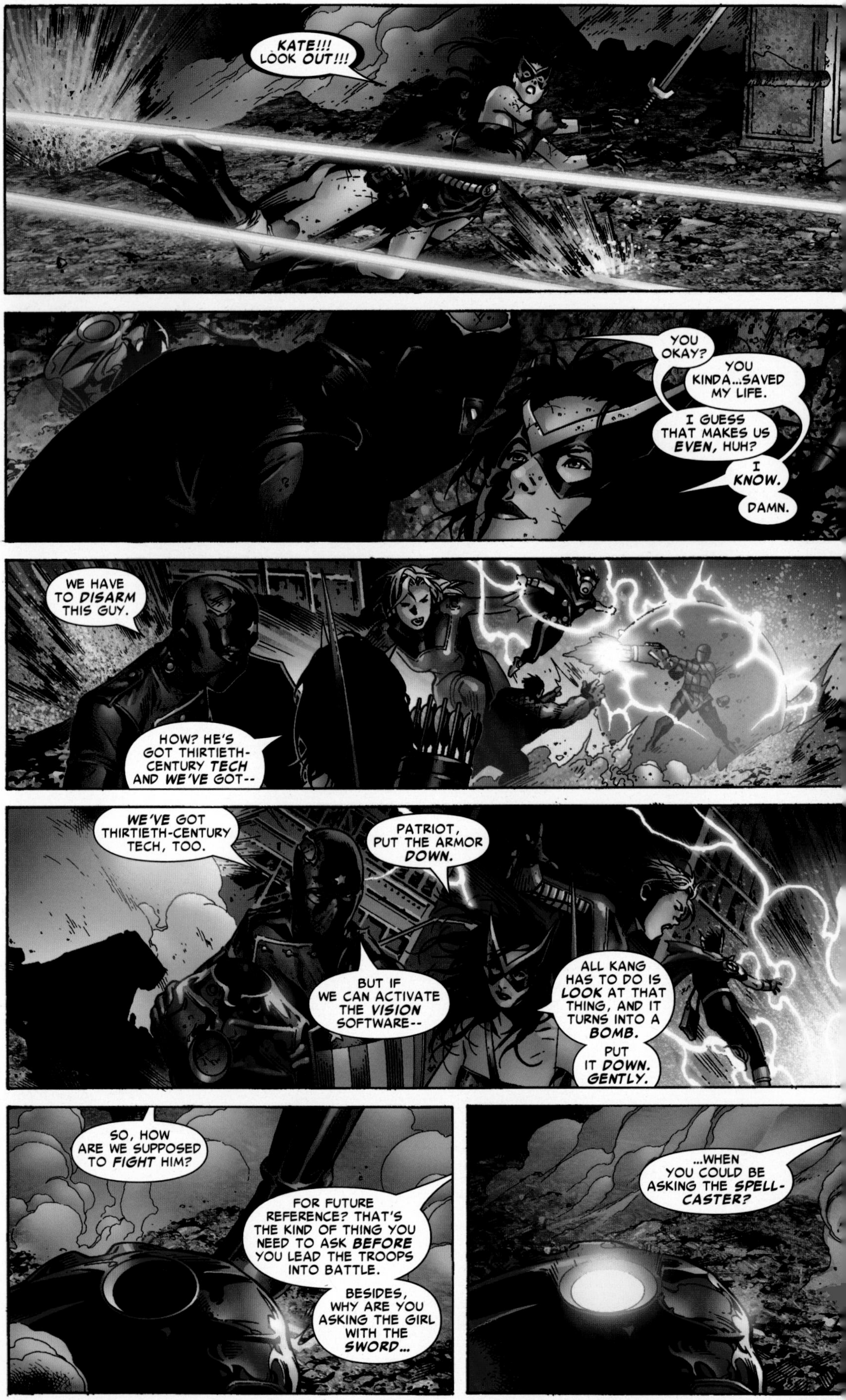
KATE!!! LOOK OUT!!!
YOU OKAY?
YOU KINDA...SAVED MY LIFE.
I GUESS THAT MAKES US EVEN, HUH?
I KNOW.
DAMN.
WE HAVE TO DISARM THIS GUY.
HOW? HE'S GOT THIRTIETH-CENTURY TECH AND WE'VE GOT--
WE'VE GOT THIRTIETH-CENTURY TECH, TOO.
PATRIOT, PUT THE ARMOR DOWN.
BUT IF WE CAN ACTIVATE THE VISION SOFTWARE--
ALL KANG HAS TO DO IS LOOK AT THAT THING, AND IT TURNS INTO A BOMB.
PUT IT DOWN. GENTLY.
SO, HOW ARE WE SUPPOSED TO FIGHT HIM?
FOR FUTURE REFERENCE? THAT'S THE KIND OF THING YOU NEED TO ASK BEFORE YOU LEAD THE TROOPS INTO BATTLE.
BESIDES, WHY ARE YOU ASKING THE GIRL WITH THE SWORD...
...WHEN YOU COULD BE ASKING THE SPELL-CASTER?

HOW AM I SUPPOSED TO CONCENTRATE ON **SPELL-CASTING?** I'M A LITTLE PRE-OCCUPIED TRYING TO STAY **ALIVE.**

CASSIE AND I'LL DISTRACT KANG. JUST DO WHAT YOU NEED TO DO.

THAT'S THE **THING.** I'M **NEW** AT THIS...

...I DON'T **KNOW** WHAT I NEED TO DO.

YES, YOU **DO.** WE **PRACTICED** THIS.

DON'T FOCUS ON THE **PROBLEM.** FOCUS ON WHAT YOU **WANT.**

I WANT TO DISABLE KANG'S FORCE FIELD.

SAY IT **AGAIN.**

I WANT TO DISABLE KANG'S FORCE FIELD. I WANT TO DISABLE KANG'S FORCE FIELD...

GOOD. NOW IMAGINE WHAT IT'S GONNA **FEEL** LIKE **WHEN** YOU DISABLE KANG'S FORCE FIELD.

I WANT TO DISABLE KANG'S FORCE FIELD. I WANT TO DISABLE KANG'S FORCE FIELD...

WOW...

WHERE'D YOU GUYS **LEARN** THAT? A WICCAN MANUAL?

NO. ONE OF MY MOM'S SELF-HELP BOOKS.

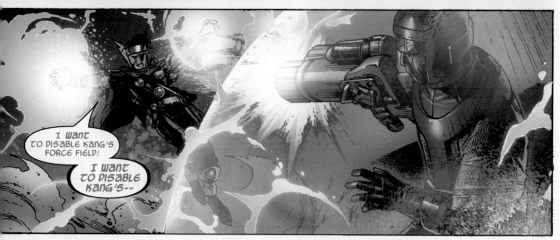

I WANT TO DISABLE KANG'S FORCE FIELD!

I WANT TO DISABLE KANG'S--

BILLY!!!

FOOOM!

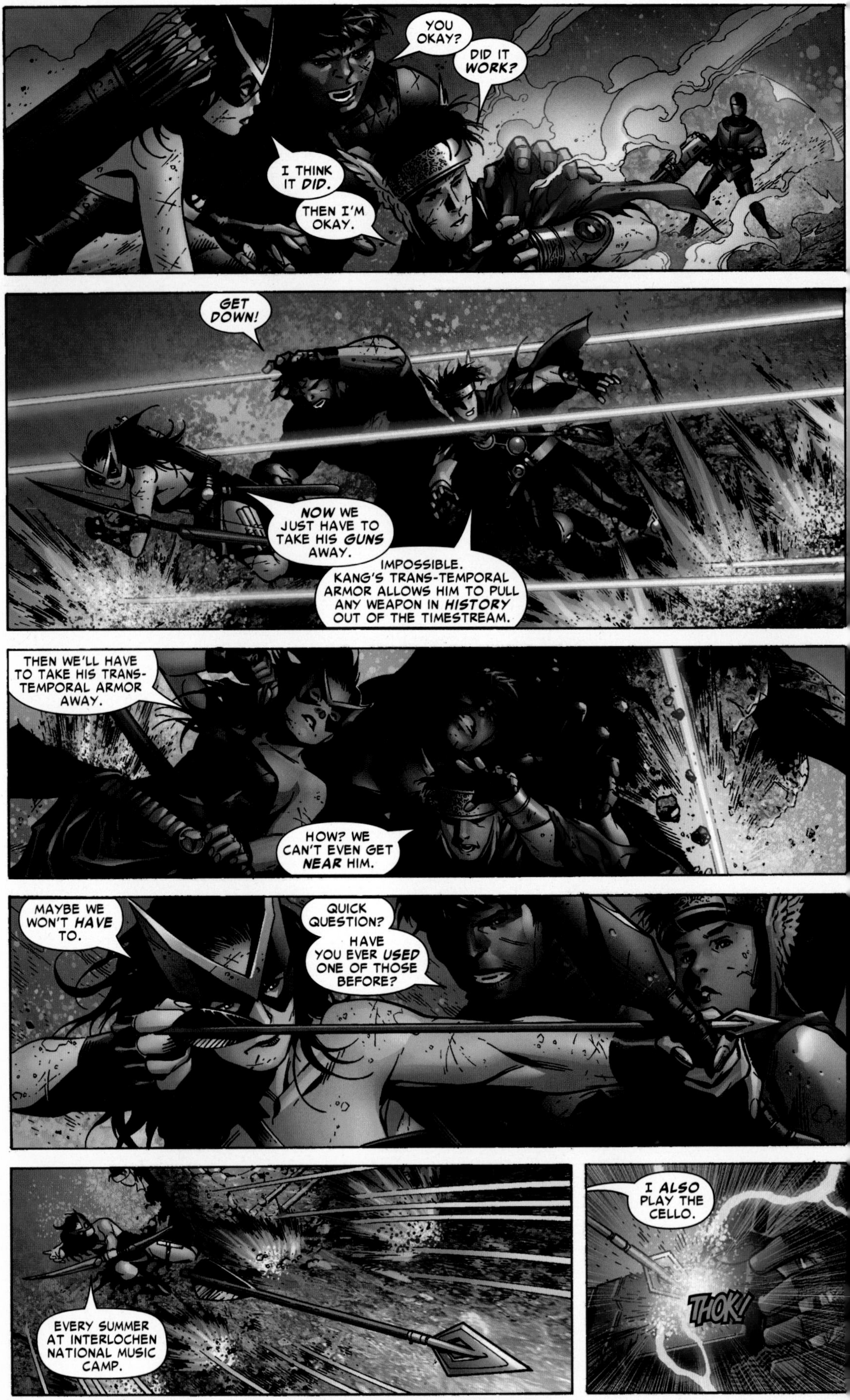
YOU OKAY?
DID IT WORK?
I THINK IT DID.
THEN I'M OKAY.
GET DOWN!
NOW WE JUST HAVE TO TAKE HIS GUNS AWAY.
IMPOSSIBLE. KANG'S TRANS-TEMPORAL ARMOR ALLOWS HIM TO PULL ANY WEAPON IN HISTORY OUT OF THE TIMESTREAM.
THEN WE'LL HAVE TO TAKE HIS TRANS-TEMPORAL ARMOR AWAY.
HOW? WE CAN'T EVEN GET NEAR HIM.
MAYBE WE WON'T HAVE TO.
QUICK QUESTION?
HAVE YOU EVER USED ONE OF THOSE BEFORE?
EVERY SUMMER AT INTERLOCHEN NATIONAL MUSIC CAMP.
I ALSO PLAY THE CELLO.
THOK!

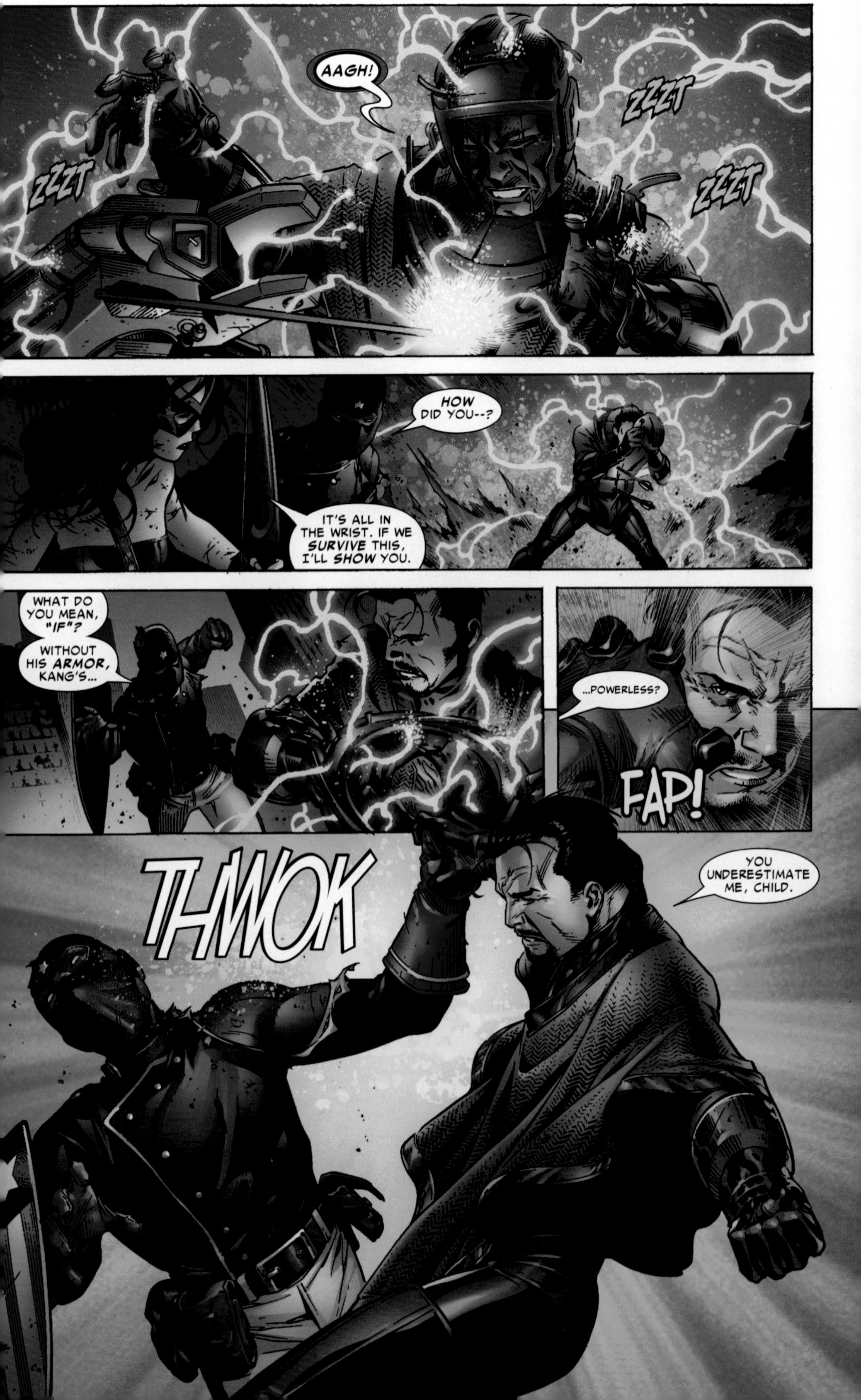
AAGH!
ZZZT
ZZZT
ZZZT
HOW DID YOU--?
IT'S ALL IN THE WRIST. IF WE SURVIVE THIS, I'LL SHOW YOU.
WHAT DO YOU MEAN, "IF"?
WITHOUT HIS ARMOR, KANG'S...
...POWERLESS?
FAP!
THWOK
YOU UNDERESTIMATE ME, CHILD.

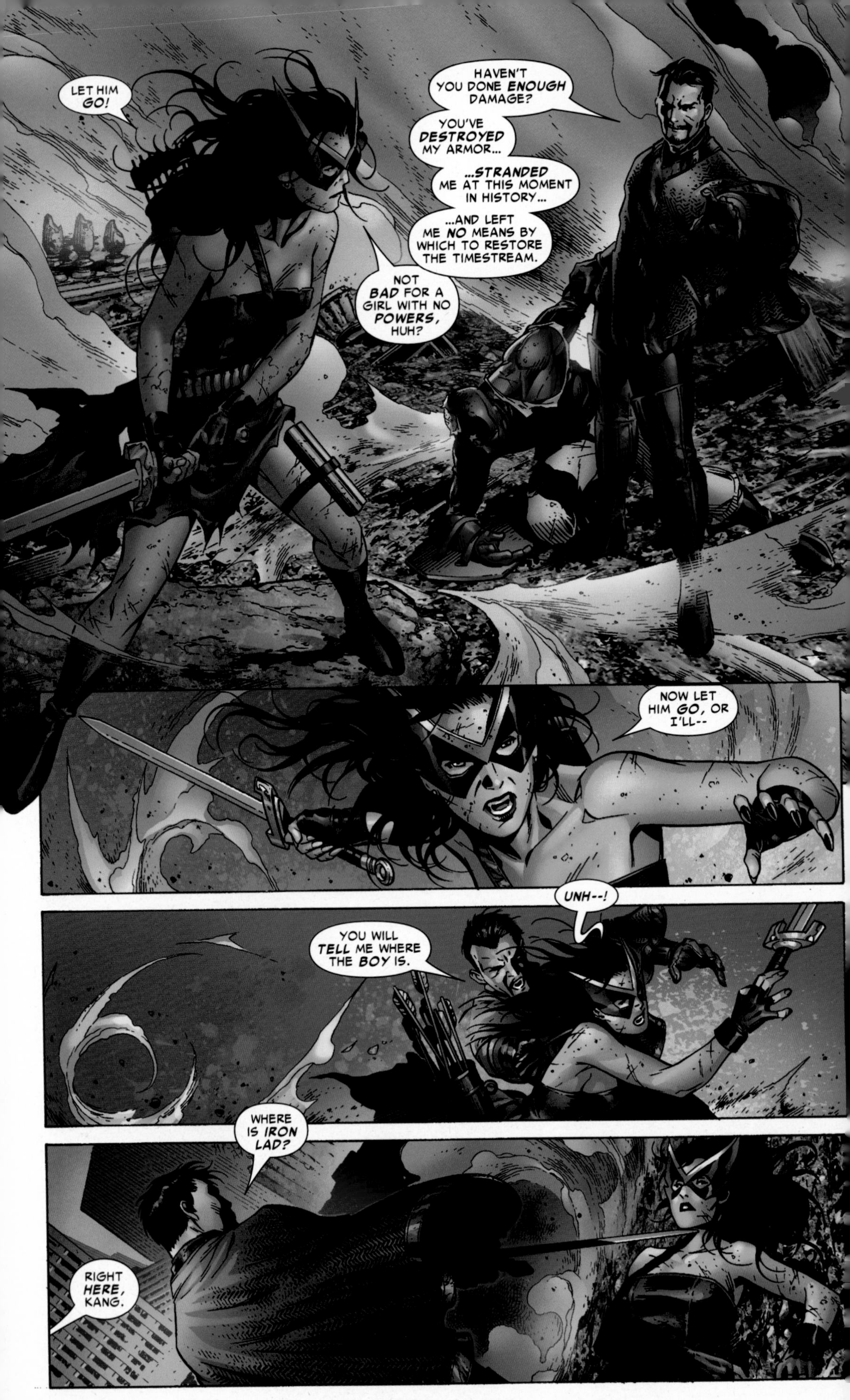
LET HIM GO!
HAVEN'T YOU DONE ENOUGH DAMAGE?
YOU'VE DESTROYED MY ARMOR...
...STRANDED ME AT THIS MOMENT IN HISTORY...
...AND LEFT ME NO MEANS BY WHICH TO RESTORE THE TIMESTREAM.
NOT BAD FOR A GIRL WITH NO POWERS, HUH?
NOW LET HIM GO, OR I'LL--
UNH--!
YOU WILL TELL ME WHERE THE BOY IS.
WHERE IS IRON LAD?
RIGHT HERE, KANG.

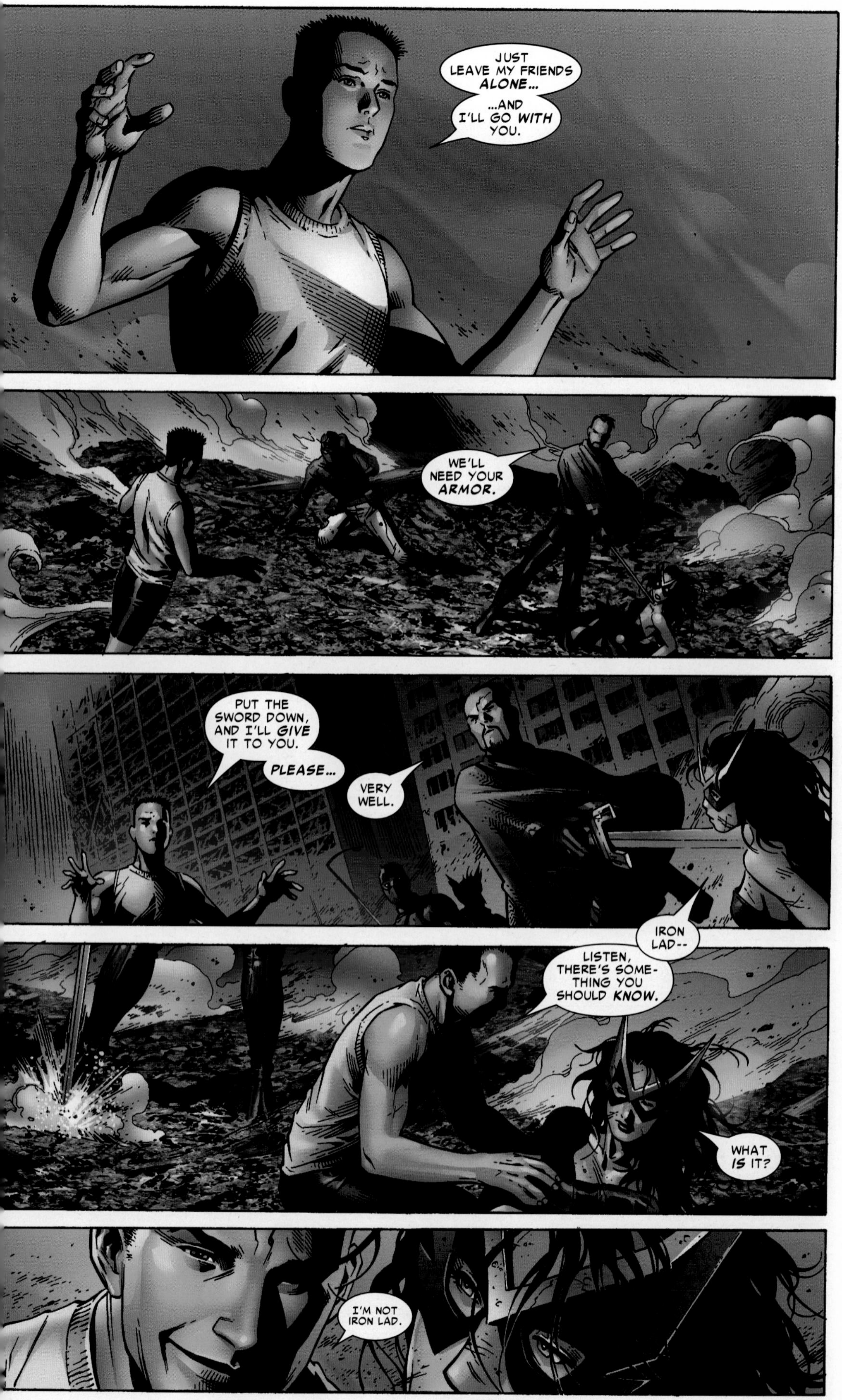
JUST LEAVE MY FRIENDS ALONE...
...AND I'LL GO WITH YOU.
WE'LL NEED YOUR ARMOR.
PUT THE SWORD DOWN, AND I'LL GIVE IT TO YOU.
PLEASE...
VERY WELL.
IRON LAD--
LISTEN, THERE'S SOME-THING YOU SHOULD KNOW.
WHAT IS IT?
I'M NOT IRON LAD.

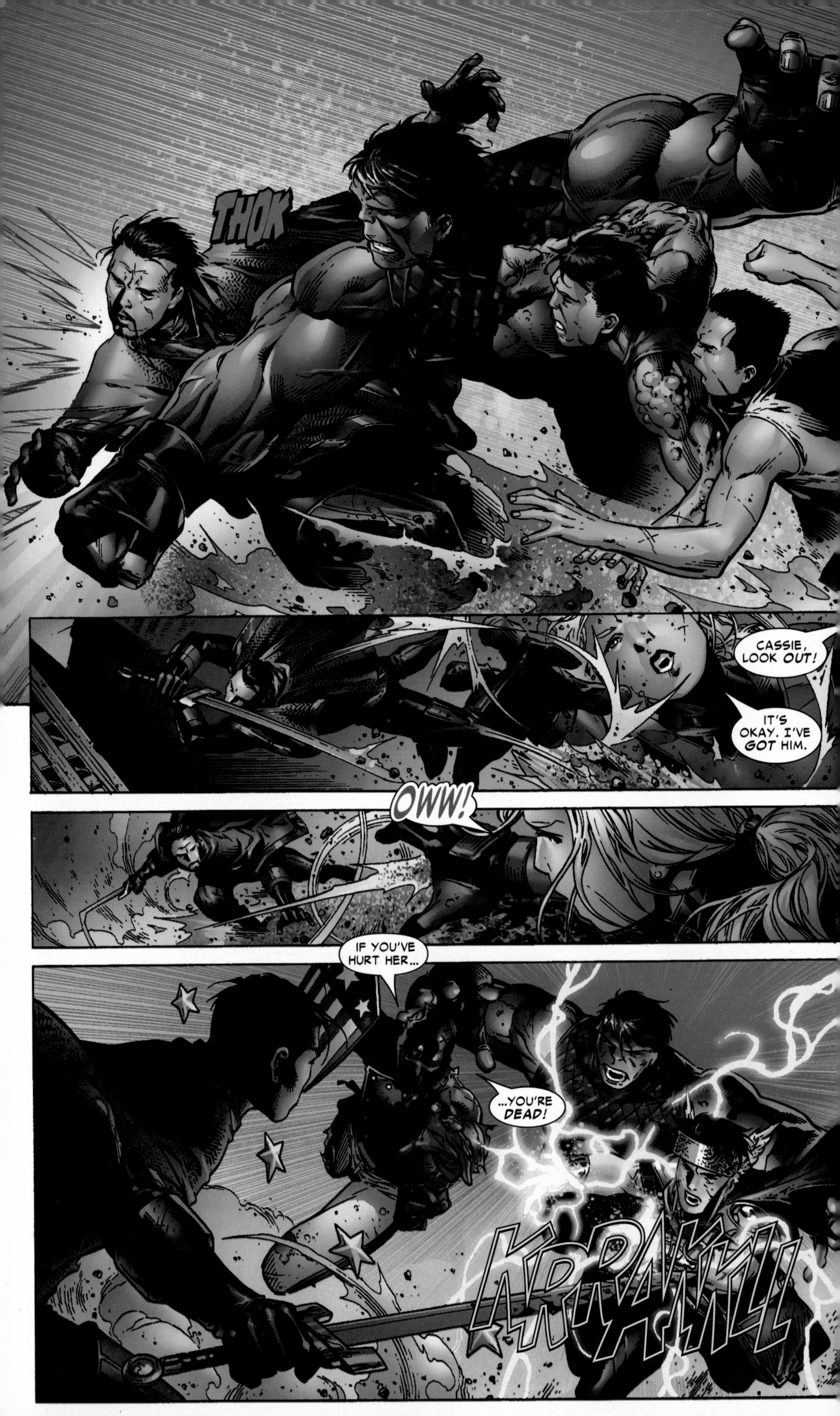
THOK
CASSIE, LOOK OUT!
IT'S OKAY. I'VE GOT HIM.
OWW!
IF YOU'VE HURT HER...
...YOU'RE DEAD!
KRAKKLL

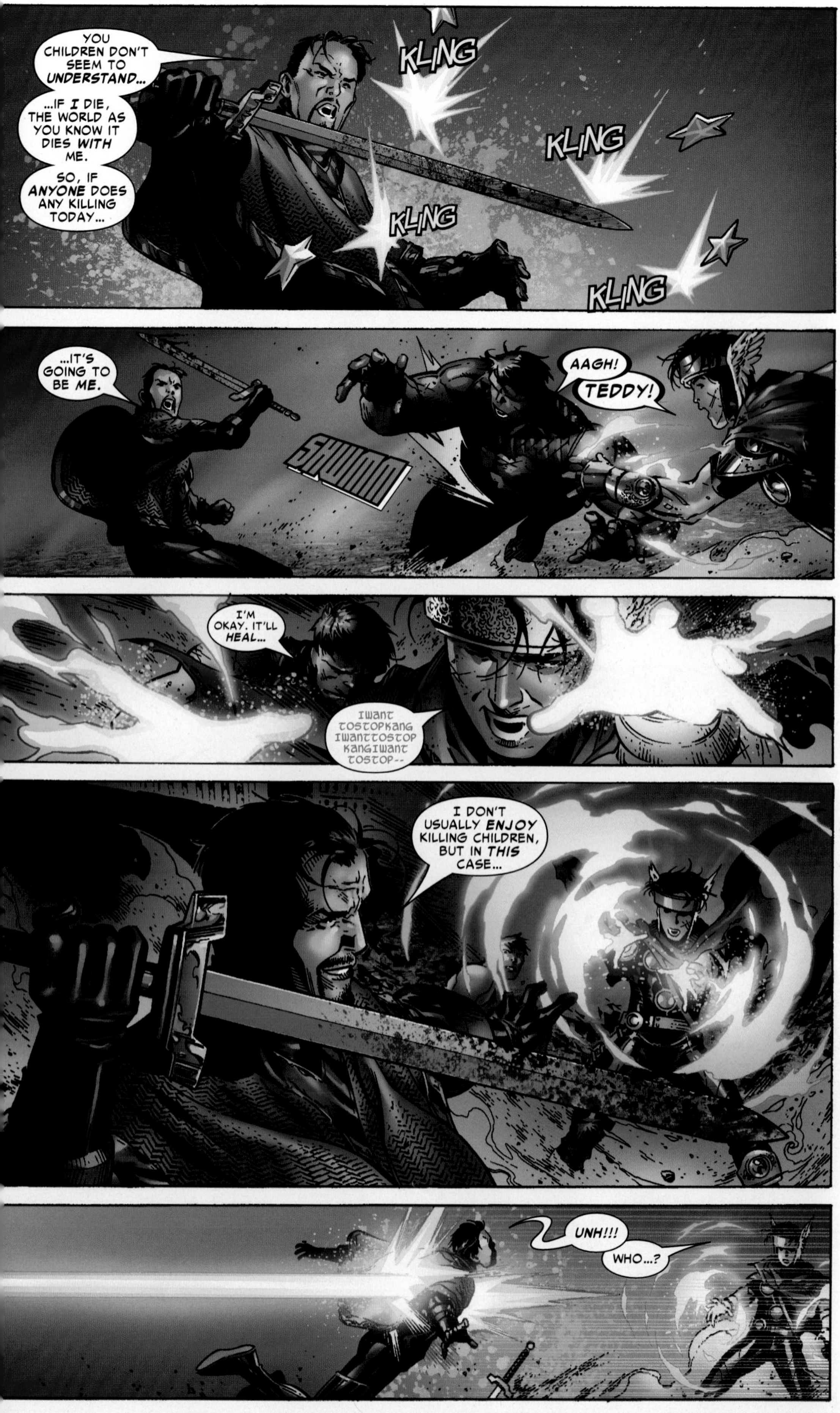
YOU CHILDREN DON'T SEEM TO UNDERSTAND...
...IF I DIE, THE WORLD AS YOU KNOW IT DIES WITH ME.
SO, IF ANYONE DOES ANY KILLING TODAY...
KLING
KLING
KLING
KLING
...IT'S GOING TO BE ME.
SHUNNN
AAGH!
TEDDY!
I'M OKAY. IT'LL HEAL...
IWANT TOSTOPKANG IWANTTOSTOP KANGIWANT TOSTOP--
I DON'T USUALLY ENJOY KILLING CHILDREN, BUT IN THIS CASE...
UNH!!!
WHO...?

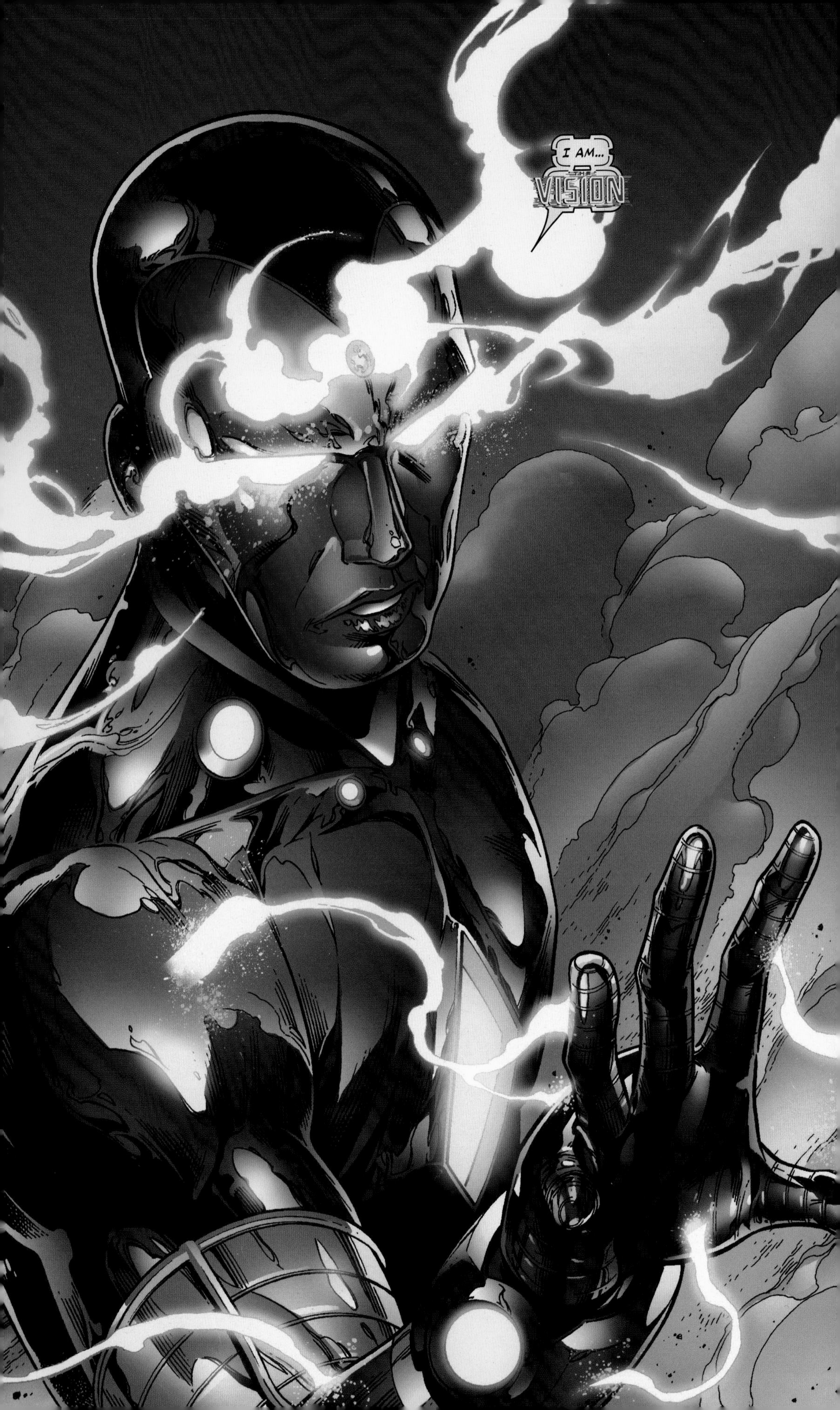
I AM...
THE VISION

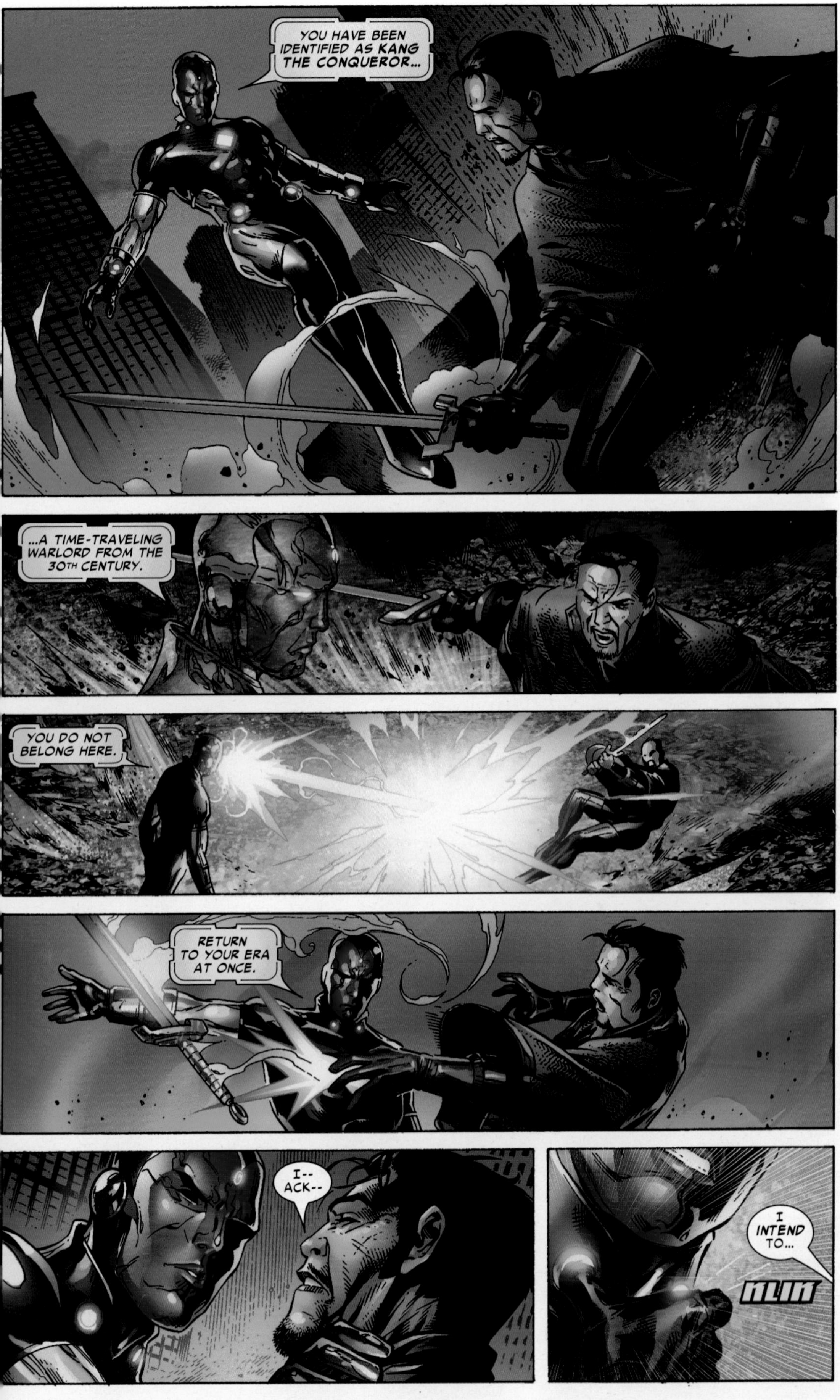
YOU HAVE BEEN IDENTIFIED AS KANG THE CONQUEROR...
...A TIME-TRAVELING WARLORD FROM THE 30TH CENTURY.
YOU DO NOT BELONG HERE.
RETURN TO YOUR ERA AT ONCE.
I-- ACK--
I INTEND TO...

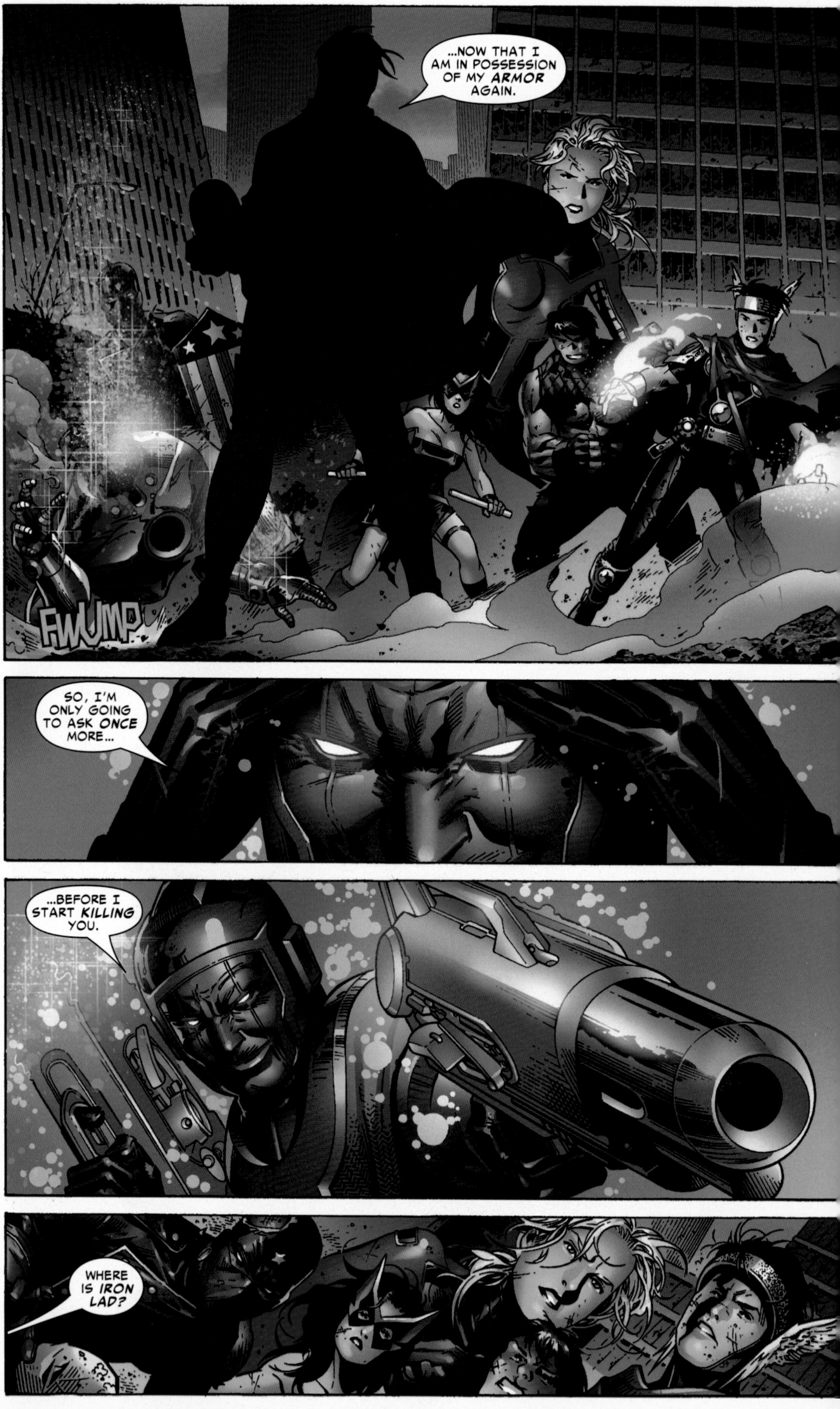
...NOW THAT I AM IN POSSESSION OF MY ARMOR AGAIN.
FWUMP
SO, I'M ONLY GOING TO ASK ONCE MORE...
...BEFORE I START KILLING YOU.
WHERE IS IRON LAD?

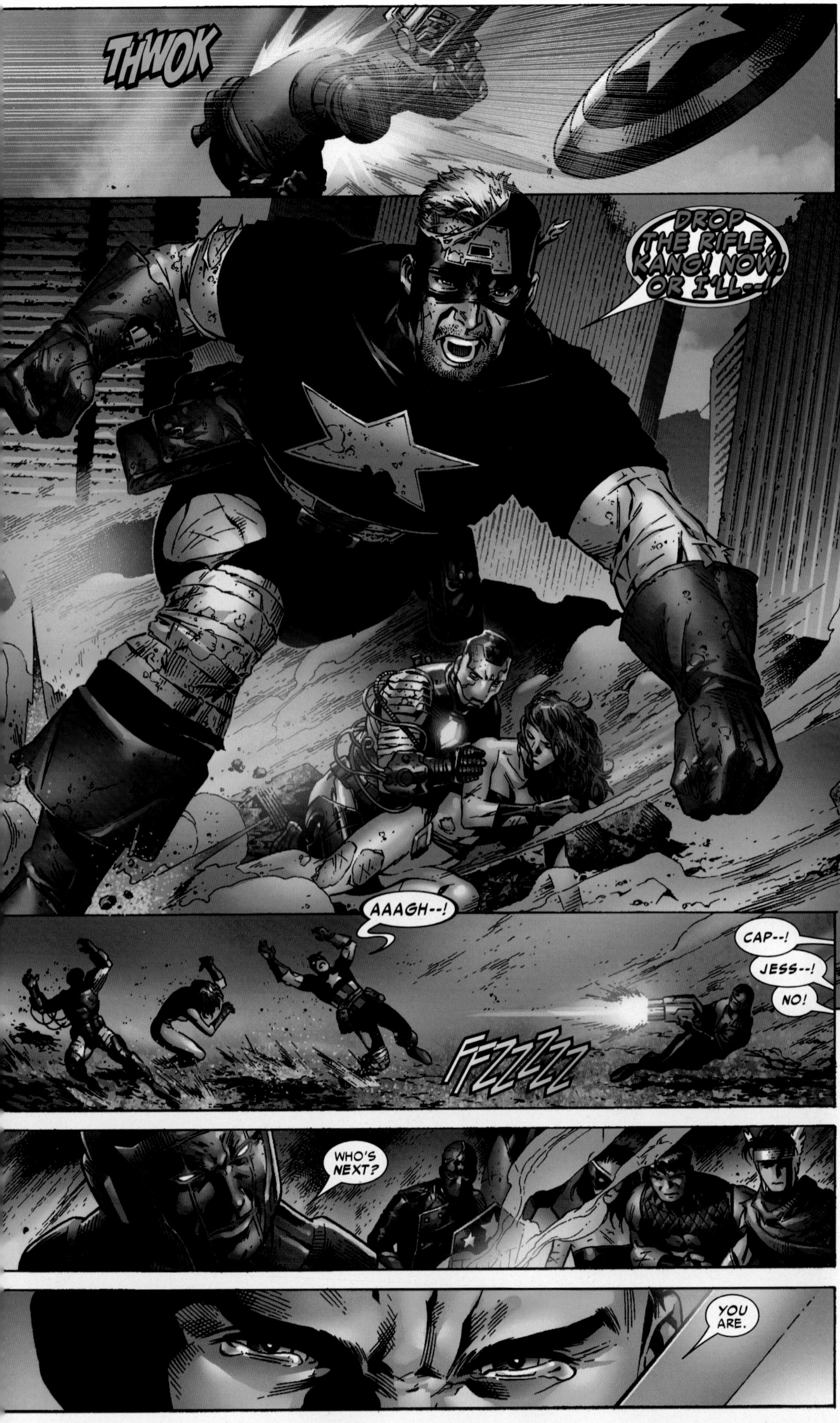
THWOK
DROP THE RIFLE, KANG! NOW! OR I'LL--!
AAAGH--!
CAP--!
JESS--!
NO!
FFZZZZZ
WHO'S NEXT?
YOU ARE.

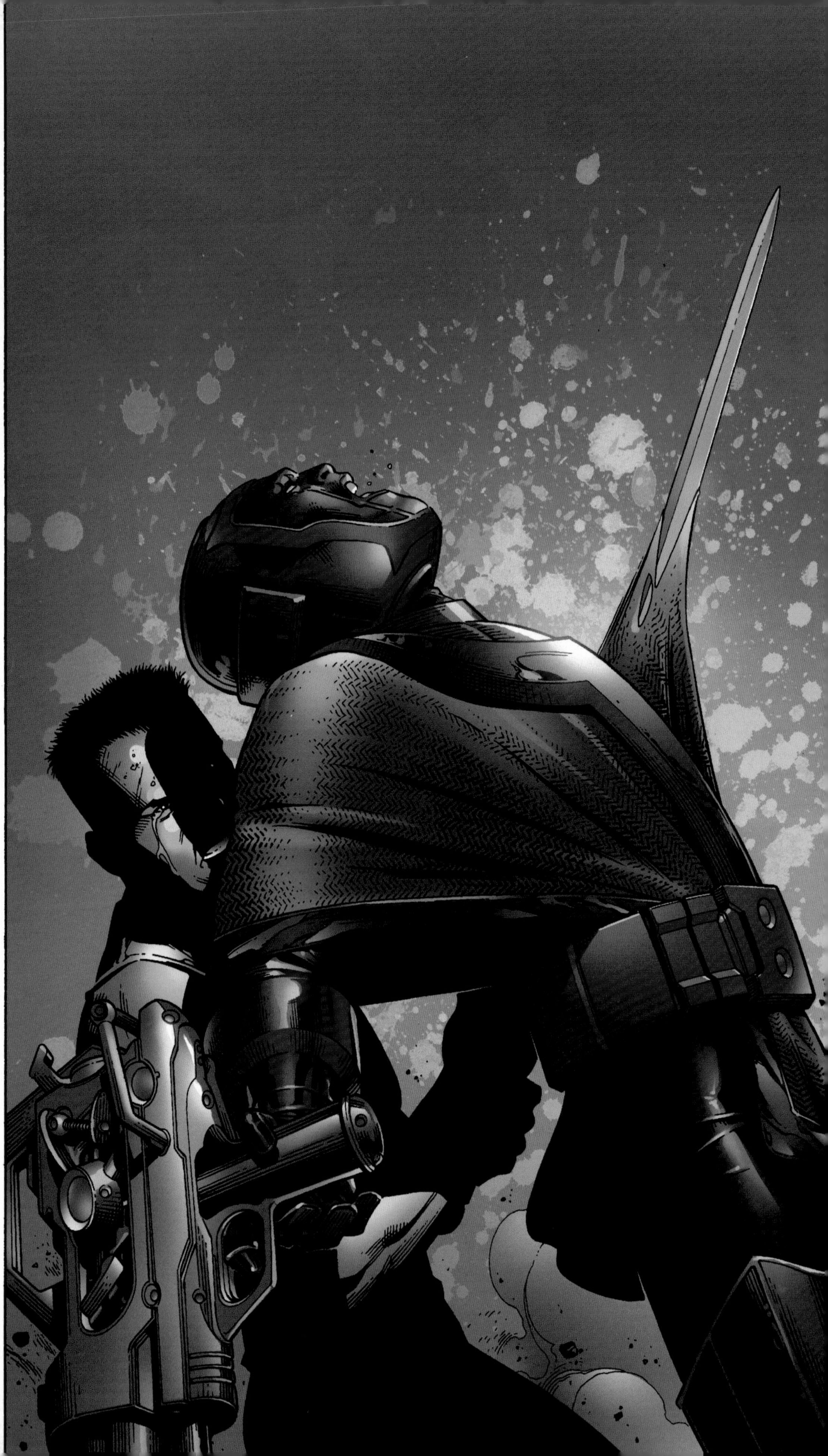

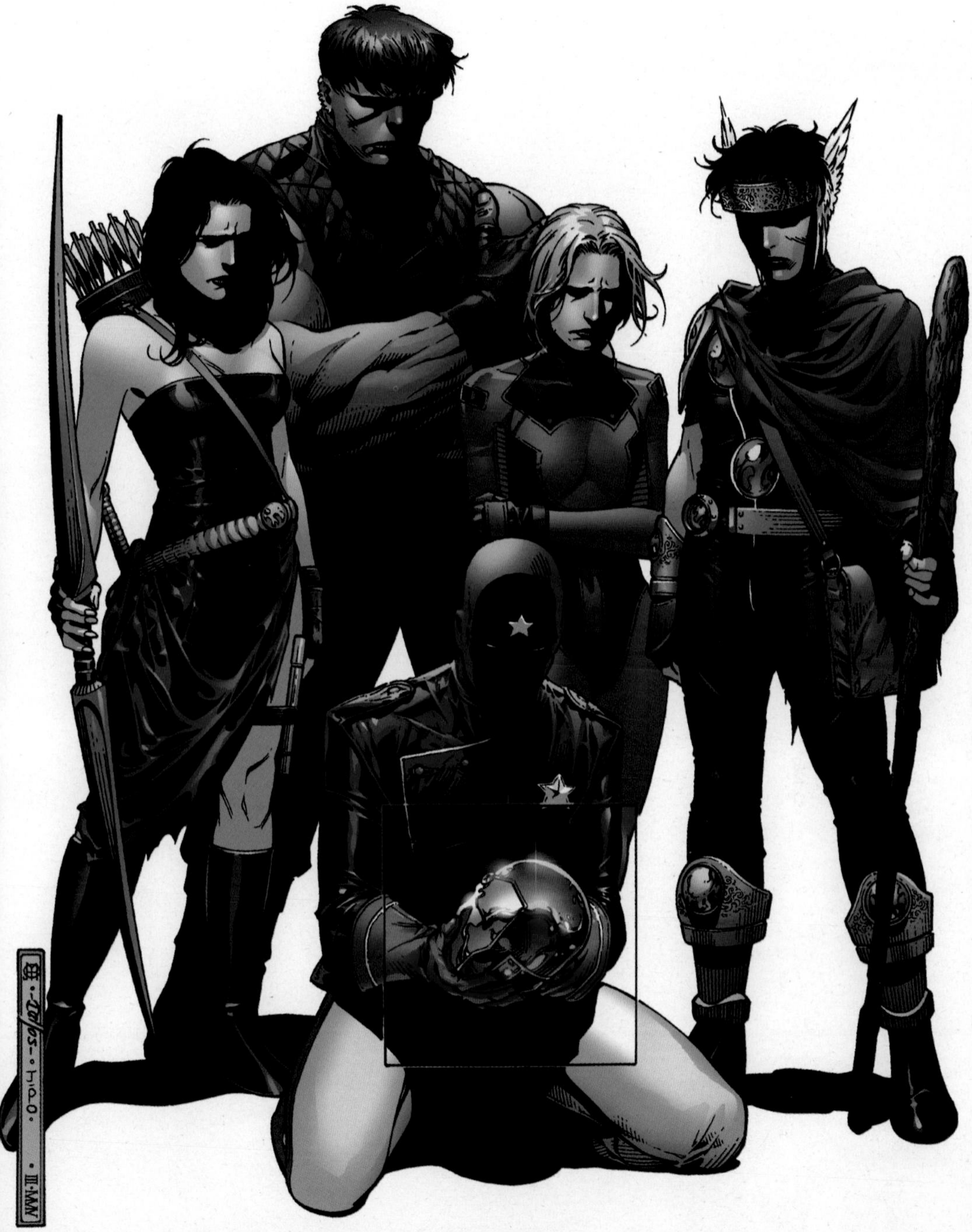

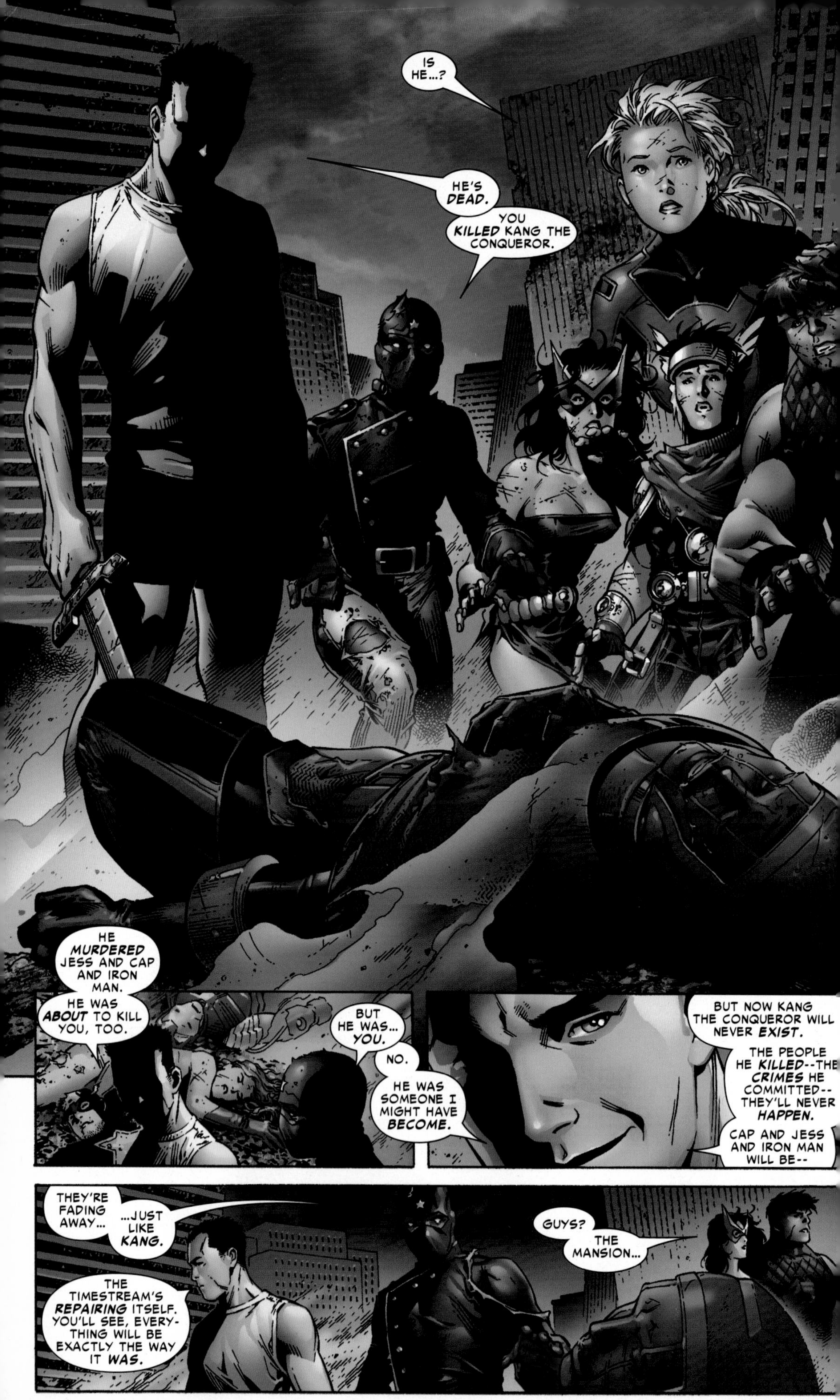
IS HE...?
HE'S DEAD.
YOU KILLED KANG THE CONQUEROR.
HE MURDERED JESS AND CAP AND IRON MAN.
HE WAS ABOUT TO KILL YOU, TOO.
BUT HE WAS... YOU.
NO.
HE WAS SOMEONE I MIGHT HAVE BECOME.
BUT NOW KANG THE CONQUEROR WILL NEVER EXIST.
THE PEOPLE HE KILLED--THE CRIMES HE COMMITTED--THEY'LL NEVER HAPPEN.
CAP AND JESS AND IRON MAN WILL BE--
THEY'RE FADING AWAY...
...JUST LIKE KANG.
THE TIMESTREAM'S REPAIRING ITSELF. YOU'LL SEE, EVERY-THING WILL BE EXACTLY THE WAY IT WAS.
GUYS?
THE MANSION...

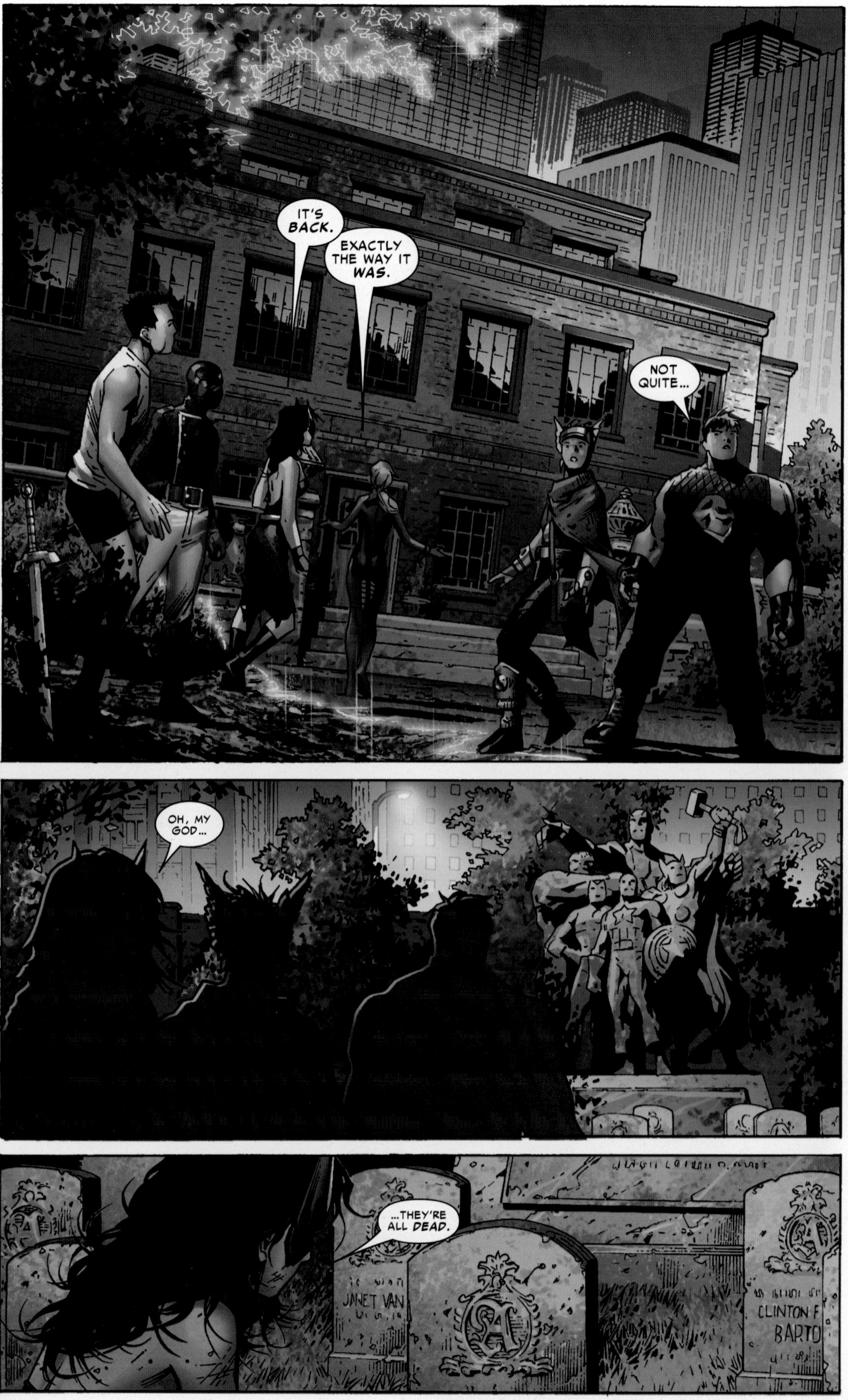
IT'S BACK.
EXACTLY THE WAY IT WAS.
NOT QUITE...
OH, MY GOD...
...THEY'RE ALL DEAD.
JANET VAN
CLINTON F
BARTO

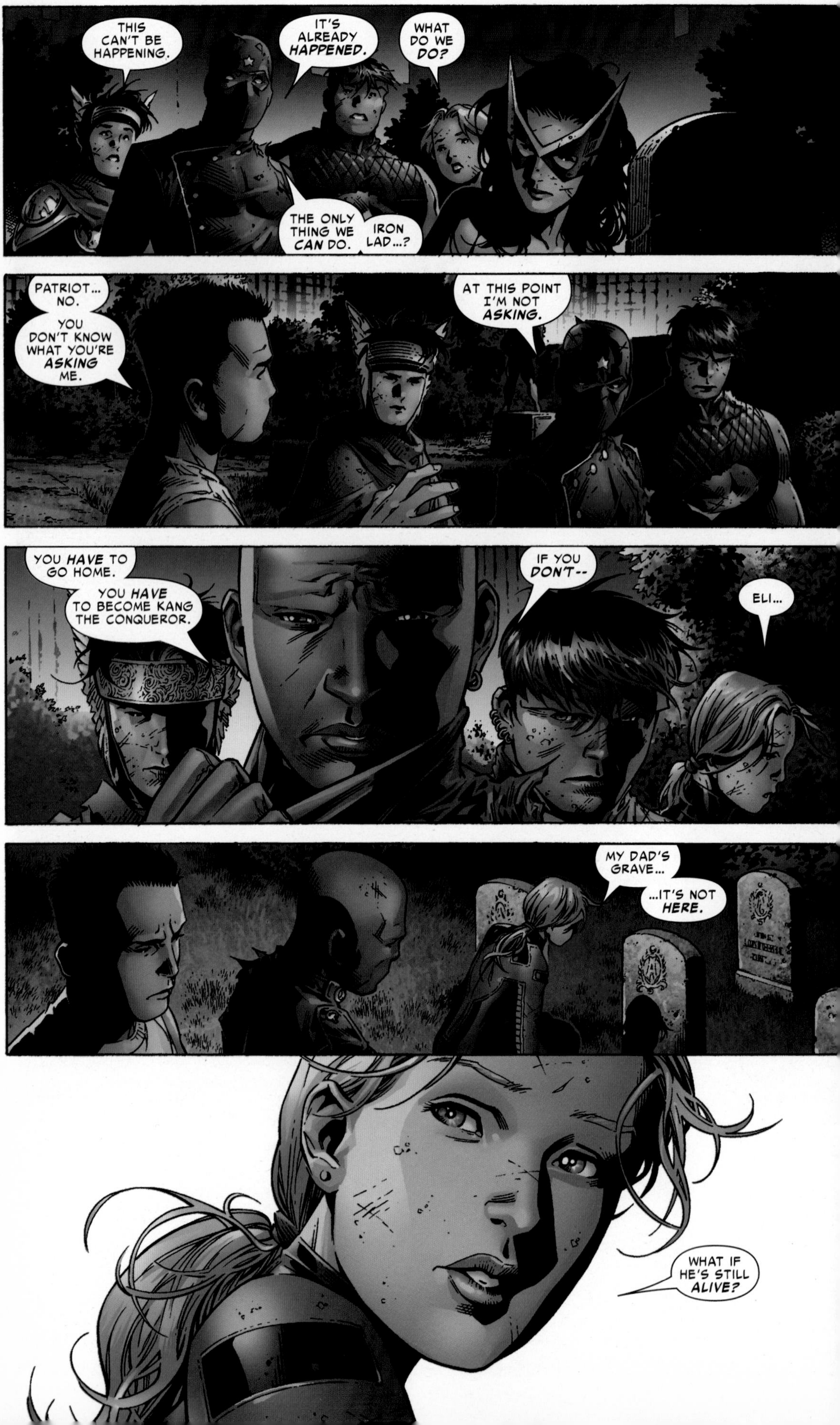
THIS CAN'T BE HAPPENING.
IT'S ALREADY HAPPENED.
WHAT DO WE DO?
THE ONLY THING WE CAN DO.
IRON LAD...?
PATRIOT... NO.
YOU DON'T KNOW WHAT YOU'RE ASKING ME.
AT THIS POINT I'M NOT ASKING.
YOU HAVE TO GO HOME.
YOU HAVE TO BECOME KANG THE CONQUEROR.
IF YOU DON'T--
ELI...
MY DAD'S GRAVE...
...IT'S NOT HERE.
WHAT IF HE'S STILL ALIVE?

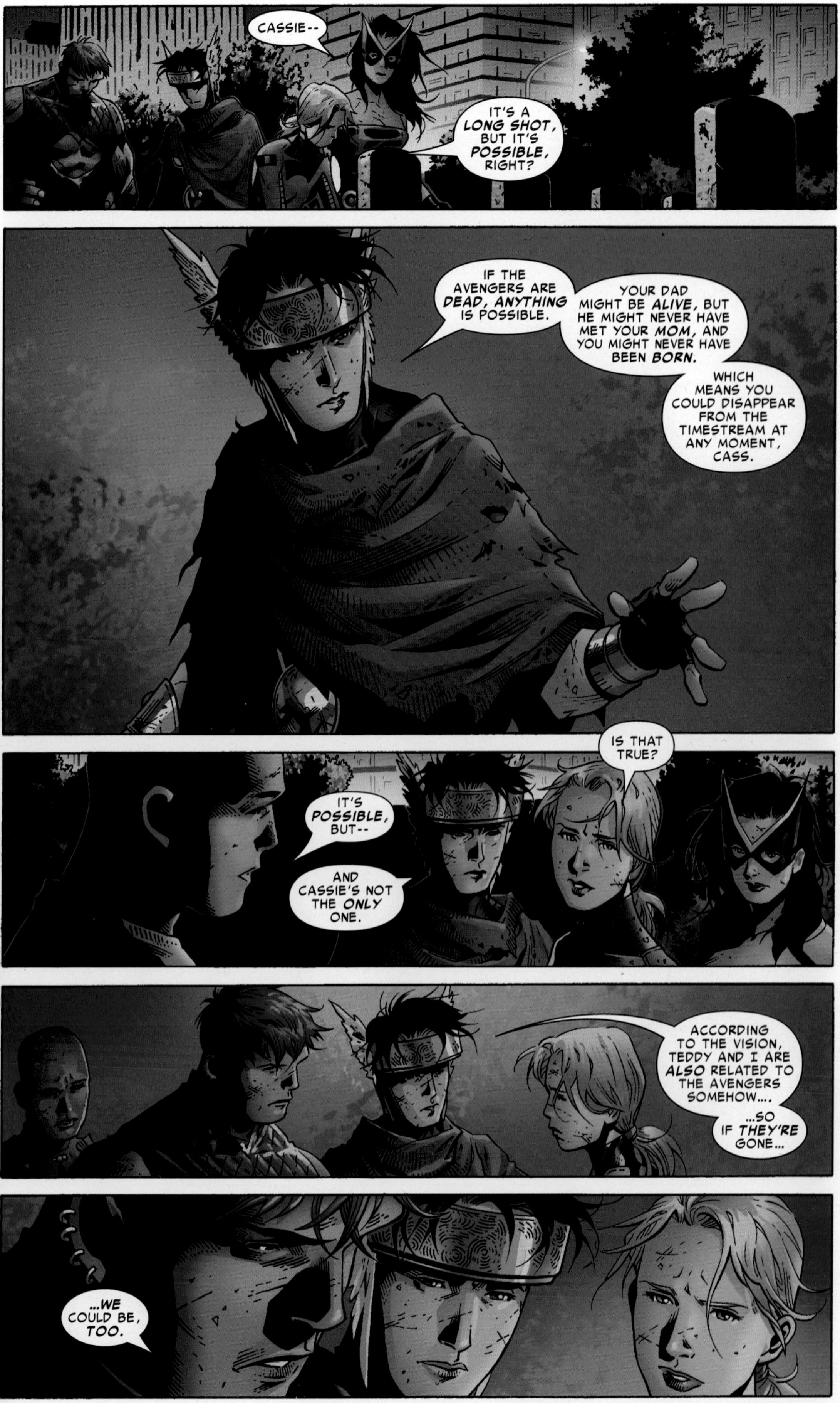
CASSIE--
IT'S A LONG SHOT, BUT IT'S POSSIBLE, RIGHT?
IF THE AVENGERS ARE DEAD, ANYTHING IS POSSIBLE.
YOUR DAD MIGHT BE ALIVE, BUT HE MIGHT NEVER HAVE MET YOUR MOM, AND YOU MIGHT NEVER HAVE BEEN BORN.
WHICH MEANS YOU COULD DISAPPEAR FROM THE TIMESTREAM AT ANY MOMENT, CASS.
IS THAT TRUE?
IT'S POSSIBLE, BUT--
AND CASSIE'S NOT THE ONLY ONE.
ACCORDING TO THE VISION, TEDDY AND I ARE ALSO RELATED TO THE AVENGERS SOMEHOW....
...SO IF THEY'RE GONE...
...WE COULD BE, TOO.

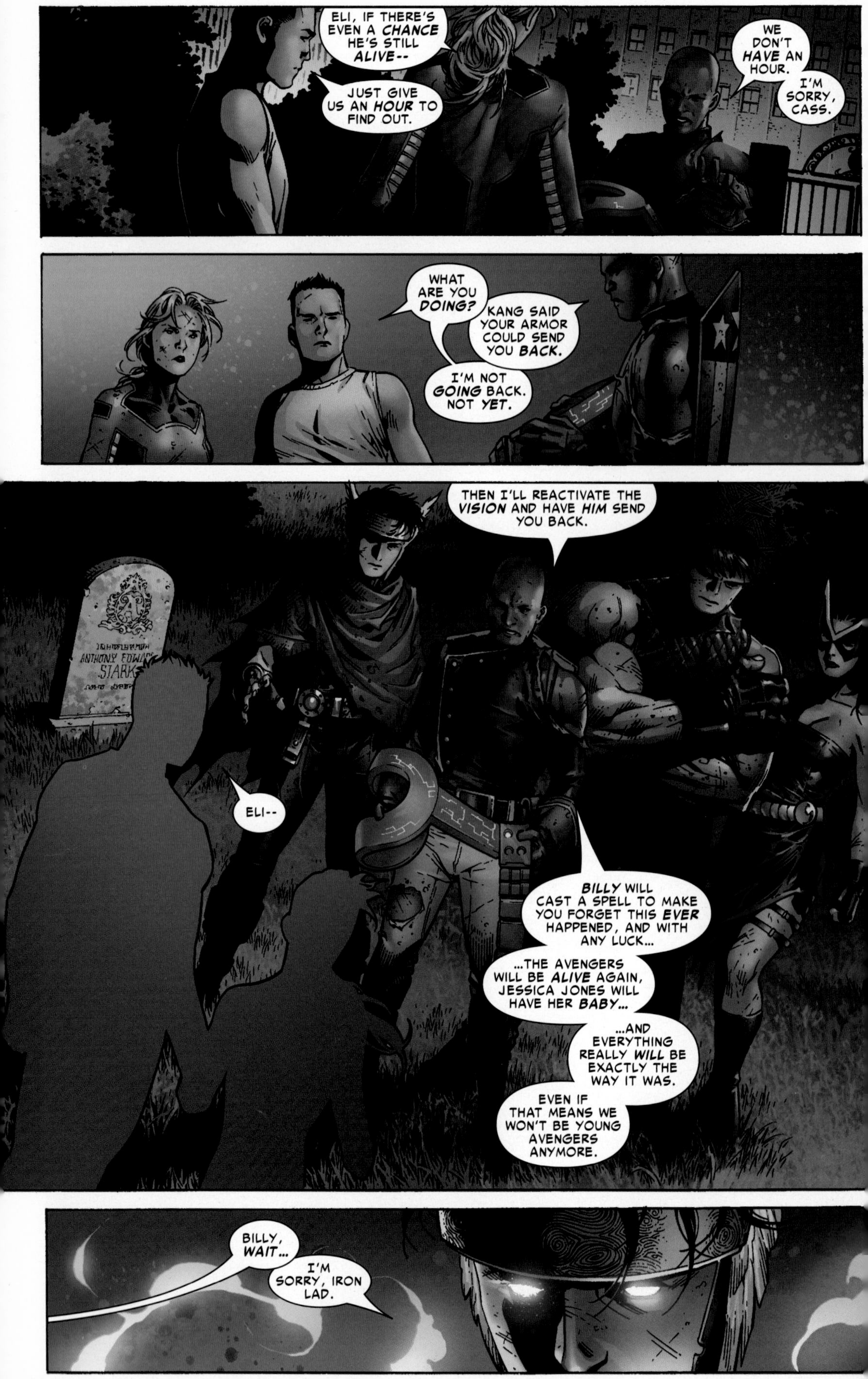
ELI, IF THERE'S EVEN A CHANCE HE'S STILL ALIVE--
JUST GIVE US AN HOUR TO FIND OUT.
WE DON'T HAVE AN HOUR.
I'M SORRY, CASS.
WHAT ARE YOU DOING?
KANG SAID YOUR ARMOR COULD SEND YOU BACK.
I'M NOT GOING BACK. NOT YET.
THEN I'LL REACTIVATE THE VISION AND HAVE HIM SEND YOU BACK.
ELI--
BILLY WILL CAST A SPELL TO MAKE YOU FORGET THIS EVER HAPPENED, AND WITH ANY LUCK...
...THE AVENGERS WILL BE ALIVE AGAIN, JESSICA JONES WILL HAVE HER BABY...
...AND EVERYTHING REALLY WILL BE EXACTLY THE WAY IT WAS.
EVEN IF THAT MEANS WE WON'T BE YOUNG AVENGERS ANYMORE.
BILLY, WAIT...
I'M SORRY, IRON LAD.

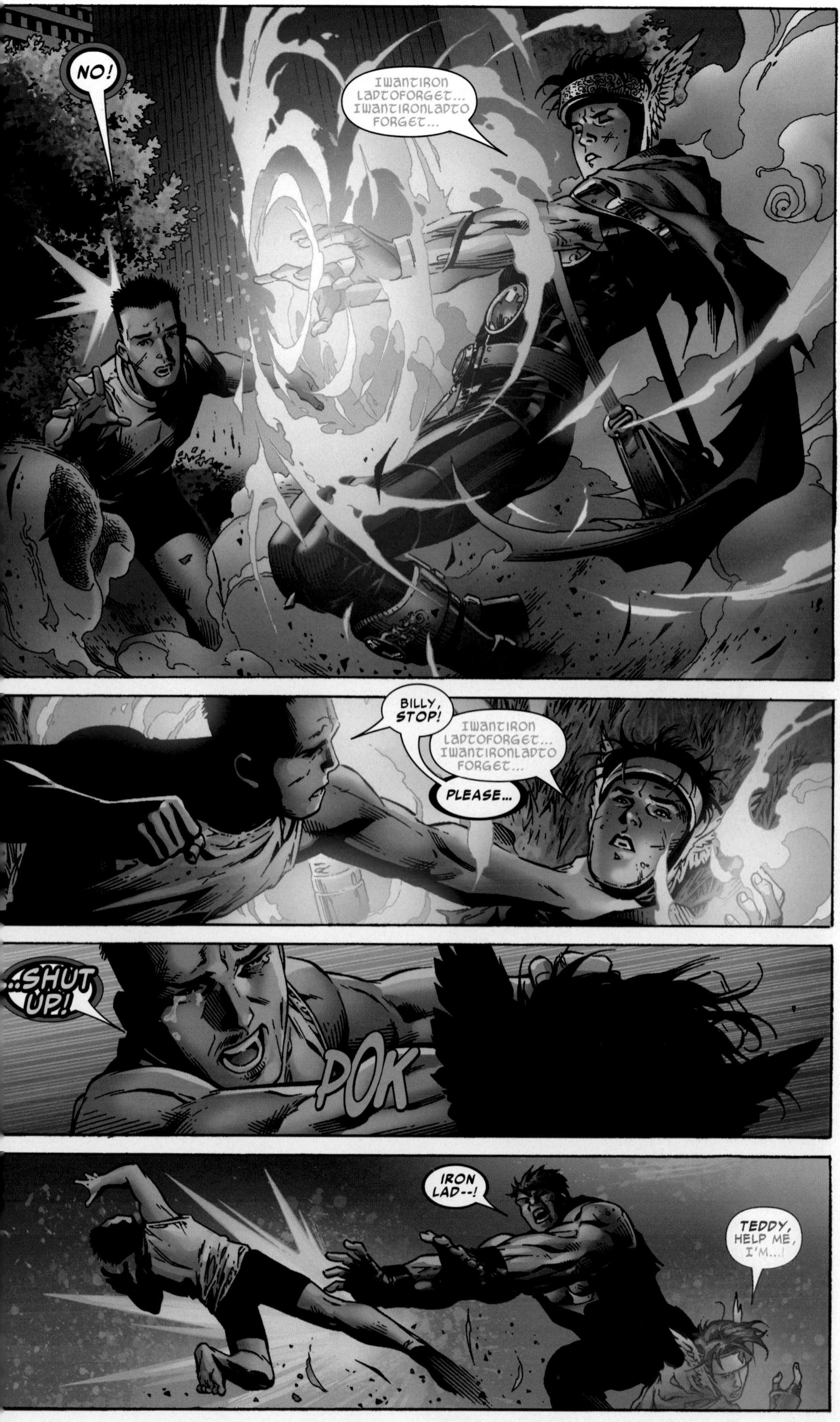
NO!
IWANTIRON LADTOFORGET... IWANTIRONLADTO FORGET...
BILLY, STOP!
IWANTIRON LADTOFORGET... IWANTIRONLADTO FORGET...
PLEASE...
..SHUT UP!
POK
IRON LAD--!
TEDDY, HELP ME, I'M...!

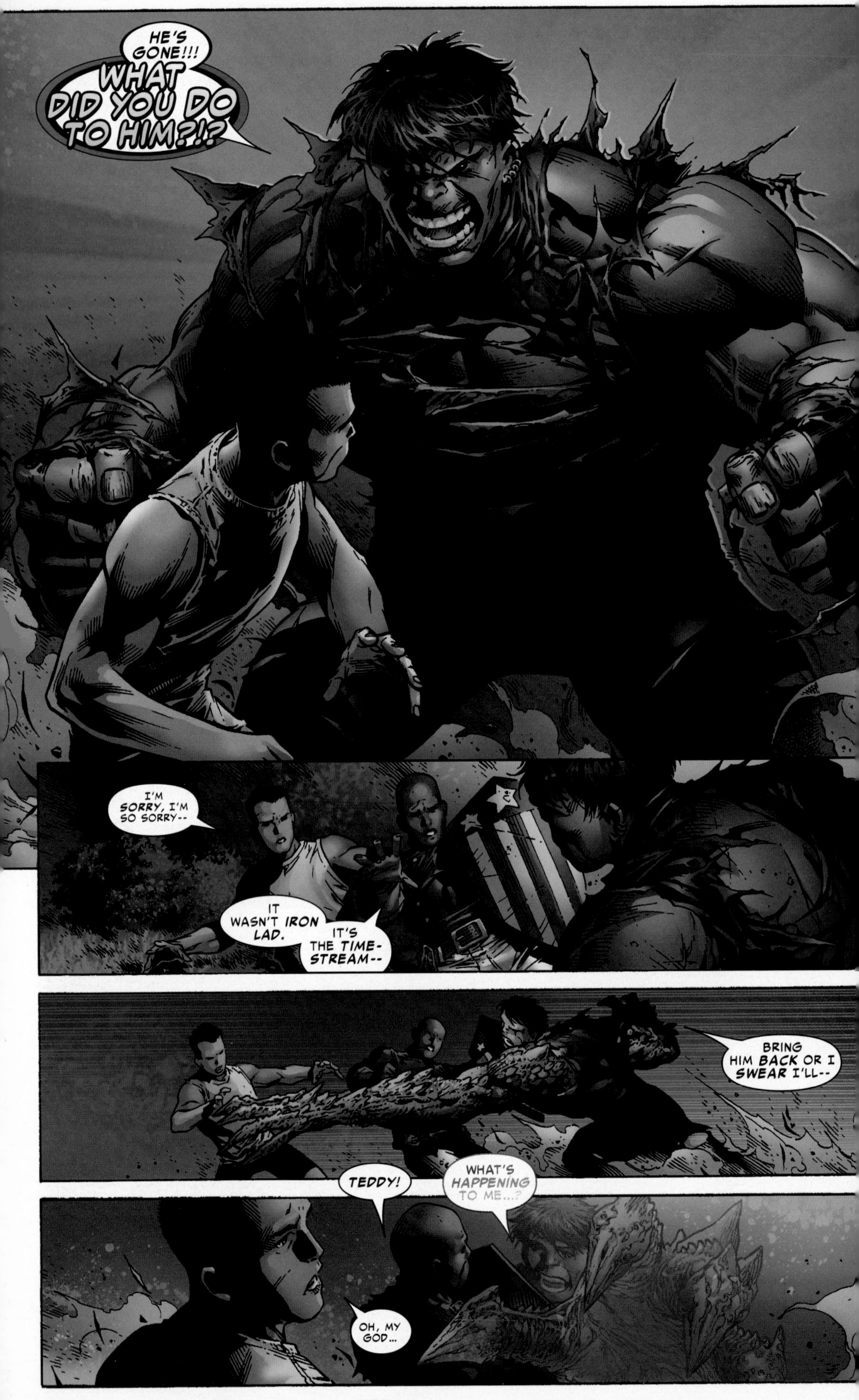
HE'S GONE!!! WHAT DID YOU DO TO HIM?!?
I'M SORRY, I'M SO SORRY--
IT WASN'T IRON LAD.
IT'S THE TIME-STREAM--
BRING HIM BACK OR I SWEAR I'LL--
TEDDY!
WHAT'S HAPPENING TO ME...?
OH, MY GOD...

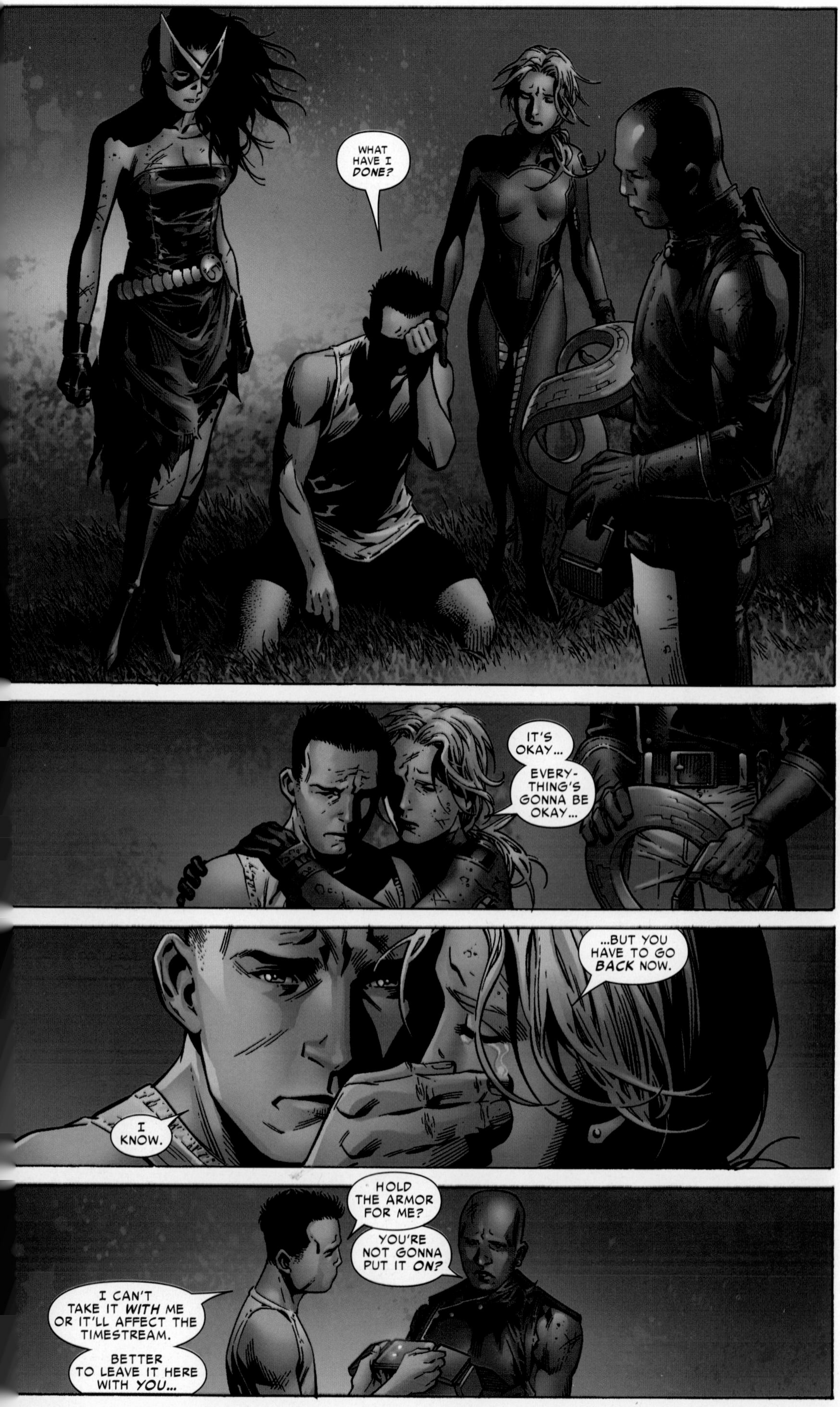
WHAT HAVE I DONE?
IT'S OKAY...
EVERYTHING'S GONNA BE OKAY...
...BUT YOU HAVE TO GO BACK NOW.
I KNOW.
HOLD THE ARMOR FOR ME?
YOU'RE NOT GONNA PUT IT ON?
I CAN'T TAKE IT WITH ME OR IT'LL AFFECT THE TIMESTREAM.
BETTER TO LEAVE IT HERE WITH YOU...

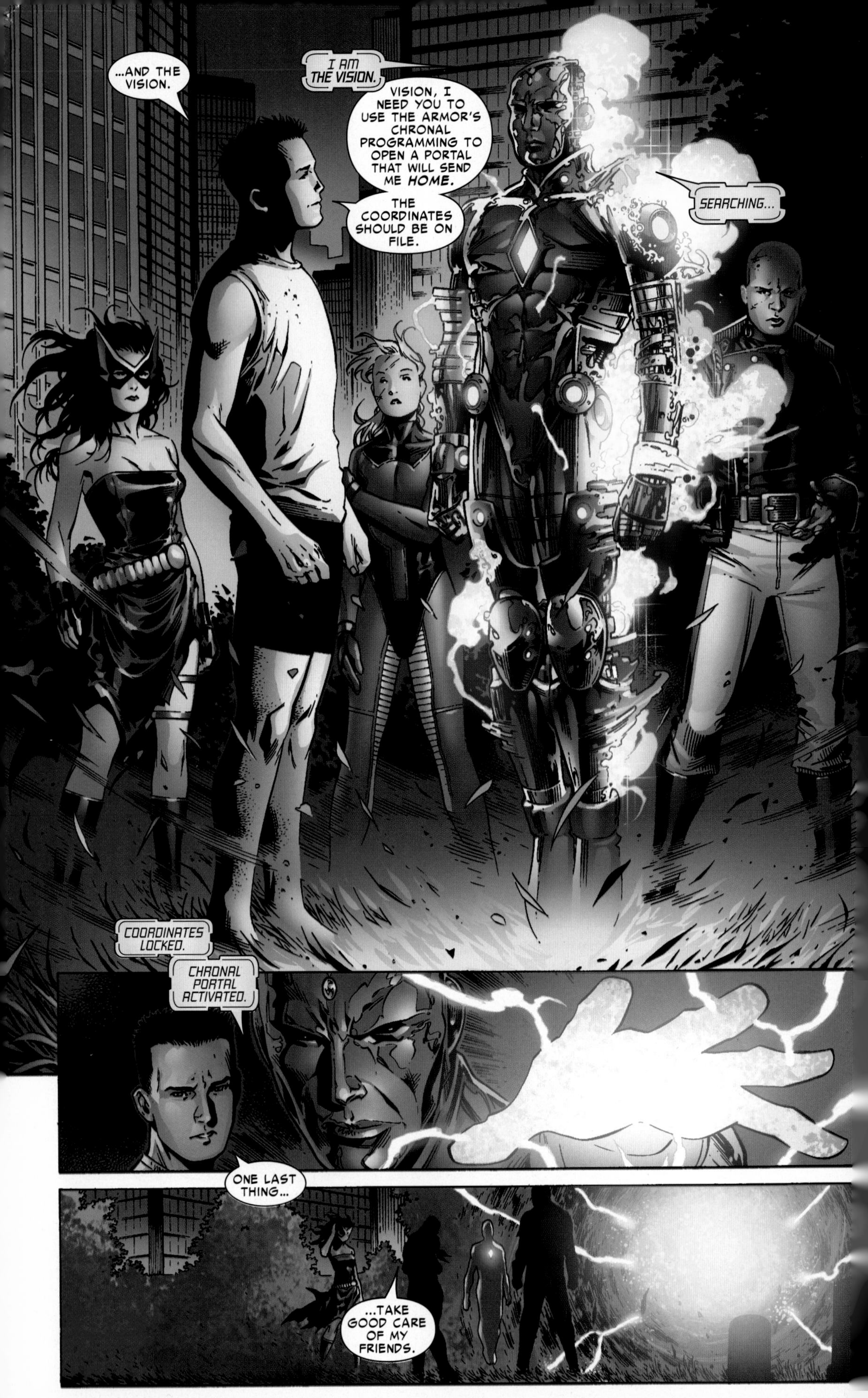
...AND THE VISION.
I AM THE VISION.
VISION, I NEED YOU TO USE THE ARMOR'S CHRONAL PROGRAMMING TO OPEN A PORTAL THAT WILL SEND ME HOME.
THE COORDINATES SHOULD BE ON FILE.
SEARCHING...
COORDINATES LOCKED.
CHRONAL PORTAL ACTIVATED.
ONE LAST THING...
...TAKE GOOD CARE OF MY FRIENDS.

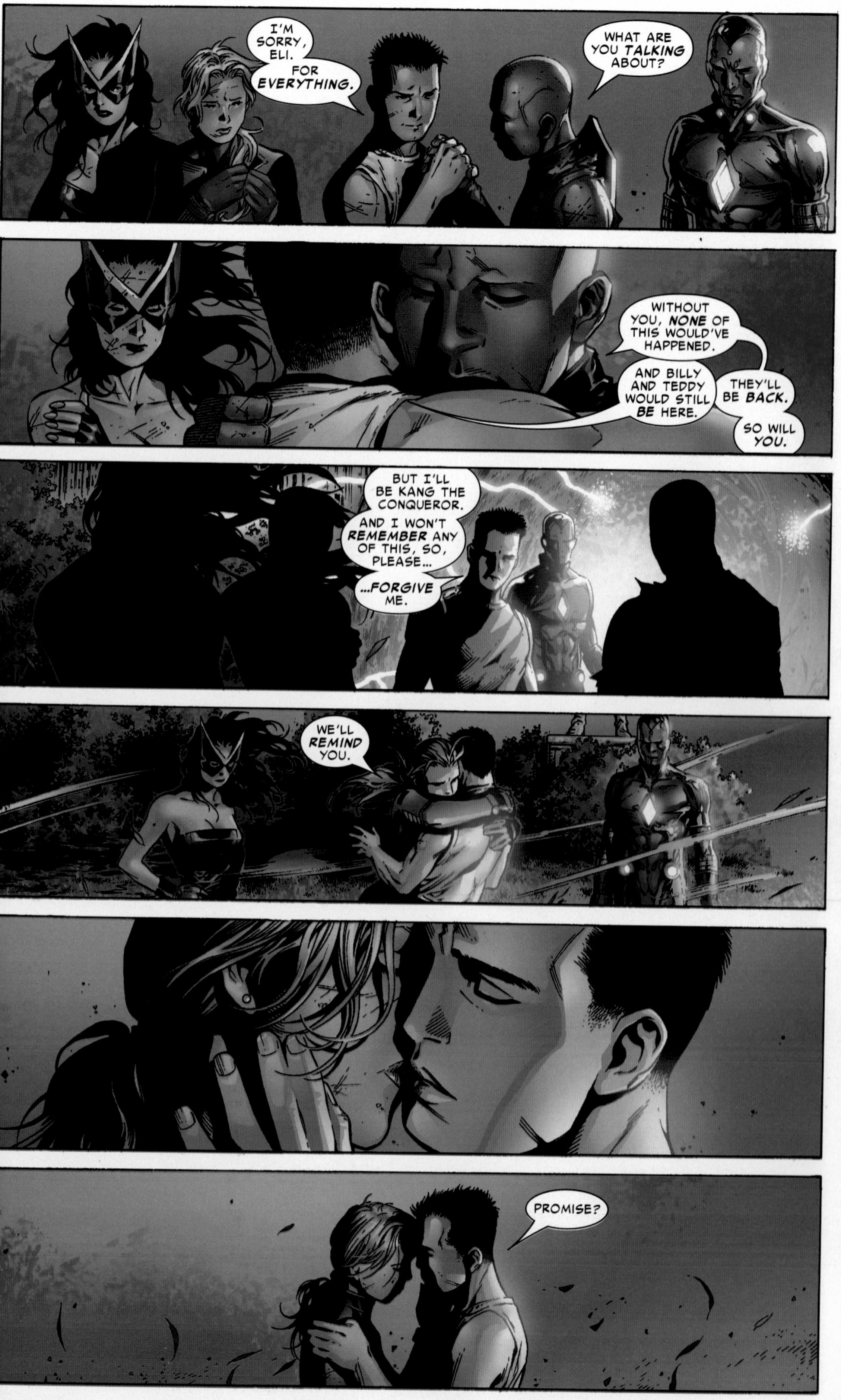

I'M SORRY, ELI.
FOR EVERYTHING.
WHAT ARE YOU TALKING ABOUT?
WITHOUT YOU, NONE OF THIS WOULD'VE HAPPENED.
AND BILLY AND TEDDY WOULD STILL BE HERE.
THEY'LL BE BACK.
SO WILL YOU.
BUT I'LL BE KANG THE CONQUEROR.
AND I WON'T REMEMBER ANY OF THIS, SO, PLEASE...
...FORGIVE ME.
WE'LL REMIND YOU.
PROMISE?

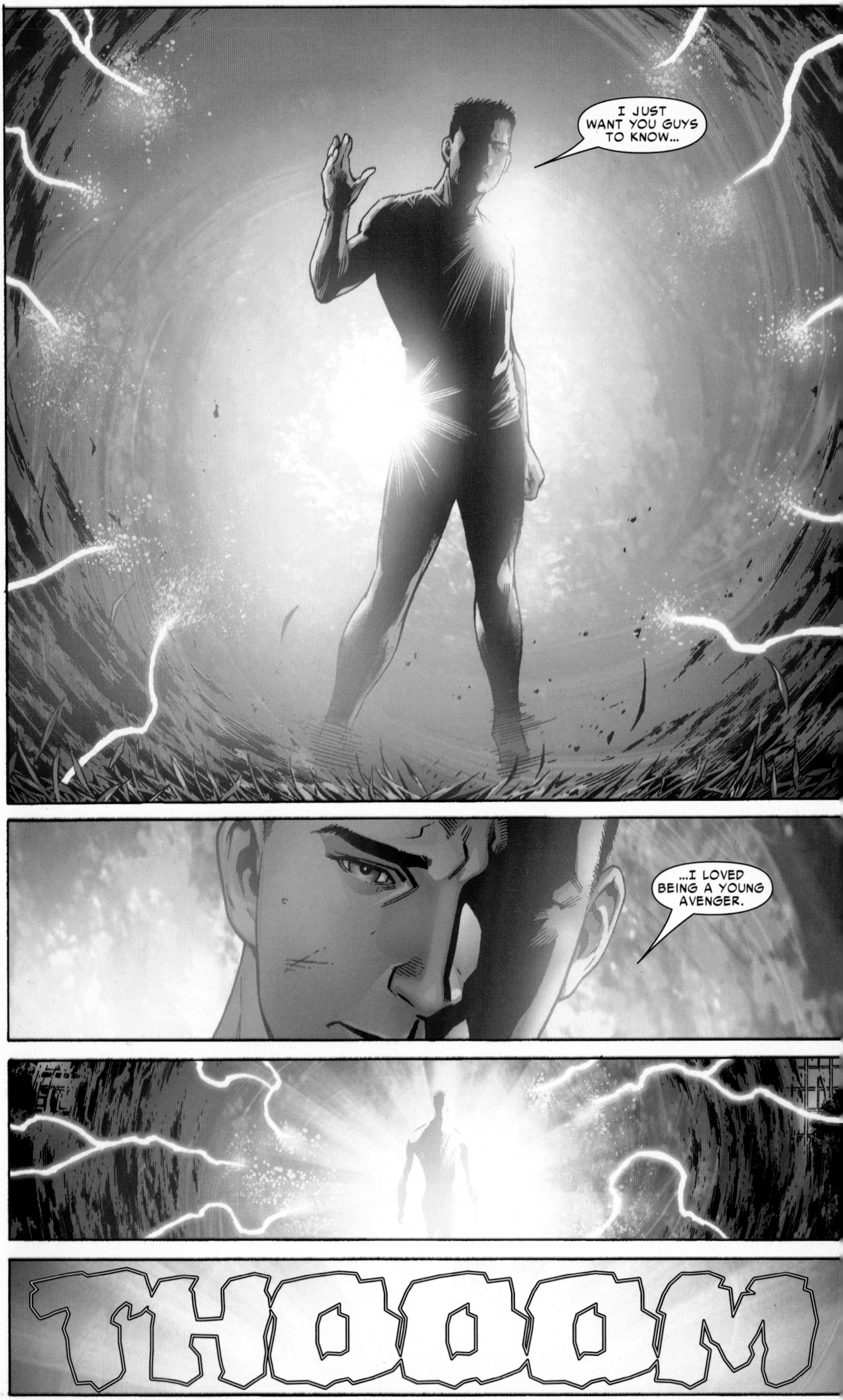
I JUST WANT YOU GUYS TO KNOW...
...I LOVED BEING A YOUNG AVENGER.
THOOOM

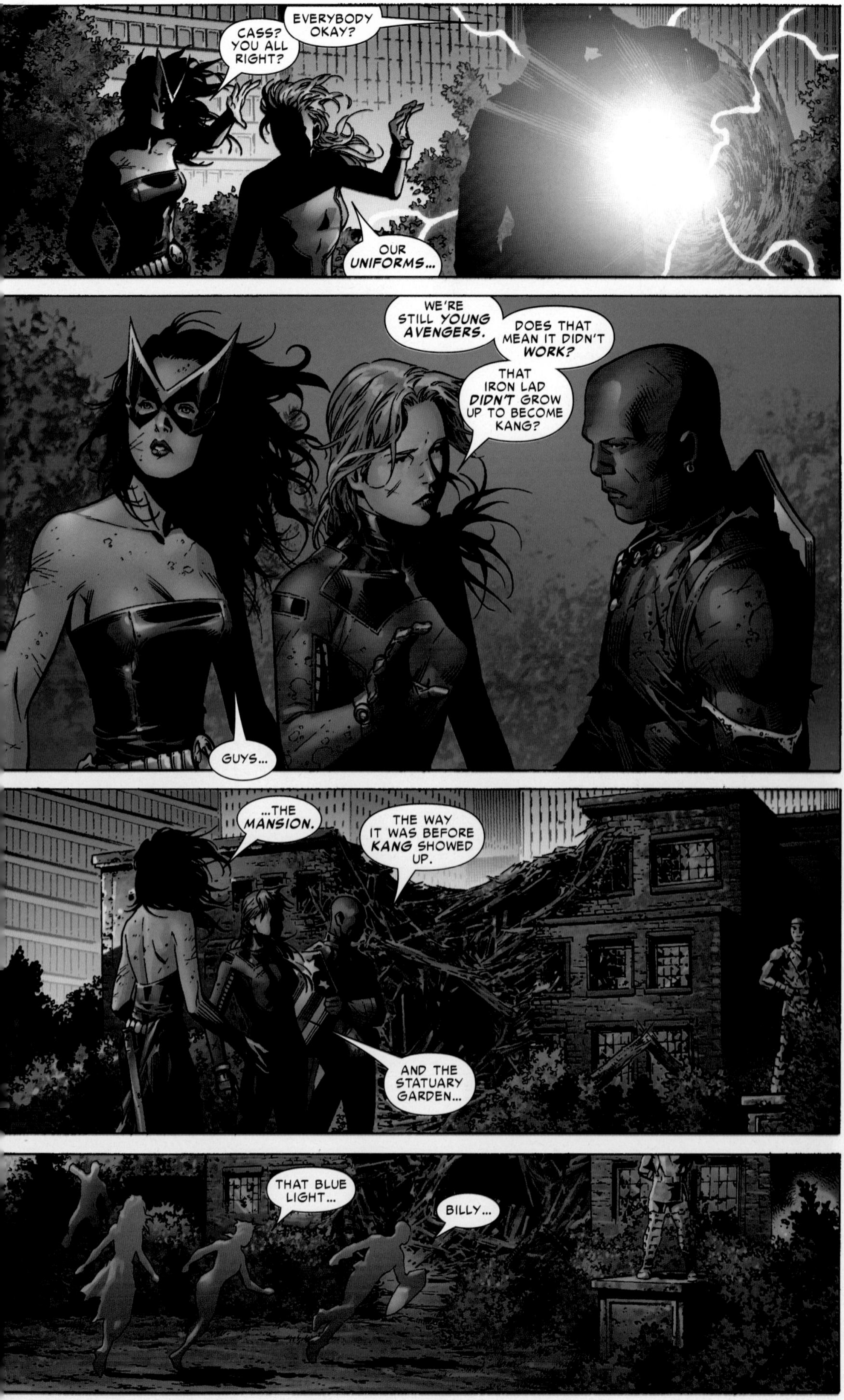
CASS? YOU ALL RIGHT?
EVERYBODY OKAY?
OUR UNIFORMS...
WE'RE STILL YOUNG AVENGERS.
DOES THAT MEAN IT DIDN'T WORK?
THAT IRON LAD DIDN'T GROW UP TO BECOME KANG?
GUYS...
...THE MANSION.
THE WAY IT WAS BEFORE KANG SHOWED UP.
AND THE STATUARY GARDEN...
THAT BLUE LIGHT...
BILLY...

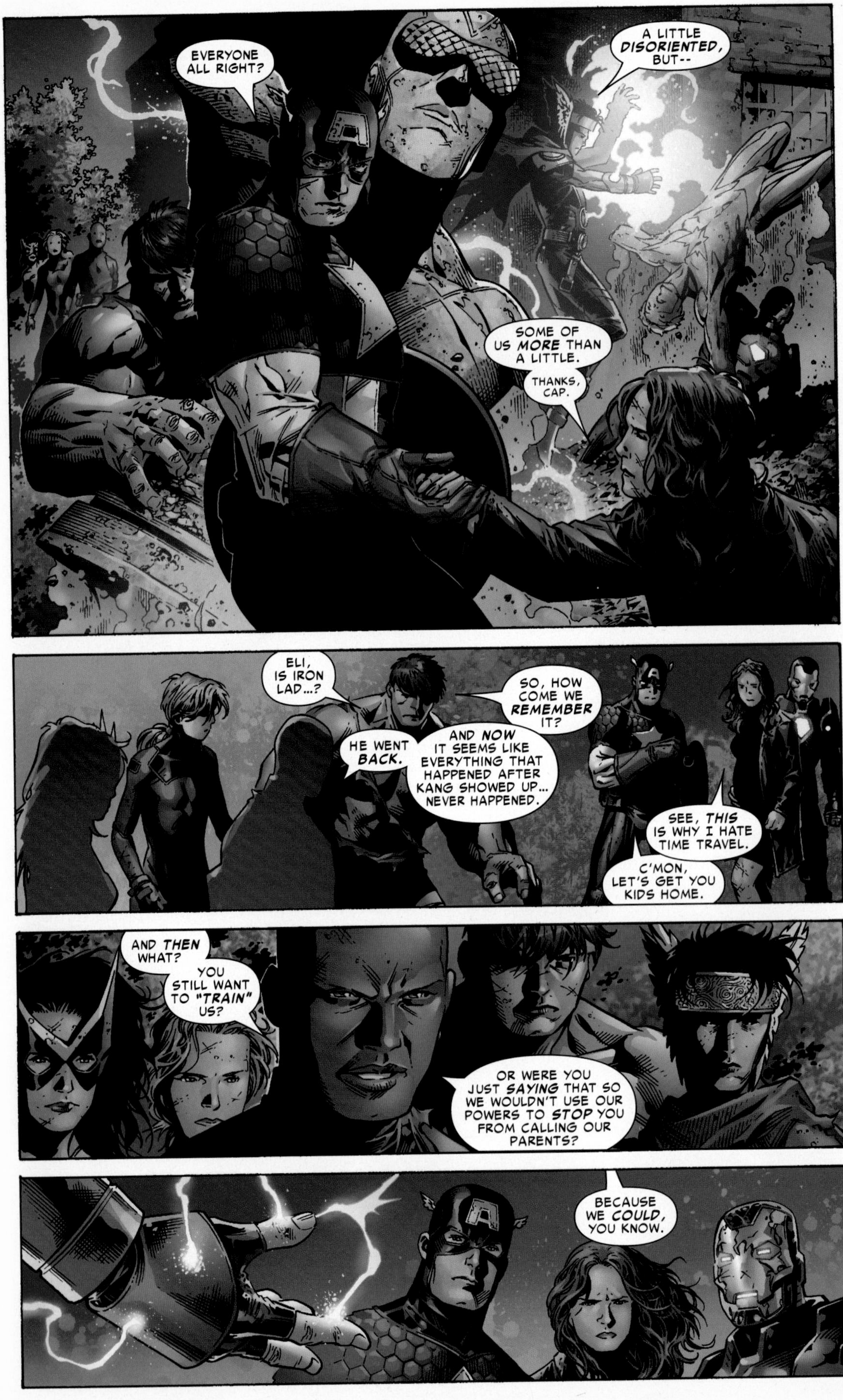
EVERYONE ALL RIGHT?
A LITTLE DISORIENTED, BUT--
SOME OF US MORE THAN A LITTLE.
THANKS, CAP.
ELI, IS IRON LAD...?
HE WENT BACK.
SO, HOW COME WE REMEMBER IT?
AND NOW IT SEEMS LIKE EVERYTHING THAT HAPPENED AFTER KANG SHOWED UP... NEVER HAPPENED.
SEE, THIS IS WHY I HATE TIME TRAVEL.
C'MON, LET'S GET YOU KIDS HOME.
AND THEN WHAT?
YOU STILL WANT TO "TRAIN" US?
OR WERE YOU JUST SAYING THAT SO WE WOULDN'T USE OUR POWERS TO STOP YOU FROM CALLING OUR PARENTS?
BECAUSE WE COULD, YOU KNOW.

IN MY OPINION, YOU KIDS HAVE *MORE* THAN PROVEN YOURSELVES HEROES TONIGHT.

BUT...

BUT...

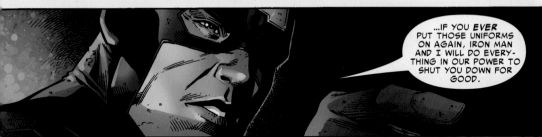

...IF YOU *EVER* PUT THOSE UNIFORMS ON AGAIN, IRON MAN AND I WILL DO EVERYTHING IN OUR POWER TO SHUT YOU DOWN FOR GOOD.

BUT WE COULD *HELP* YOU. YOU COULD *TRAIN* US.

WE CAN'T.

NOT WITHOUT YOUR PARENTS' CONSENT.

BUT IF YOU WANT US TO ASK YOUR *PARENTS*...

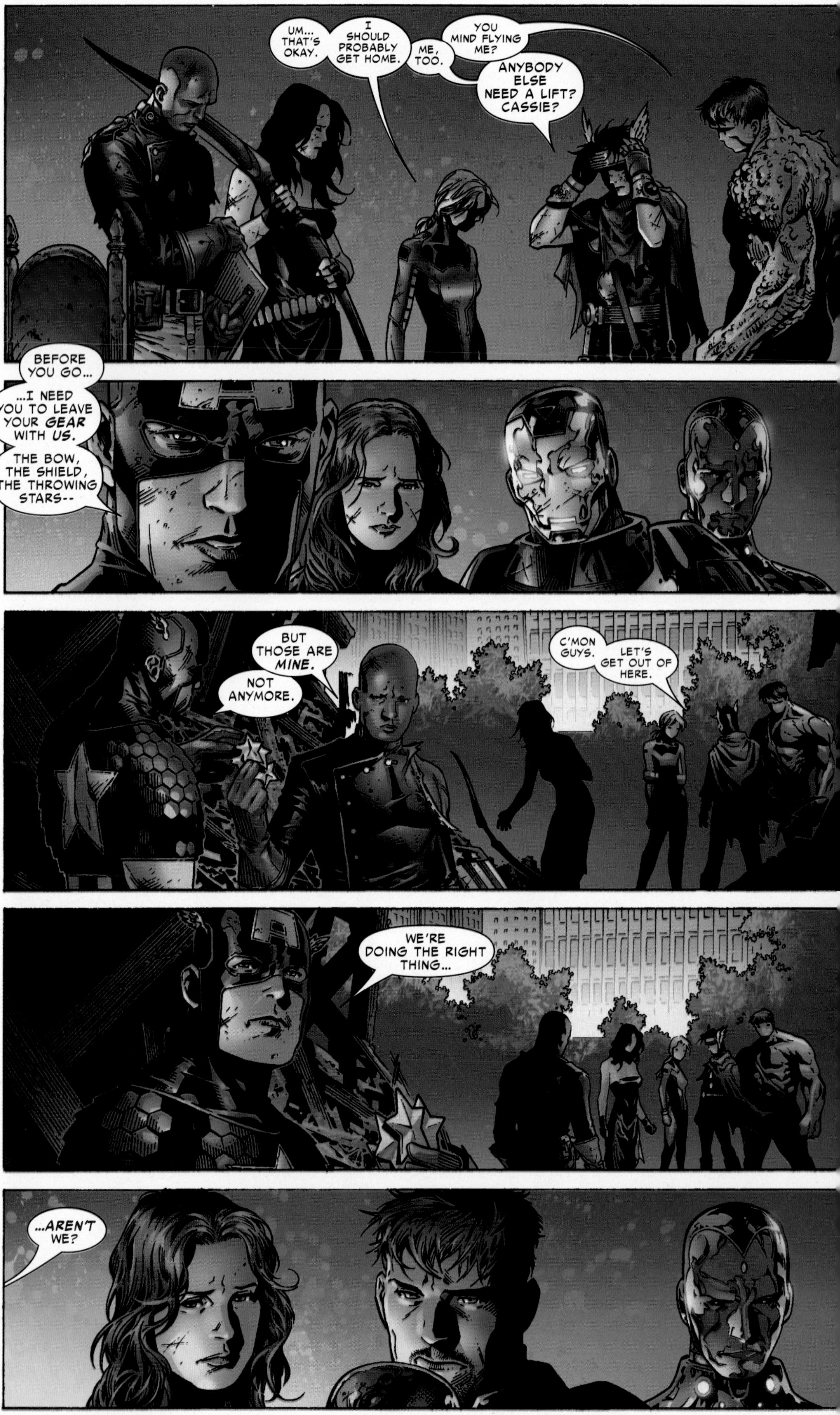
UM... THAT'S OKAY.
I SHOULD PROBABLY GET HOME.
ME, TOO.
YOU MIND FLYING ME?
ANYBODY ELSE NEED A LIFT? CASSIE?
BEFORE YOU GO...
...I NEED YOU TO LEAVE YOUR GEAR WITH US.
THE BOW, THE SHIELD, THE THROWING STARS--
BUT THOSE ARE MINE.
NOT ANYMORE.
C'MON GUYS.
LET'S GET OUT OF HERE.
WE'RE DOING THE RIGHT THING...
...AREN'T WE?

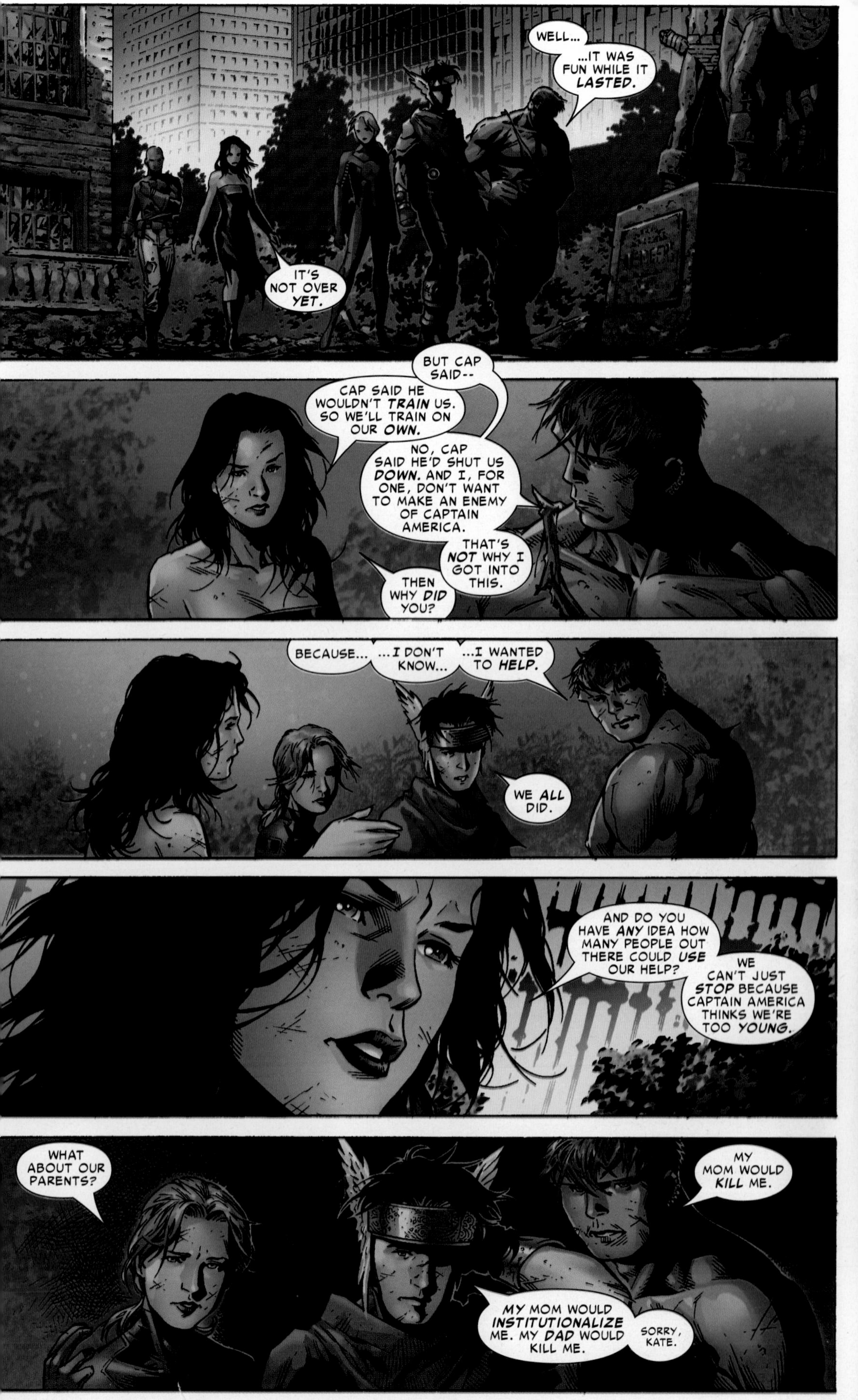
WELL...
...IT WAS FUN WHILE IT LASTED.
IT'S NOT OVER YET.
BUT CAP SAID--
CAP SAID HE WOULDN'T TRAIN US. SO WE'LL TRAIN ON OUR OWN.
NO, CAP SAID HE'D SHUT US DOWN. AND I, FOR ONE, DON'T WANT TO MAKE AN ENEMY OF CAPTAIN AMERICA.
THAT'S NOT WHY I GOT INTO THIS.
THEN WHY DID YOU?
BECAUSE...
...I DON'T KNOW...
...I WANTED TO HELP.
WE ALL DID.
AND DO YOU HAVE ANY IDEA HOW MANY PEOPLE OUT THERE COULD USE OUR HELP?
WE CAN'T JUST STOP BECAUSE CAPTAIN AMERICA THINKS WE'RE TOO YOUNG.
WHAT ABOUT OUR PARENTS?
MY MOM WOULD KILL ME.
MY MOM WOULD INSTITUTIONALIZE ME. MY DAD WOULD KILL ME.
SORRY, KATE.

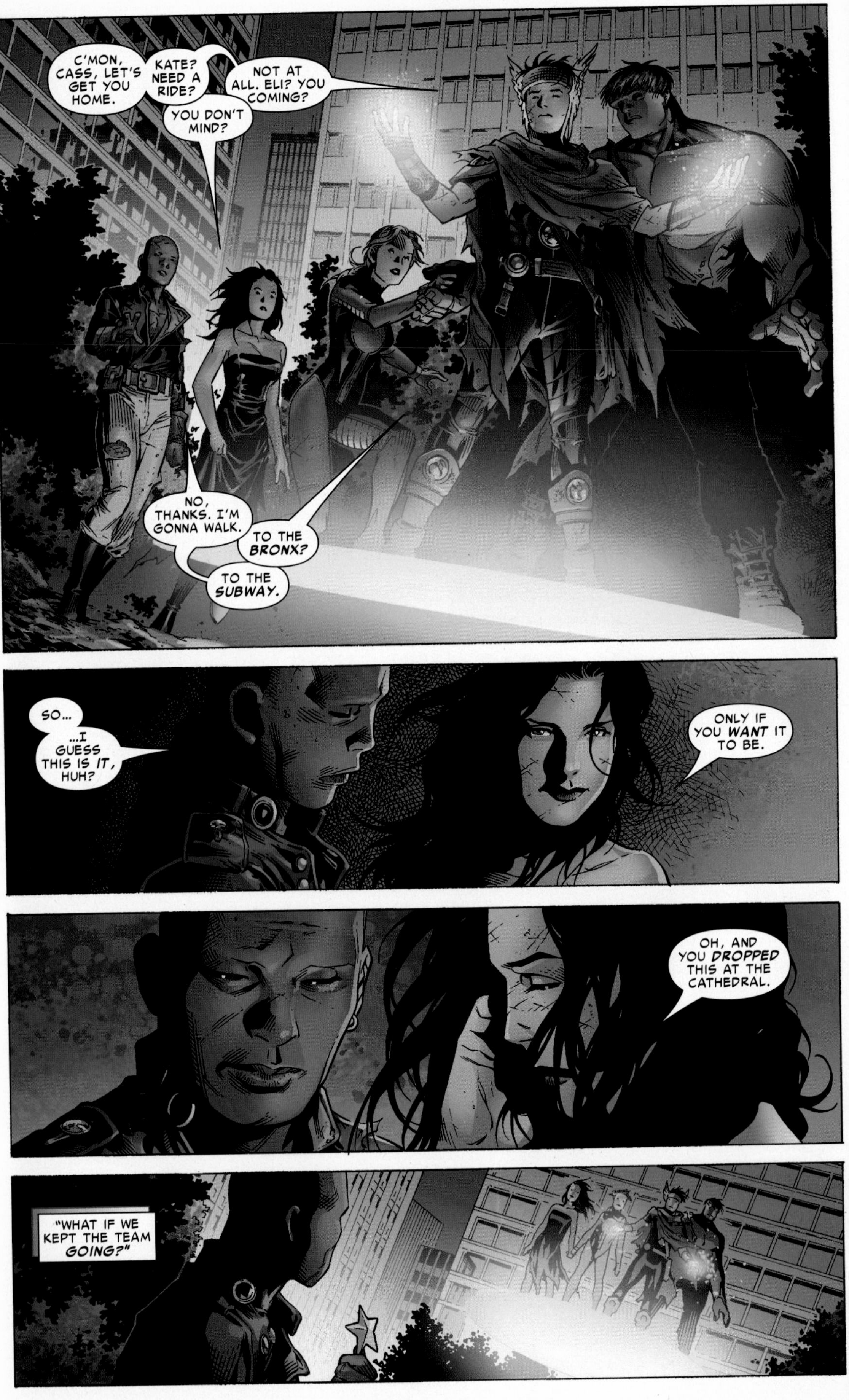

C'MON, CASS, LET'S GET YOU HOME.
KATE? NEED A RIDE?
YOU DON'T MIND?
NOT AT ALL. ELI? YOU COMING?
NO, THANKS. I'M GONNA WALK.
TO THE BRONX?
TO THE SUBWAY.
SO...
...I GUESS THIS IS IT, HUH?
ONLY IF YOU WANT IT TO BE.
OH, AND YOU DROPPED THIS AT THE CATHEDRAL.
"WHAT IF WE KEPT THE TEAM GOING?"

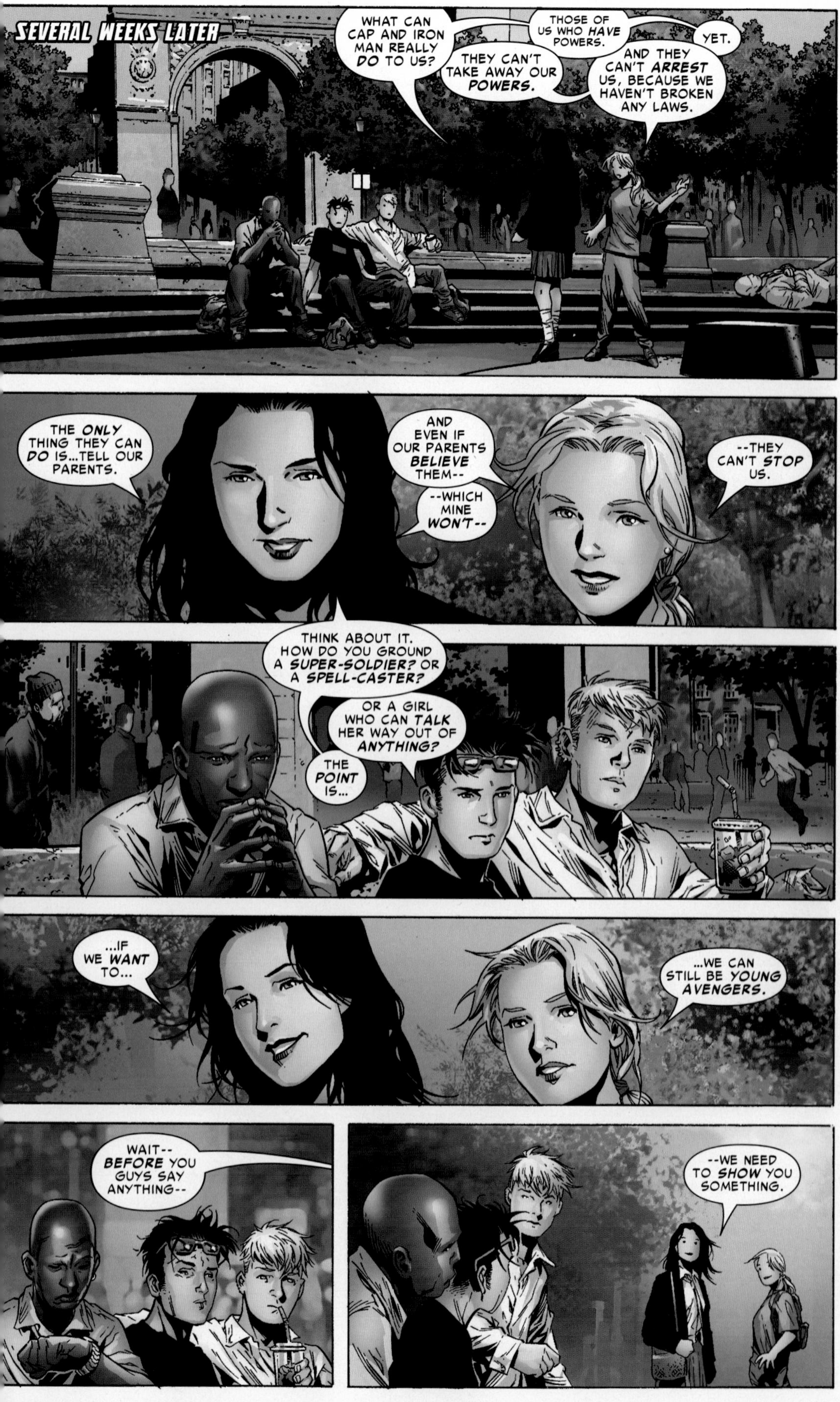
SEVERAL WEEKS LATER
WHAT CAN CAP AND IRON MAN REALLY DO TO US?
THOSE OF US WHO HAVE POWERS.
YET.
THEY CAN'T TAKE AWAY OUR POWERS.
AND THEY CAN'T ARREST US, BECAUSE WE HAVEN'T BROKEN ANY LAWS.
THE ONLY THING THEY CAN DO IS...TELL OUR PARENTS.
AND EVEN IF OUR PARENTS BELIEVE THEM--
--WHICH MINE WON'T--
--THEY CAN'T STOP US.
THINK ABOUT IT. HOW DO YOU GROUND A SUPER-SOLDIER? OR A SPELL-CASTER?
OR A GIRL WHO CAN TALK HER WAY OUT OF ANYTHING?
THE POINT IS...
...IF WE WANT TO...
...WE CAN STILL BE YOUNG AVENGERS.
WAIT-- BEFORE YOU GUYS SAY ANYTHING--
--WE NEED TO SHOW YOU SOMETHING.

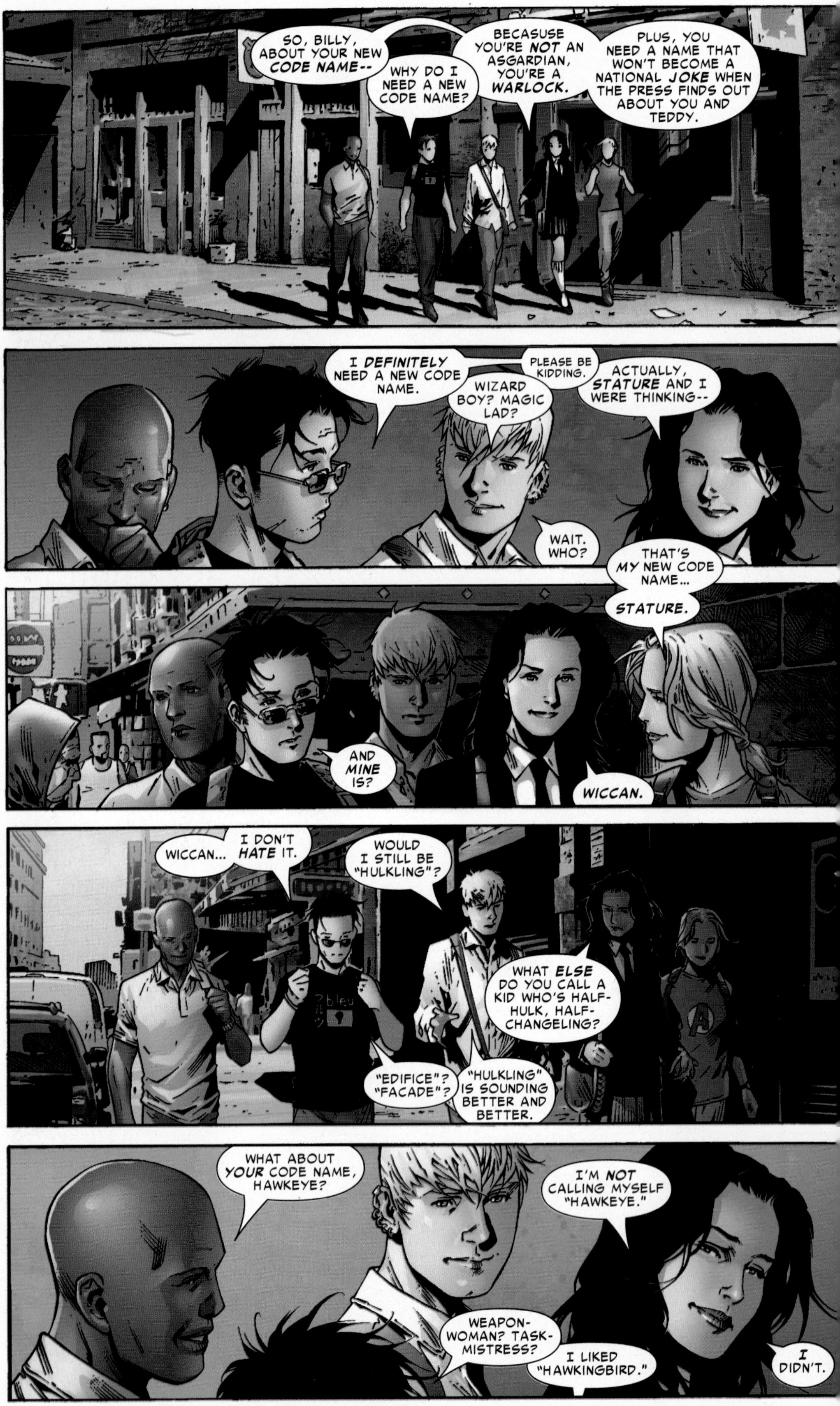
SO, BILLY, ABOUT YOUR NEW CODE NAME--
WHY DO I NEED A NEW CODE NAME?
BECASUSE YOU'RE NOT AN ASGARDIAN, YOU'RE A WARLOCK.
PLUS, YOU NEED A NAME THAT WON'T BECOME A NATIONAL JOKE WHEN THE PRESS FINDS OUT ABOUT YOU AND TEDDY.
I DEFINITELY NEED A NEW CODE NAME.
PLEASE BE KIDDING.
WIZARD BOY? MAGIC LAD?
ACTUALLY, STATURE AND I WERE THINKING--
WAIT. WHO?
THAT'S MY NEW CODE NAME...
STATURE.
AND MINE IS?
WICCAN.
WICCAN... I DON'T HATE IT.
WOULD I STILL BE "HULKLING"?
WHAT ELSE DO YOU CALL A KID WHO'S HALF-HULK, HALF-CHANGELING?
"EDIFICE"? "FACADE"?
"HULKLING" IS SOUNDING BETTER AND BETTER.
WHAT ABOUT YOUR CODE NAME, HAWKEYE?
I'M NOT CALLING MYSELF "HAWKEYE."
WEAPON-WOMAN? TASK-MISTRESS?
I LIKED "HAWKINGBIRD."
I DIDN'T.

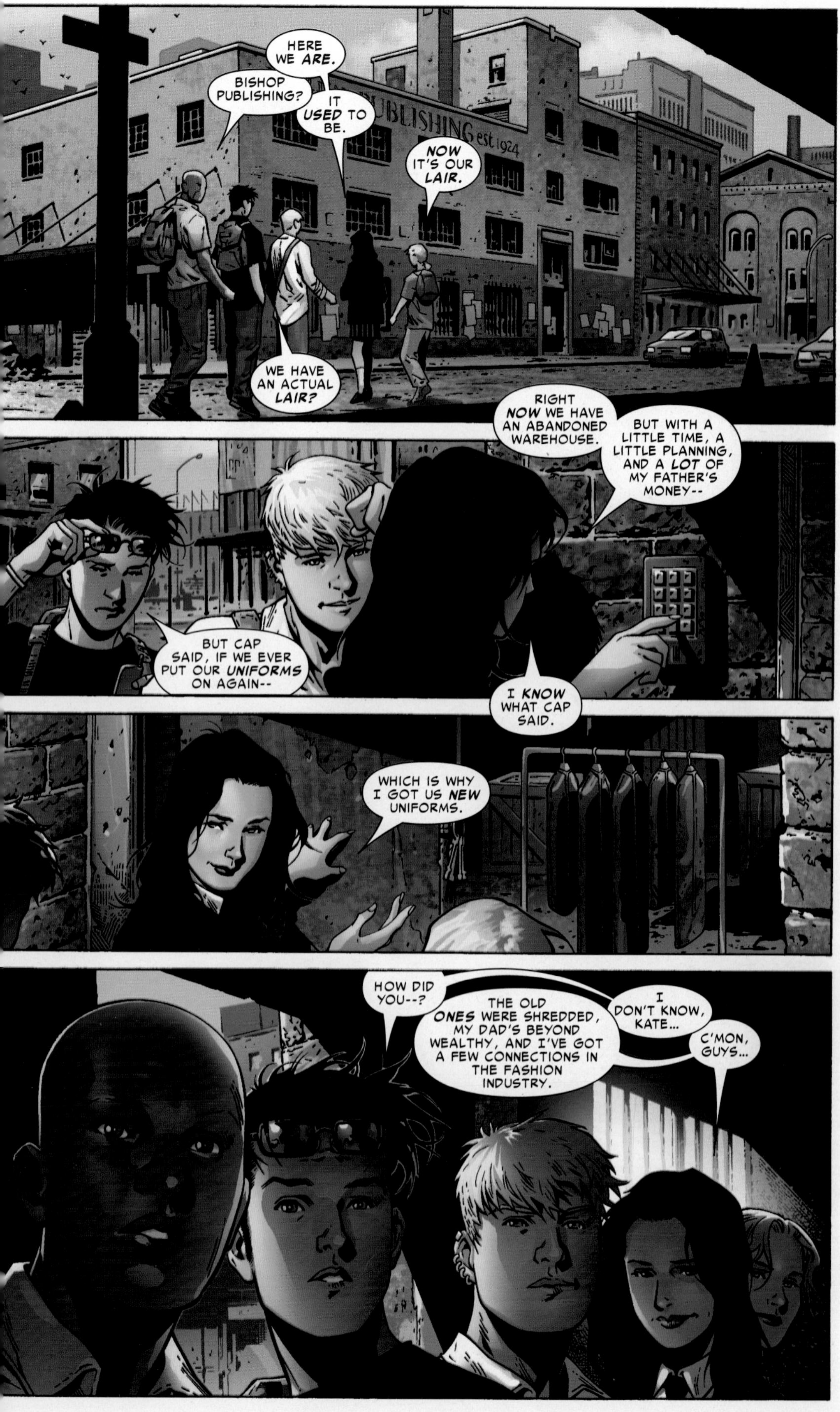

HERE WE ARE.
BISHOP PUBLISHING?
IT USED TO BE.
NOW IT'S OUR LAIR.
WE HAVE AN ACTUAL LAIR?
PUBLISHING est 1924
RIGHT NOW WE HAVE AN ABANDONED WAREHOUSE.
BUT WITH A LITTLE TIME, A LITTLE PLANNING, AND A LOT OF MY FATHER'S MONEY--
BUT CAP SAID, IF WE EVER PUT OUR UNIFORMS ON AGAIN--
I KNOW WHAT CAP SAID.
WHICH IS WHY I GOT US NEW UNIFORMS.
HOW DID YOU--?
I DON'T KNOW, KATE...
THE OLD ONES WERE SHREDDED, MY DAD'S BEYOND WEALTHY, AND I'VE GOT A FEW CONNECTIONS IN THE FASHION INDUSTRY.
C'MON, GUYS...

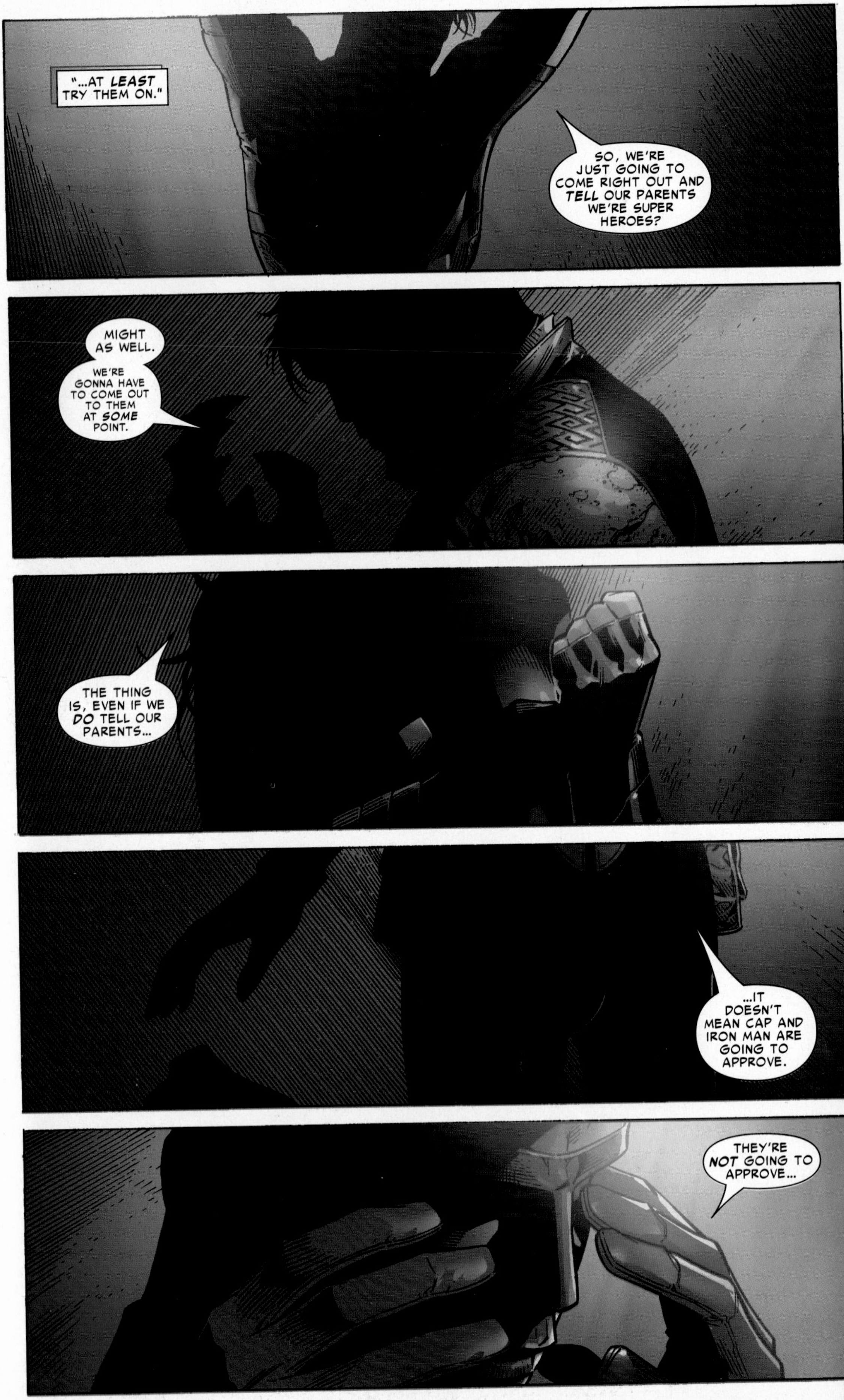
"...AT LEAST TRY THEM ON."
SO, WE'RE JUST GOING TO COME RIGHT OUT AND TELL OUR PARENTS WE'RE SUPER HEROES?
MIGHT AS WELL.
WE'RE GONNA HAVE TO COME OUT TO THEM AT SOME POINT.
THE THING IS, EVEN IF WE DO TELL OUR PARENTS...
...IT DOESN'T MEAN CAP AND IRON MAN ARE GOING TO APPROVE.
THEY'RE NOT GOING TO APPROVE...

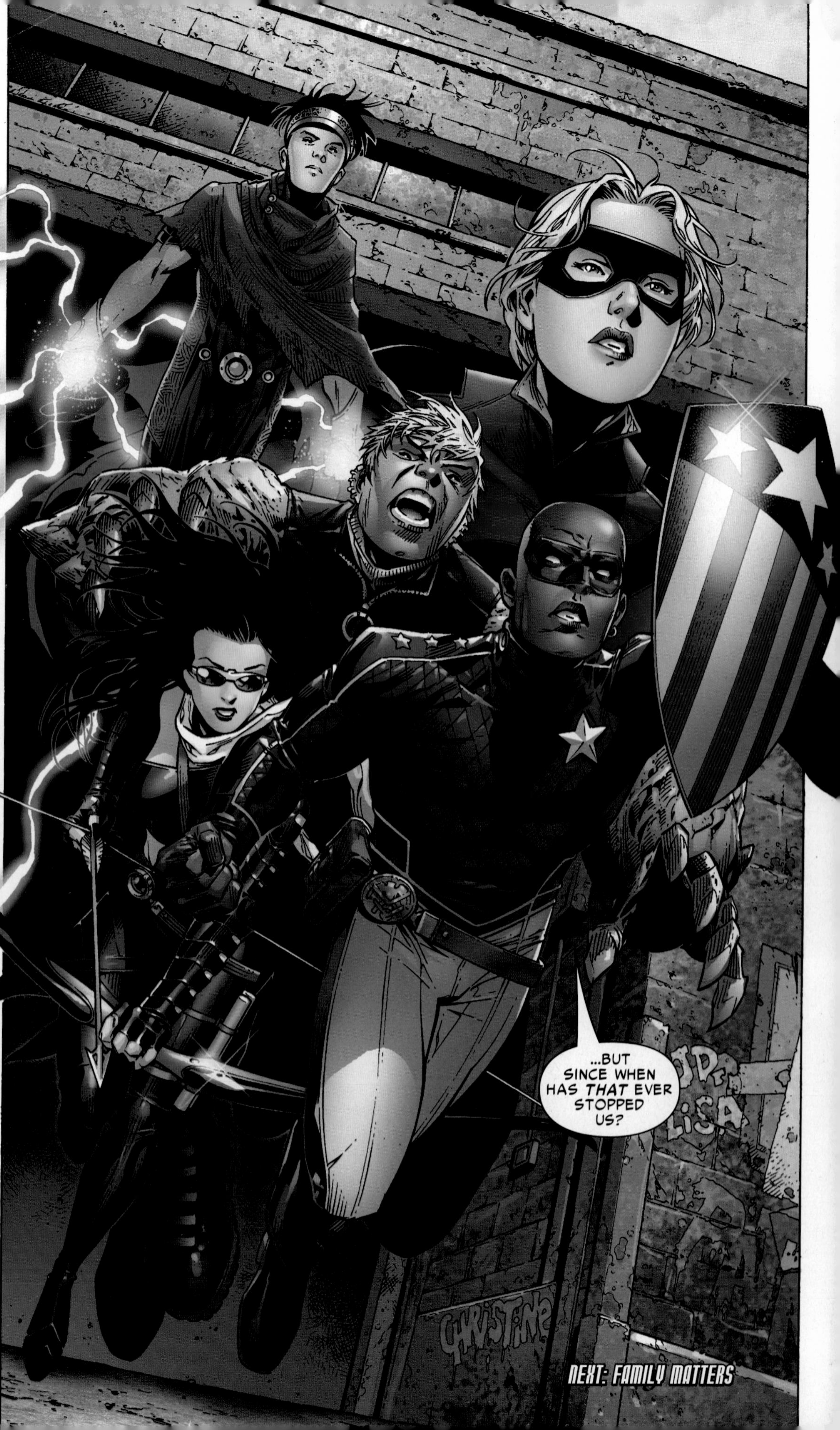
...BUT SINCE WHEN HAS *THAT* EVER STOPPED US?
CHRISTINE
NEXT: FAMILY MATTERS

CHARACTER DESIGNS BY JIM CHEUNG

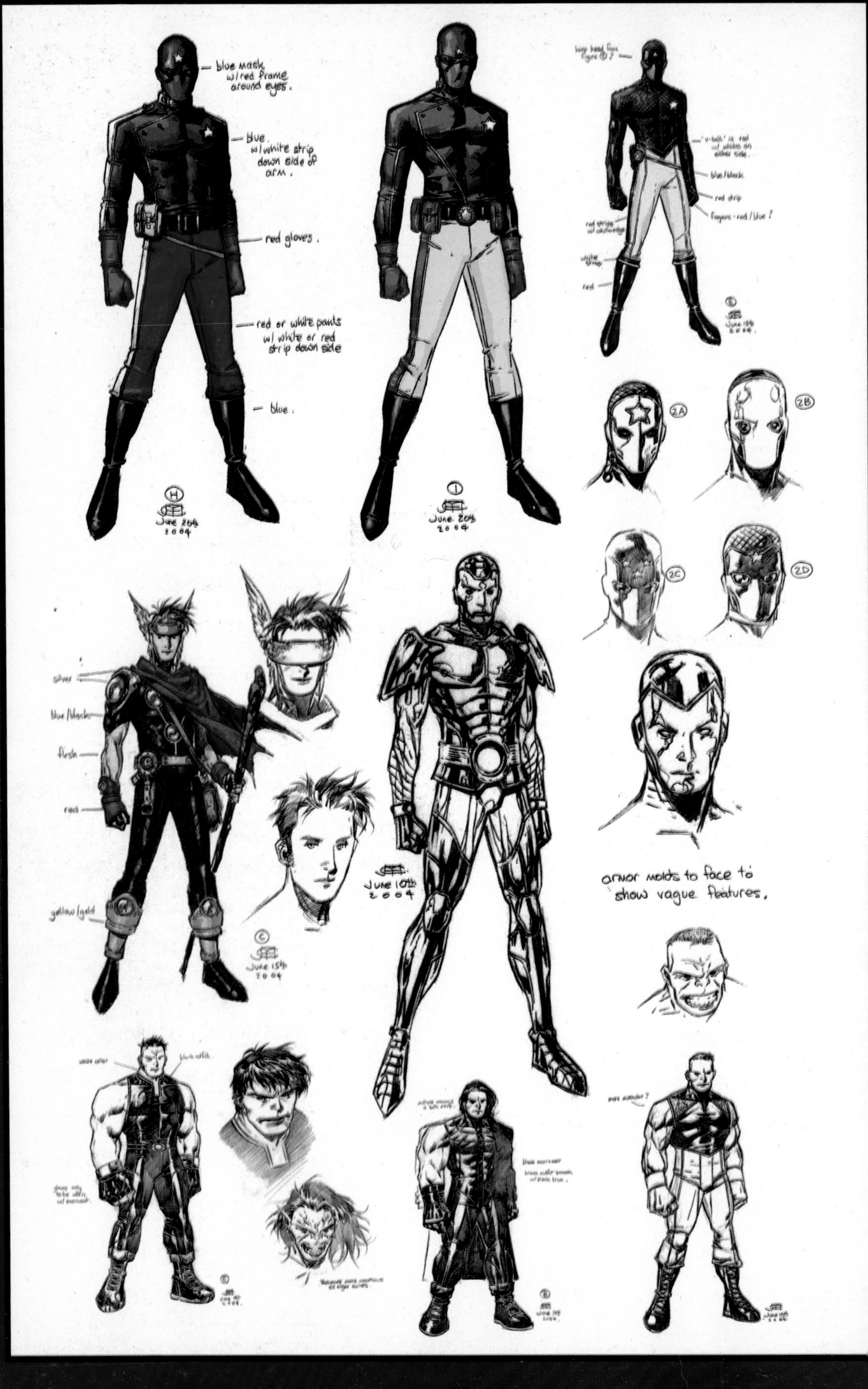
blue mask w/red frame around eyes.
blue w/white strip down side of arm.
red gloves.
red or white pants w/ white or red strip down side
blue.
H
June 26th 2004
1
June 20th 2004
2A
2B
2C
2D
silver
blue/black
flesh
red
yellow/gold
C
June 15th 2004
June 10th 2004
armor molds to face to show vague features.